The Accidental Diplomat

The Autobiography of **Maurice Baker**

Maurice Baker

NEW JERSEY · LONDON · SINGAPORE · BEIJING · SHANGHAI · HONG KONG · TAIPEI · CHENNAI

Published by

World Scientific Publishing Co. Pte. Ltd.
5 Toh Tuck Link, Singapore 596224
USA office: 27 Warren Street, Suite 401-402, Hackensack, NJ 07601
UK office: 57 Shelton Street, Covent Garden, London WC2H 9HE

National Library Board, Singapore Cataloguing-in-Publication Data
Baker, Maurice, 1920–
    The accidental diplomat : the autobiography of Maurice Baker / by Maurice Baker ; edited by Edmund Baker. -- Singapore : World Scientific, 2014.
    pages cm
  ISBN: 978-981-4618-30-4 (hardcover)
  ISBN: 978-981-4618-31-1 (paperback)
  1. Baker, Maurice, 1920–   2. Ambassadors -- Singapore -- Biography.
3. College administrators -- Singapore -- Biography. I. Baker, Edmund. II. Title
JX1664
327.2092--dc23

                                                          OCN 881509045

British Library Cataloguing-in-Publication Data
A catalogue record for this book is available from the British Library.

Copyright © 2015 by World Scientific Publishing Co. Pte. Ltd.

All rights reserved. This book, or parts thereof, may not be reproduced in any form or by any means, electronic or mechanical, including photocopying, recording or any information storage and retrieval system now known or to be invented, without written permission from the publisher.

For photocopying of material in this volume, please pay a copying fee through the Copyright Clearance Center, Inc., 222 Rosewood Drive, Danvers, MA 01923, USA. In this case permission to photocopy is not required from the publisher.

Typeset by Stallion Press
Email: enquiries@stallionpress.com

for Barbara

FOREWORD

AS A STUDENT at the University of Malaya in Singapore in the 1950s, I had heard of a Maurice Baker — a Queen's Scholar — who was due to return from London, having completed his studies. He joined the University's small team of local academics in 1955.

It was only many years later, when I joined the Ministry of Foreign Affairs, that my friend the late Professor Wong Lin Ken introduced him to me. Then, it was because Maurice Baker was heading the local staff association in its negotiations with the University authorities on staff remuneration and terms of service. Before that, I had heard of him as head of the Department of Extra-Mural Studies at the University, where my friend Joseph Conceicao was also engaged.

It was in 1967, when he was about to take up the position of Singapore's high commissioner to the Republic of India, that I began a close association with him which has lasted to this day. He turned out to be a remarkable product of our times of political consciousness and struggle. Later, he turned out to be a most distinguished diplomat too.

As I got to know him closely, I found him to be full of humour, and possessed of a special grace. As a literary scholar, his command of the English language and the way in which he used it in his written communications and in his diplomatic engagements was impressive, to say the least, for someone like me who had had limited education.

In his diplomatic exchanges, he used his humour and his engaging skills to great advantage to canvass support, even from those who disagreed with him. From his reports I saw how these interlocutors, who did not hold favourable views about Singapore, its leaders or its policies, responded to his persuasions. They not only listened but also gave their full attention to his persuasive arguments.

Once he embarked on his diplomatic career, his commitment to it overcame his deep affection for teaching, and he took seriously the need to connect with anyone — high or low — in diplomatic circles who facilitated his diplomatic engagements. He ably harnessed his energies to fulfil the mission he was asked to undertake in the countries to which he was posted.

In the course of his diplomatic career, he stood at the crossroads of many happenings and crises in our early post-independence days. He ably forged relationships that stood the test of time. When our embassy in Jakarta was sacked by demonstrators and our relations with Indonesia were at a low ebb, his friendship with the Indonesian diplomatic staff in New Delhi helped both sides to bear no animosity over these unfortunate developments, providing an example of diplomacy at its best.

I am certain that readers of Maurice Baker's memoirs will be entertained by his many experiences during the years he spent as a diplomat in India, the Philippines and Malaysia. The book is filled with many illuminating anecdotes from these varied postings. He recounts them with candour and in ways most entertaining. Wherever he served, he invested much time and energy building ties for Singapore with ministers, politicians, maharajahs, sultans, scholars and laymen. His encounters with outstanding personalities in the countries in which he served, and his recollections of their conversations with him, are what make his memoirs worth more than a single read. Above all, they reflect the rare qualities of a school master who successfully became a diplomat.

S. R. Nathan
Sixth President of the Republic of Singapore

Message

I have known Maurice Baker for almost 60 years. I first met him in 1954 when he was a teacher in Victoria School. He was the class master of Form 5 (Arts), and I was in Form 5 (Science) — the level which prepared students for the then Senior Cambridge Examination (equivalent to today's GCE O-Levels). Though I was not in his class, I got to know him as Adviser to the Literary and Debating Society of which I was the Secretary.

Later when I was admitted to the University of Malaya in 1956, I came to know him better. English literature was one of my major subjects and he was my lecturer in English Drama. More than being my teacher, he was an angel in disguise in my life. He had time and a ready ear for me. He was someone I could drop in and see in his office at any time to seek advice and confide in. He helped me financially and he played a decisive role, as he recounts in this book, to help me pursue Economics instead of English for my honours degree.

As a teacher, he was infectious in his love for English poetry and drama. That has shaped my own love for poetry and the poetic word. He had an ear for the spoken word which was evident in his ambassador's reports that I was to read many years later. When I visit him, he still remembers and loves to quote the great poets, even at his present age of 94. He always impressed me as a soft spoken gentleman and it came as a surprise to me when I later learnt of his political activities in London. These activities got him into the black book of the official British establishment even though he was a Queen's Scholar. It is only when I read the draft of this book that I learnt of his part in promoting the interests of the local staff in a university dominated and controlled by expatriates. In all my interactions with him he never came across as an angry revolutionary in a constant state of war against the colonial masters or the establishment. He was a quiet and soft-spoken nationalist.

We had a lot more interaction with each other in the 1980s when he was Singapore's Ambassador to the Philippines and Malaysia during my term as the Minister for Foreign Affairs.

It is a practice in the Ministry for ambassadors to file periodic reports on developments in their countries of posting. Obviously these reports had to be more than a recounting of events and happenings of the kind one could read in the newspapers and journals. The ambassador and diplomatic staff were expected to move around in the circles of policy and opinion makers to glean insights, which would give a more accurate understanding than media reports.

At that time, these reports came as hard copies, typed in the embassy and sent by secured diplomatic bags. Snail mail was probably much more secure than the encrypted emails of today which are child's play for the NSA to break into. Moreover as they had to be typed manually, they were probably more carefully thought out and scripted than today's instant email reports.

Every day I read reports from the staff of our Singapore foreign diplomatic offices. Sadly most of these made for dry, uninteresting reading. However there were a few ambassadors whose reports I eagerly looked forward to reading. Ambassador Baker was among them. It was not just his literary style and choice of words that stood out. This was expected of an English Literature academic. He showed a keen ability to identify local personalities who would have views and a take on events that gave a better and more accurate understanding of the important developments in the country. It was his choice of the people with whom he talked and the particular views of such personalities that he thought worthwhile to record and comment on, that made his reports so very interesting and valuable.

As I read this book, I found myself immersed again in the atmosphere of my times in the Ministry of Foreign Affairs. There are glimpses and vignettes of the history and issues of Singapore's relationship with our neighboring counties, which revived my memory. They give a feel for the fabric of our relationship with our neighbors, especially Malaysia. Our neighbours and ourselves have changed beyond recognition. In certain fundamentals that shape relationships, things have not changed that much after all.

This book is a personal account of one man for some of the events from the start of the Japanese Occupation of Malaya and Singapore to the end of the 1990s. A proper understanding of history requires more than a reading of objective facts. It is very questionable if there can ever be such a thing as objective facts about past events as the very selection of facts is shaped by the personal bias of the writer. Personal accounts like Maurice Baker's breathe life into accounts of the past. This is a very readable narrative covering a significant period of our history. It should appeal to all Singaporeans who want a richer understanding of our past.

S. Dhanabalan
Former Minister for Foreign Affairs

Acknowledgements

I would like to thank my friends, S. R. Nathan and S. Dhanabalan for writing the Foreword and the Message respectively, and Lee Kuan Yew, Tommy Koh, Bilahari Kausikan, Kirpal Singh and Robert Yeo for writing the endorsements.

I am most fortunate to have the assistance of Ms Jill Quah, retired University Librarian, National University of Singapore (NUS), who was my former student. She took charge of the project, seeing to the typing of my manuscripts, proof-reading them, verifying facts pertaining to historical events mentioned, in case my recollections were clouded after so many years in retirement. Later, as I got older, Parkinson's disease made it impossible for me to write due to its debilitating effect, she took to taping me as I talked and then transcribing the recordings so that I can revise them before sending them for typing. She selected from my collection of photographs relevant ones to match the text, and provided the caption information for each photograph. Furthermore, she undertook the task of checking and correcting the proofs, being very familiar with my manuscripts. I am greatly indebted to her for her unstinting support, for her painstaking effort and the countless hours she spent getting my memoirs ready for publication.

I am most grateful to Mrs Daisy Hwang and Mrs Gan Yong Chuen for typing the manuscripts and the transcribed texts; Mr Tim Yap Fuan, in charge of the Singapore/Malaysia Collection of the NUS Libraries for providing the information I needed; and Ms Sylvia Yap, University Librarian, NUS for providing the facilities to produce the CDROM version of my memoirs.

There are many people I must also thank for helping me one way or another over the years, particularly the staff who worked for me during my various diplomatic postings, but their numbers are too many for me to name individually.

Last but not least, I dedicate these memoirs to my dear wife, Barbara, for her love and support.

Maurice Baker

CONTENTS

Foreword by S. R. Nathan — vii
Message by S. Dhanabalan — ix
Acknowledgements — xiii
Introduction — xvii

Part 1 — 1

Chapter 1 Cameron Highlands, Malaya — 3
March 1942–August 1945

Chapter 2 University College, Leicester and King's College, University of London — 39
October 1947–August 1952

Chapter 3 Return to Singapore — 75
September 1952–June 1967

Part 2 — 95

Chapter 4 High Commissioner to India — 97
July 1967–August 1969

Chapter 5 High Commissioner to Malaysia and Return to Academia — 151
August 1969–August 1971 and 1972–June 1977

Chapter 6	Ambassador to the Republic of the Philippines *June 1977–August 1980*	201
Chapter 7	Return to Malaysia *September 1980–April 1988*	231
Chapter 8	Retirement in Singapore *1988–present*	277

INTRODUCTION

"*There's a divinity that shapes our ends,*
Rough-hew them how we will –"
Hamlet, Act V Scene II

IN THE COURSE of my long life I have found how true this observation is, because the most important events in my life were never planned.

Motivated by my love for English literature, I wanted to be a school teacher and prepared myself by attending Raffles College, acquiring a diploma after three years. The extra year I spent studying for an education diploma was disrupted by the Japanese attack on 8 December 1941 which prevented the examination from taking place. I was awarded a war diploma instead. I was inspired by my good teachers, both local and American, at the Anglo-Chinese School (ACS) in Ipoh. I taught at the Choon Guan School (now called Presbyterian Boys) for a year before leaving for England. On my return from England I taught at two secondary schools, Bartley and Victoria, for three years. I was then unexpectedly asked by Professor Roy Morrell, head of the Department of English at the University of Malaya in Singapore, to help out by tutoring final-year undergraduates part-time because one of his lecturers had suddenly quit. Subsequently I was offered a lectureship although I never applied for it.

That I became a diplomat was accidental. When Singapore separated from Malaysia in 1965, there was a shortage of matured and qualified people to head its diplomatic missions abroad. I was invited to be Singapore's first high commissioner to India in 1967. Apart from the privilege to serve Singapore, I accepted the appointment because I was acquainted with several People's Action Party (PAP) cabinet ministers and I did not want to let them down. Subsequently, after the 1969 May 13 riots in Malaysia, I was asked to return at very short notice to move to Kuala Lumpur. This was because Tun Abdul Razak, who was a good friend of mine both at Raffles College and in England when we were students, was then the deputy prime minister of Malaysia.

I felt it my mission to do what I could to iron out difficulties and resolve misunderstandings between the governments of Singapore and Malaysia. Both prime ministers appreciated my honest efforts though one or two of Singapore's ministers were critical of my attitude. They thought I was too sympathetic towards the Malaysians. As I had been born in British Malaya, brought up and educated there, it was natural that I should love the country although I owed allegiance to my adopted country Singapore and served her as high commissioner. Tunku Abdul Rahman, who knew I was born in Alor Star, Kedah, wondered how I had become Singapore's high commissioner to Malaysia. He would, from time to time, tease me about it and even called me a "traitor" in jest.

Professor D.J. Enright suddenly resigned from the University of Singapore's Department of English in 1970. I was asked to return home to head the department. Subsequently in June 1977, I was again recalled by the Ministry of Foreign Affairs and posted as ambassador to the Republic of the Philippines.

The changes in my career from being a school teacher, university lecturer and head of the Department of Extra-Mural Studies to being the high commissioner to India and to Malaysia and later head of the University's Department of English were followed by two more diplomatic stints, in the Philippines and once again in Malaysia.

All these career moves took place without any planning on my part. I thought that my experience both as a teacher at school and university, and especially my experience as a diplomat, would be of interest, hence this book.

I have already written an account of my happy school days at the Anglo-Chinese School in Ipoh and elsewhere, my years in Raffles College before the Japanese invasion of Malaya and Singapore and up to the fall of Singapore in a book entitled *A Time of Fireflies and Wild Guavas* (Federal Publications, 1995). With this book I continue with my life as a farmer in Cameron Highlands during the Japanese Occupation (1942–1945). I left for England in 1947 to continue my education, taking up the Queen's Scholarship awarded to me in 1941. By sheer coincidence, Professor L.F. Casson, who had taught me at Raffles College, got me into King's College, University of London when I was placed in University College, Leicester because places at Cambridge University — where Queen's Scholars were supposed to be admitted — were reserved for soldiers returning from the war. The war interfered in my career and life. Indeed the war changed my whole life, as it did for many others of my generation.

During my four diplomatic postings I had the privilege of meeting many eminent political personalities and the pleasure of becoming friends with some of them.

In India, besides Prime Minister Indira Gandhi, Presidents Zahir Husain and Shri V.V. Giri as well as Deputy Prime Minister Moraji Desai, one of my most enjoyable calls was on the then Chief Justice of India, Mohamad Hidayatullah, who obtained his first degree in English literature at Cambridge. He later returned to England to read law and was eventually appointed a judge. But English literature remained his first love.

Prominent among my diplomatic colleagues were Chester Bowles, American ambassador on his second tour of duty in India, the scholarly Prince Prem Purachatra of Thailand and Octavio Paz, the dean of the diplomatic corps, who was a famous Mexican poet. Octavio Paz was awarded the Nobel Prize for Literature in 1990.

In Malaysia, the friendship of former schoolmates and Raffles College graduates was of great help to me in my two difficult years there. Apart from Tun Razak, Tan Sri Kadir Yusof, attorney-general, Tan Sri Raja Mohar, secretary-general of the Ministry of Commerce and Industry, and Tan Sri Ghazali Shafie (from London days) for instance, were very helpful and always accessible when I needed to see them. During my second term,

I met the Tunku and Tun Hussein Onn regularly. Both former prime ministers in their retirement were approachable, so I was able to listen to their views from time to time and report back their comments on the political and economic developments in Malaysia. The most important friendship I made was with Daim Zainuddin as he was always helpful and informative. He was the best source on the intricacies of Malaysian politics that a diplomat could have.

In the Philippines, General Carlos Romulo, the foreign secretary, made no secret that the Association of Southeast Asian Nations (ASEAN) ambassadors were a favoured lot. He was the soul of wit and humour. He had a distinguished career representing his country at the United Nations. He was the greatest Filipino I was privileged to meet. Other important personalities, besides President Ferdinand Marcos and his beautiful wife Imelda, were the fearless Cardinal Jaime Sin and General Fidel Ramos. But one of the most fascinating personalities I met during my three years in the Philippines was the famous guerrilla leader Luis Taruc, commander-in-chief of the Hukbalahap (The People's Anti-Japanese Army, called "Huks" for short), who served 15 years in prison after his surrender which had been negotiated by a young journalist, Benigno Aquino, during the administration of President Ramon Magsaysay.

My second term in Malaysia lasted more than seven years, the longest in my diplomatic career. Many important events and some very serious and sensitive issues occurred that affected relations between the two countries. I had chosen to focus on those that had a significant impact, directly or indirectly, on bilateral ties. Two incidents proved to be the most difficult in my diplomatic career: the Israeli President Chaim Herzog's state visit to Singapore in November 1986 and Minister of Trade and Industry Brigadier-General (Res) Lee Hsien Loong's remarks about Malays in the Singapore Armed Forces (SAF) in early 1987, created a furore across the Causeway causing youths from the United Malays National Organisation (UMNO), in particular, to be up in arms. The severe reactions had a detrimental impact on bilateral ties.

My memoirs cover more than 46 years of my life, from 1942 to 1988 when I retired. I wrote these memoirs over a long period, on and off. Fortunately, I wrote extensively about the early years, and the first and second diplomatic postings while memories were still fresh. After 1996, the manuscripts were revised and I went on to write about the later postings to the Philippines and Malaysia.

By the time I started writing about my return to Malaysia, it was more than 12 years since I retired. I thus had to rely on press reports and other information sources in order to recount events and issues affecting Singapore — Malaysia relations with accuracy. These sources also served as a trigger, helping me recall incidents and the part I played in helping to strengthen the ties between the two nations.

I had the rare honour of representing Singapore during the years 1969 to 1971 and 1980 to 1988, when the first four Malaysian prime ministers — Tunku Abdul Rahman, Tun Abdul Razak, Tun Hussein Onn and Tun Dr Mahathir Mohamad — held office.

Part 1

Chapter 1
Cameron Highlands, Malaya
March 1942–August 1945

3

Chapter 2
University College, Leicester and
King's College, University of London
October 1947–August 1952

39

Chapter 3
Return to Singapore
September 1952–June 1967

75

Chapter 1

Cameron Highlands, Malaya
March 1942–August 1945

I LEFT SINGAPORE for Cameron Highlands in early March 1942 after seeing my English father before he went into internment during the Japanese Occupation. I returned to Cameron Highlands to be with my Indian mother and younger brother Leonard. My sister Margaret had left earlier for India. My father owned a small estate of about 60 acres (24 ha), a quiet retreat about a mile (1.6 km) from the main road and bounded by the mountain stream, Sungei Habu, which he had kept clean of weeds and whose banks he had reinforced by rock walls at the bends, made of stones taken out of the stream. All day and night, the sound of the stream fell on one's ears, a pleasant lullaby along with the jungle noises of the night. My father, who found social intercourse invariably difficult, found peace in the tranquil atmosphere of the green forested hills of Cameron Highlands.

Some parts of the land my father had leased from the government were used to grow tea, while other parts were given to vegetable and fruit cultivation. Grapefruit, oranges, strawberries, grapes and South American seedless guava abounded; the grapes failed and the strawberries were not sweet and mostly eaten by birds. He also experimented with a variety of temperate vegetables including kohlrabi, asparagus, swedes and turnips. But in the main, he grew cabbages, carrots and the more easily saleable Chinese cabbages and tomatoes. He had a thriving vegetable business, dispatching weekly baskets to Alor Star (Alor Setar) in the north, to Ipoh and Kuala Lumpur and even to Singapore, I think. His pet buffaloes which he loved had been sold by my mother who feared the Japanese would confiscate them but a cow was wisely retained for milk.

The Japanese had stuck a notice in red on the house claiming it as "Enemy Property" along with the whole estate but had removed nothing, not even the thousands of books in the house. This gave me time to hide the most valuable books before removal lorries arrived to cart away the symbols of Western culture! However, unlike the front line troops in Singapore who destroyed many of the books in the Raffles College library, the Japanese civilian administration merely deposited the books in the Ipoh town library.

The Japanese came no more than three times to the house in all the years of occupation, chiefly because they feared getting off the main road and exposing themselves to the dangers of an ambush. For a few months, one or two officers made use of the Battensby bungalow nearby to which they brought their Chinese mistresses, but they soon gave it up as a risky business because of communist guerrillas and perhaps the ghost! (The bungalow's former owner, Battensby, together with his wife and his father, were killed when the Japanese bombed the Tapah Road railway. The story was that the house was haunted. The ghost of the old man walked around at night.) On one of their visits to my house, I was fortunate to be found literally labouring in the field where I had been planting sweet potatoes. I came up to the house in singlet and shorts, *changkol* (a type of hoe) in hand, mud on my feet and sweat on my face. This certainly impressed the Japanese who believed I was contributing heartily to their Co-prosperity Sphere. I was certainly producing food, and though in the first few weeks my palms blistered and my arms ached, life in the open was a healthy one and I was never ill — not for a single day — what with plenty of work and a simple diet. It was food growing that saved me from being interned every time there was a round-up of Eurasians — the final occasion being in 1944 when all 'direct descendants', meaning all those whose fathers were English, were taken down to Singapore and locked up in Changi gaol. I was packed and ready but no one came to collect me. Two of us, Patrick Bewsher and I were, I think, the only so-called 'direct descendants' who never saw the inside of a prison.

We used to meet at least once a month, Pat and I, to compare notes, share a meal and chuckle over his father's collection of *La Vie Parisienne* magazines. There were also good friends in the neighbouring Veterinary Sanatorium for racehorses belonging to Captain Bloxham, who had left for England before the Japanese arrived, leaving "Doc" John Rodgers, a friendly Indian in his thirties, in charge. Doc was a well-known veterinarian who perforce also became the local doctor in the area. "What's good for the horses is good for men — in smaller doses, of course" was the basis of his free medical practice. Many of us farmers in the area remain indebted to him for his help during those years. He was joined by Tommy Acton from Ipoh, a phlegmatic young man of great charm whose coolness in all situations helped us to bear the worst with equanimity. Both Pat and Tommy had Siamese (Thai) mothers. We trusted each other completely, and the three of us spent many evening hours talking of the future. They made the task of survival that much more pleasant. Towards the end of the war came Cecil Wong and his family from Singapore to take refuge in the Highlands. In his house I enjoyed not only the good company of his parents and of his lovely friend Kismet Fung, but also had a taste of genuine cake in 1944 when wheat flour was more difficult to acquire than diamonds even on the black market. I used to sell eggs and milk to Cecil who also paid to have a whole hillside cultivated with sweet potatoes in 1945. Before he could harvest his crop, the Japanese had surrendered.

 I took to chicken rearing with gusto as I was fond of birds from my childhood days. My mother had invariably reared a few hens which I found friendly except when they were brooding over their eggs. They were also fierce in defence of their fluffy chicks. Doc Rodgers presented me with a few Rhode Island Reds and a cockerel which gave me a good start. Using local hens to hatch the Rhode Island eggs (Rhode Island Red hens rarely go broody as they have been bred to be layers and table birds), I built up a small flock of about 30 layers which were fed on *jagung* (maize) and sweet potatoes. These I kept confined in a large pen to protect them from "ranikets", a dreaded killer of a disease which can wipe out a flock in a few days. Soon I got to know most of the pullets and decided to name them after all the girls I had known in Raffles College. The prettiest pullets were named after the best looking "chicks", so I had my Rosie, Lan Eng, Swee Lian, Nellie, Chanlet, Swee Eng and so on. I noticed that the rooster shared my taste in beauty and bestowed his favours as I would have done myself had I been born a cockerel! It is true that normally only male birds are clothed in resplendent feathers, but a pullet can be delicately shaped and attractive with its bright red comb and wattles, its yellow curved beak and brilliant eyes.

The intelligence of chickens is, I think, underrated and even the intelligence of other birds and beasts is only recently being scientifically studied and evaluated. Man in his arrogance, assuming that he is the pride of creation, has been content to kill, eat and feel superior at will. Chickens, I discovered, can be extremely friendly, sometimes mischievous, and they easily recognise you and come when you call. Anyone who has got to know chickens will never be able to breed battery hens, which are confined in small cages and treated as laying machines, or produce table birds, rushed from egg to slaughter in a few weeks, never having felt the sun or run on the green grass. Poets have bemoaned the inhumanity of man to man, but few have spared a thought for the cruelty of man to the birds and animals in the wild or when domesticated. I once read a moving passage in a book by the South African author Laurens van der Post entitled *The Night of the New Moon* in which that sensitive writer observed, "I had often in the past seen dumb domestic animals in Africa so aware of the secret intent of the people who had bred and reared them and earned their trust that they could hardly walk, knowing they were being led to a distant place of slaughter." But of course, man must deny this as he cannot otherwise justify his taste for beef. I have often thought that actual scenes of the slaughter of animals on cinema and television screens are likely to lead to a significant decrease in meat eating. Soya bean steak can be eaten with a good conscience and science can make it taste excellent as well as ensuring that it has all the nutritive values. I hope this will happen one day because of the sheer impossibility of feeding the world's multiplying mouths.

But to return to the Japanese Occupation. The day began with feeding the chickens and ducks and setting off to the field after breakfast, *changkol* in hand. I shall always remember the fresh smell of the earth in the morning sun as the mist lifted and how happy I was to see that the seeds had sprouted into tiny leaves above ground. How carefully I scratched round the young shoots to dig up bugs that could decapitate them. I crushed the pests as I would have liked to crush the Japanese! In 1942, I could grow very large cabbages (Chinese and English) and a variety of other vegetables. But the prices were low. Once, thinking I might get a better price in Tapah, which was more than 30 miles (50 km) away and nearly 4,000 ft (1,200 m) lower at the foot of Cameron Highlands, I cycled down with a big load. It was easy most of the way down but I got only a couple of cents more per kati (approximately 625 g). It wasn't worthwhile as the way back uphill was back-breaking. Nightfall caught me still some miles from home plodding up in a gathering misty darkness and riding whenever the gradient was not too steep. In the back of my mind there was the fear of encountering a tiger on the hunt, remote though such a possibility was. The darkness of a lonely forest road inspires numerous terrors of the imagination no matter how rational one is. No wonder aborigines dwelling in the jungles fear the spirit of the trees and will not mention the tiger by name for fear that he would materialise! "Lord of the jungle" or "he with stripes" is more respectful and safer if you must voice your fears to a companion. But on this journey I had none to speak to — only my thoughts which kept turning to the king of the jungle. I made up my mind to stand still and not panic should he appear but fortunately my resolution was not put to the test!

One valuable lesson of my experience over the years of manual work was that I understood, as I had never done before, what it was to be a labourer. For the first time, my thoughts turned to the need to revise the whole system of wealth distribution, although it was obvious to me even then that no two people are born equal in intellectual or physical capability though they may be equal in the eyes of God. I was convinced that it was not right that anyone who toiled hard all day as a labourer should earn so little. I had seen Tamil labourers, "coolies" as they were called, earning no more than $15 a month on which they had to support a family and even send some money back to India to their relatives. Most of the time they ate plain rice, salted fish, chillies and brinjals, the vegetables being home-grown. I think it was this experience which made a "socialist" of me after the war and during my student days in England. There I was a passionate supporter of the Labour Party.

Morning was the best time for work whether it was weeding, planting or harvesting, because it usually gets drizzly in the afternoons in the Highlands. On such afternoons I read, rather at random, from my father's rich treasury of books. I recall delving into contemporary issues like the Spanish Civil War but the most pleasurable hours were spent with Thomas Hardy, Anthony Trollope and Charles Dickens, my father's favourite novelists. All their works, along with the comic masterpieces of P.G. Wodehouse, were on the shelves. Hardy certainly suited my melancholy disillusioned mood. I felt the futility of struggling against the unpredictable and arbitrary destiny that shapes one's ends. All my hopes for the future seemed dashed and it had been no fault of mine. Perhaps the "President of the Immortals", as Hardy called him, had designed it that way. I was intrigued by the contrast between the social concern of Dickens and his efforts to rouse his countrymen to reform the factories, the prisons and the law courts, and make the life of the poor better with the placidity of Trollope's interests in England's upper middle class. Dickens used literature to do some good in the world while it entertained and brought him a good income. Subsequently, I came to accept that Bernard Shaw's belief that literature should be functional could be justified. This is especially true for developing countries, I think.

I also kept track of the way the war was going. My father had many good atlases. The best of these I concealed in the chicken coop for fear of a Japanese raid. Once a week I made a trip to Ringlet, the nearest village 4 miles (6 km) away, where the postmaster, a Mr Tara Singh, was no lover of the Japanese, unlike many of his countrymen. Even when the Indian National Army was formed to fight alongside the Japanese in their march to "free" India, he remained unmoved. The only available newspaper was the *Syonan Shimbun*, but even this was good enough to glean the truth from by studying the shifting battle fronts in Europe, Africa and the Pacific. Often I returned home with the paper and studied the positions of the Allied and Axis armies which confronted each other. Through 1942 it was gloomy geography but with the prolonged battle in Guadalcanal in the Solomon Islands, the failure of the Japanese hordes to break through to Port Moresby in New Guinea, and the indecisive battle of the Coral Sea, there were grounds for hope. The Japanese had been halted, at any rate, in their phenomenal advances. Although the Japanese claimed a great naval victory at Midway Island, it became obvious before long that they had lost as they did not take the island. Little did we realise that they had suffered a major disaster with the loss of four aircraft carriers and that the tide in the Pacific had turned. The success of General Montgomery at

El Alamein in North Africa against General Rommel, whose tank corps had got to within 70 miles (110 km) of Cairo, boosted my morale, along with the failure of the great German war machine before Moscow, and later Stalingrad, where it ground to a halt in ice and snow in the face of determined Russian resistance. I was grateful for the military genius of Zhukov, Montgomery and later Eisenhower and MacArthur. Ultimately the future of all of us in Southeast Asia seemed to depend on them.

1943–1945

Sometime in 1943, my agricultural routine was pleasantly interrupted by the arrival of two young girls in their late teens on a fortnight's holiday in Cameron Highlands. Both Vivie and Moira from Ipoh were acquaintances of my good friend Tommy Acton who was then living in the Veterinary Sanatorium. Captain Bloxham's spacious wooden bungalow was occupied by Doc Rodgers and Tommy. The girls shared a room in this bungalow to which I was a frequent visitor as it was within walking distance from my house.

Vivie, the taller of the two girls, was a fair graceful Chinese and Moira was a honey-coloured vivacious Filipina with a glint of mischief in her smiling dark eyes set in a flawless moon face so beloved by the author of the *Arabian Nights*. She had an eye-catching figure, really breathtaking. Her hair, dark and naturally wavy, reached down to her shoulders. Like many Filipinos, she had Spanish blood in her veins and she had charm and an individuality of her own. Her parents had long settled in Malaya. I was instantly attracted to her. It was intoxication at first sight. I sensed that she liked me. In time of war with all its threats and uncertainties, love, or infatuation if you like, blooms rapidly. For me the darkness lifted momentarily and it seemed to be roses, roses all the way. The landscape blossomed into tropical radiance in her presence. I felt that, like Shakespeare's Beatrice in *Much Ado About Nothing*, a star danced when Moira was born. I revelled in her smile and my life shifted into higher gear, into a different exciting dimension in her presence. She insisted that I learn to dance and taught me the foxtrot in Captain Bloxham's sitting room while a 78 rpm record on a small gramophone played a song entitled "Body and Soul" which had a lilting rhythm. The dance steps were not complicated or too difficult and soon I was holding her close enough, but not too close! I had resisted all blandishments to dance in Raffles College but I was in the right mood now!

I took to visiting Ipoh as often as I dared. As a direct descendant of an English father I was considered an enemy alien and had to wear a red armband whenever I left home. However, I discarded it in Ipoh to pass off as an Indian. One of my Malay friends at Raffles College was a magistrate in Ipoh so I stayed with him in his government bungalow. The house was empty while he was away at work so Moira and I embraced with delight. For the first time in my life I lost myself in the delectable curves and subtle lines of the female form, exploring its mysterious convexities and concavities. There is a famous poem of the 17th-century poet John Donne entitled *To His Mistress Going to Bed* which celebrates the joys of love-making in geographical imagery. The poet appeals to his beloved:

> "Licence my roving hands, and let them go
> Before, behind, between, above, below
> My America, my new found land,
> My kingdom, safeliest when with one man manned,
> My mine of precious stones, my empery,
> How blessed am I in this, discovering thee!
> To enter these bonds, is to be free,
> Then where my hand is set, my seal shall be:
> Full nakedness, all joys are due to thee.
> As souls embodied, bodies unclothed must be,
> To taste whole joys …"

And so it proved.

Moira's lovely face and figure reminded me of the famous Renaissance artist Titian's painting *The Venus of Urbino* which is perhaps a perfect image of feminine beauty, especially the appealing face and graceful form. Beautiful women have captured the imagination of painters and poets who have immortalised them in art and poetry all through history. Perhaps there is nothing more beautiful in the world than a beautiful woman.

Dear reader, you must excuse these poetic recollections of moments of happiness and beauty in my life more than half a century ago! Time glorifies the joys of the past and erases its miseries!

We moved around town on a bicycle, me peddling and Moira perched uncomfortably on the cross-bar, my arms around her. She did the steering. One day while we were cycling along chatting happily, we failed to notice a Japanese sentry standing under a tree some distance away. He bellowed at us for passing by without bowing to him. When we drew near at his imperious signal and dismounted he gave me a stinging slap. He tried to snatch the gold chain from Moira's neck but the timely approach of a Japanese officer in his car deterred the sentry. He dismissed us abruptly. This was the only occasion that I was hit by a Japanese sentry. It was a common occurrence in Malaya and Singapore, the soldiers intent on teaching us good Japanese manners. Sometimes a passerby was ordered to hold a large stone for several hours over his head as an alternative punishment for failing to observe Japanese courtesy. Sometimes the victim was beaten up badly. It all depended on the temper of the sentry — the Koreans being far more brutal than the Japanese, as prisoners of war have testified in their stories after the Occupation.

Our relationship was sustained by frequent letters and occasional meetings which brightened my otherwise "vegetable" life, to quote Andrew Marvell.[1] Moira was the only positive factor in a negative existence. I quoted Marvell's poem "To his Coy Mistress" conscious that "Time's winged chariot was hurrying near" so we should "gather our strength up into one ball" if not to make "the sun stand still, to make it run". I discovered the power of poetry, for all women love poems in praise of their beauty. Poetry may succeed when even diamonds fail! Anyway, as I've never been able to afford gems I've had to rely on Shakespeare's sonnets, on John Donne's and Andrew Marvell's love poems. If any beauty I did see which I desired and got, it was thanks to great love poetry.

Strangely enough, both Moira and I knew that the road we were on would lead nowhere as I had a girlfriend who had fled to India and she had a boyfriend who was abroad as well as another older man her parents wished her to marry. All these did nothing to cool our ardour as we seized upon present joys, ignoring the future. In any case, we rationalised, would

---

[1] From Andrew Marvell's 'To His Coy Mistress':
"My vegetable life should grow
Vaster than empires, and more slow"

there be a future? What's to come was still unsure so present mirth had present laughter. Youth was a stuff that would not endure, so we kissed and we cuddled. This mutually happy affair of ours lasted till the end of the war. I am grateful to Moira for dancing into my life and dispelling the darkness with the glow of her beauty during the final years of the war. After the war she married the older man, an engineer, chosen by her parents. She later wrote to me in England that if she had known my Chinese girlfriend would reject me she would have waited for me! It was a touching compliment.

For the last months of the Japanese Occupation I kept a diary which is before me now as I write after over 50 years. It shows the growing excitement day by day as the war drew to an end. I noticed that I had headlined 1945 as "Liberation Year", an accurate forecast. Apart from personal matters and the sale of milk at $5 a bottle on 12 January (milk from my faithful cow which kept the family provided for most of those years), I have written,

> "With the New Year the Allies have launched a terrific offensive in the Pacific and have begun landing in Luzon. The Allied armies are converging on Mandalay in Burma. Yesterday five B29s' flew overhead in formation westwards. Even earlier than this American planes (B24s' and B29s'), like silver pencil streaks in the sky, flew over the Cameron Highlands on the way to bomb Singapore. No interception was ever attempted by the Japs in this area. How overjoyed we were to see the planes!"

Despite my confidence that the war would end soon I noted that I was practical enough to "plant 1,000 cuttings of sweet potato" on the 15th! Just in case things went wrong I suppose. The *Syonan Shimbun* dated 18 January indicated that the final Russian winter offensive had broken into Poland, captured Warsaw and reached a point within 15 miles (25 km) of the German border. "The Germans now face their final and fatal crisis," I predicted, adding that the Germans would be finished by the end of March. Actually they lasted into May. In the Pacific I noted "big air-raids over Hong Kong, China and Philippines coastal areas and Taiwan to isolate Luzon where the advance southward is beginning. In Burma it seems Akyab (now Sittwe) was evacuated on 31 December. Things look very hopeful now."

But hopes were dashed on 4 February when Pat Bewsher and I were summoned to Tapah police station. We both expected to be interned for the rest of the war. I wrote my farewell messages which sound sentimental now, full of self-pity: but the summons turned out to be a fortunate anti-climax. It was a mere roll-call and we returned safe on the 5th by lorry as usual. But we would have been glad to walk back the 33 miles (53 km)!

15 February 1945

By 15 February — always to be a significant day as Singapore had surrendered on that day three years before — there was desperate fighting in Manila street by street, the Japanese making one of their dreaded "to the last man" defences and slaughtering every citizen in sight in the process. Malaya was bombed — as expected — on that day by American planes and again on the 19th. "I hope it will be all over by June down here," I recorded. "Rice has gone up to $2,000 a pikul (and everything has doubled and trebled in price). Dried prawns $40 per kati; pork $20 per kati is the cheapest meat. Poultry is $37 per kati. It seems that over Chinese New Year cabbage was sold at $90 per kati in Ipoh. Normal price $45." It looks as if the Chinese retailers are forever relentless in their exploitation of their fellow men in festive seasons, war or no war! There has been no change in the last 40 years. I am sure this incorrigible habit has disappeared under the Communist regime in China — if so, it should be acclaimed a good thing.

24 February

On 24 February I counted 20 American B29s' overhead and read later that over 130 had bombed Singapore and 60 had flown over Penang. The numbers were certainly impressive. I expected British landings in Malaya after the fall of Rangoon but hoped the Japanese "decide to give up at the Imperial Diet Session now about to begin."

I made only two entries in the diary in March mentioning a party we had in Tanah Rata when my old friend Lim Kean Siew arrived from Penang with his wife and Cecil Wong joined us too. Meanwhile the Japanese bastion of Iwo Jima fell and the Allies crossed the Rhine. No doubt we quietly celebrated the impending end of the war.

6 April

I got news that all "direct descendants" of English parents had been interned in Ipoh. I expected to be summoned and once again packed a bag but nothing happened. Meanwhile we celebrated at Yap Neng Chew's house (he became an engineer and permanent secretary in the Singapore civil service) and at Cecil Wong's and with another friend of mine, Boon Lay, who managed the Shum Yip Leong Tea Estate.

Meanwhile the price of everything went up further — chickens being $50 a kati and a cup of coffee cost $2.50. That was an enormous sum as we used to pay no more than 5 cents a cup before the war.[2] Besides, it was no longer coffee — merely ersatz. "Japanese dollars are rapidly becoming useless. Nothing can stop its slide now," I noted in my diary.

12 April

The death of President Roosevelt on 12 April of cerebral haemorrhage was a blow, although I knew the war would not be affected. But it seemed such a pity that the man who had stood behind Britain in her darkest hours with every support short of actually declaring war on the Germans, and who had brought the United States together in the face of the disaster of Pearl Harbor as Winston Churchill had done for Britain after Dunkirk, should not live to see the victory so nearly within his grasp. Elected for an unprecedented third term as President, Roosevelt has won his place not only in the annals of American history but in the pages of world history. Even the Japanese expressed "profound sympathy". In my diary I sound uncharitable about this, that it was merely evidence that the Japanese government no longer doubted Japan's imminent defeat and that this "is the first instance of chivalry from these skunks in this war".

3 May

The Russians had encircled and broken through into Berlin, something which the Allies could have done even earlier. But they had allowed the honour of capturing the German capital to fall to the USSR. This was a

---

[2] Initially, the Japanese government-issued dollar was at par with the Malayan dollar.

mistake, as was proved after the war by the need for a massive airlift by USA to save the international zones in the city from being starved into subjection by Stalin during the Cold War. "To all intents and purposes the war in Europe is over and now Japan alone faces the world. Severe air-raids on her big cities — already 770,000 houses have been destroyed and three million are homeless. But Japan is determined to fight on fanatically to the inevitable end. Hopeless struggle but one hopes she'll see reason soon … ." This is followed by a list of books I read in which D.H. Lawrence figured prominently.

10 May

"Hitler and Mussolini are dead. The turbulent and fateful years of their power changed Europe into a mass concentration camp and a decisive battleground in which millions of lives have been sacrificed. So this mad dictator Hitler at whose threats the world trembled; whose armies subdued Europe from the Pyrenees to Stalingrad, from Norway to the toe of Italy, where troops fought even in North Africa in a great bid to sever Britain's lifeline the Suez Canal; has been beaten to his knees. No more stab in the back for Germany to excuse defeat, no Marxist-Jewish plotters to blame! Germany has been trounced by the Russians and the Anglo-American Allied troops have swept into Germany from end to end and Berlin has fallen to the Russians. But now the capitalists and the communists who have been thrown together by the threat of Fascist Nazi Germany are growling over what remains of the corpse of the once-dominant power. Who knows what the outcome of this conflict in the offing will be?"

That piece of rhetoric which sweeps aside sentence structure and perhaps grammar reveals nonetheless my feelings at that time. And the prophetic note at the end was sound after all.

13 May

"On 1st May, British troops encircled Rangoon and landed from the sea in the town itself. By now the Burma campaign can be considered over and we are next! Next month I hope there will be landings in the Peninsula itself."

I was to discover after the war that such landings were scheduled for September 1945 and actually took place after the Japanese surrender in

August. Even so I heard it was a mess as landing boats and tanks foundered off Morib and Port Swettenham (now Port Klang). Goodness knows how much slaughter there would have been if the Japanese had manned the beaches.

The 13 May entry goes on: "Admiral Doenitz (Hitler's successor) has made a speech saying, 'all further resistance against the Anglo-Americans is senseless' and ordering surrender but insisting on fighting the Russians hoping against hope that the Soviet and the Allied armies would clash. Though the San Francisco Conference isn't going as smoothly as it should, Poland being a thorny problem, it is unlikely that there will be a trial of strength between the Soviets and the Allies so soon especially as Russia had suffered colossal damage to her industrial regions and massive battles have been fought in her territory. On the other hand the people of Britain and the USA would be unwilling to tackle the Soviets too. Besides, the Americans have still to finish off the Japs. Okinawa is in its last phase and will be captured this month. Tokyo next?"

16 May

"On the 7th May at 2.40 p.m. French time, the Germans represented by the Chief of Staff of the army unconditionally surrendered to the Allies at Rheims thus ending the second great war in Europe after a struggle of 5 years 8 months and 6 days! The Nips held an extraordinary Cabinet meeting and decided to fight on."

The postal services were still functioning as not only did the *Syonan Shimbun* arrive regularly though with news from a week to a fortnight out of date but even letters were delivered. I received one from my good-humoured friend of Raffles College days F.C. or Fred Arulanandom, who hoped, he said, to see me in August. It was his way of telling me that the war should be over by then. Fred sent me a comic poem on his racing misadventures which I found cheerful. Here it is:

TO MY FRIEND M.B.

Now listen, my friend, to my tale of woe
    They're all at the start, all ready to go
'Tis Farad on Courting and Buang on Kit
    To Night Star I plead, my fortune to wit.

They're off, they're gone, they're riding so hard
        They rise on the stirrups — (would I were bard)
To capture the rhythm of hoof upon hoof
        To wisely distinguish a jockey from "goof".

Ye Gods, behold yon mare at the start
        She capers and curvets — she's breaking my heart.
I backed her to gallop — not dance me a jig
        Though rider was frantic, she cared not a fig.

Need you be oppressed with sentiments vile
        What else could I feel, when mare did beguile
Dame Fortune did frown, my tipsters were clowns.
        If boots were but cheaper, I'd make 'em all bounce.

She wasn't a maiden, no not Miss Zipp
        She'd ne'er be Missus, if they took my tip
And Gold Dust were dust, but there was no gold
        Quisana should plough. I often have told.

Younger Ginger I picked, her breed is of Kings
        No horse could have caught her, nor Perseus on wings
My last shirt was on her (with trousers thrown in)
        She sped like Pegasus, by five lengths to win.

Dismal dejection, avaunt to the skies,
        I dreamt of roast chicken and saucy pork pies,
The sport among Kings, 'tis racing I bet,
        The thrills are divine — if they cause no debt.

Objection, objection, the dread word did sound
        My spirits that soared came crashing to ground
In malice and triumph the red cone did ride.
        In spite of my plaint, atop his white bride.

I now feed on "sambal" and "ikan bilis"
        Don't think me rude, if "bene vobis"
I use only water and think it is wine
        Price of mistaking as horses — some swine!

> So closes, my friend, my tale of woe;
> Horses are vile from nostril to toe;
> If you should encounter the horse of the track
> Stick knives in his belly and bombs on his back!

23 May

Very tersely, the papers reported the sighting of two British cruisers and three destroyers in the Straits of Malacca. This was the first time since the surrender of Singapore that British ships had come so near. The Japanese had made no attempt to intercept or bomb them, obviously because they did not have the means to do so. Meanwhile groups of us began to meet more frequently over lunch to talk things over. Our steps were more sprightly in those days, our hearts buoyant with hope. Curiously enough, I have recorded the death of one of my chicks hatched out on 17 May! It must have mattered to me then, trivial though it sounds now.

Churchill's victory speech or excerpts from it were reported. I recorded a stilted tribute to that great war leader in my diary — "among the cords of this Armageddon will be the imprint of Churchill's personality and achievements on the imperishable pages of history. 'In war resolution, in defeat defiance, in victory magnanimity and in peace goodwill'. The first half of his well-known words he has already fulfilled for what greater resolution than his to hold on when the whole of Europe was blitzkrieged to defeat in a few months? And the mighty Luftwaffe raining fire and death over London and wiping out Coventry? He was defiant in defeat but he can be magnanimous in victory in spite of Stalin?"

4 June

Churchill resigned but was asked to head a coalition until the elections in July. This and a couple of raids on Tokyo and Yokohama was all the news.

"The June of our great hope has begun with a dull grey dawn. Is it the lull before the storm or are we being bypassed? I fear it may be the latter. However the British army seems to be heading for Thailand which will certainly abandon the Japanese." Meanwhile Yugoslavia under the leadership of Tito, which had fought so gallantly against the Germans, had marched into Italian territory, Trieste and Carinthia. The Anglo-Americans ordered Tito's partisans to evacuate the disputed areas so as to prevent other such attempts to seize territory. No one could, of course, order the Russians back as became evident soon. I seem to have been naively upset by such immorality. My comment: "Hitler is hardly dead before Tito imitates him. There is no world conscience even after this disastrous war — still the same land-grabbing! Nobody is willing to make any sacrifice; everybody wants to grab whatever can be snatched. What sort of a world peace can we expect at this rate?" Well, I was soon to find out.

6 June

6 June was the first anniversary of the opening of the second front in Europe and 5 June of the evacuation at Dunkirk but all the news I recorded was the hatching of 11 chicks and the planting of two rows of sweet potatoes on the hillside. The price of pork was now $48 per kati, coconut oil $400 a tin; the cheapest salted fish $35 a kati. Most food was unobtainable anyway. But no one was ill-fed as we farmers grew our own food. There was never any danger of starvation in the countryside. Luxuries we had none but there was always enough food. We only feared the Japanese Kempeitai with their unpredictable raids and the Japanese troops.

25 June

We heard of a pamphlet raid on Tapah and of a landing in Brunei, probably because of its oilfields. I began reading H.G. Wells' *The Outline of History* and noted that Wells thought Buddha the greatest of all religious teachers. There is a mysterious entry: "Got something forbidden at a price". I wish I knew what the exciting forbidden thing was that I got. Alas! I cannot remember. I sold a couple of piglings for $7700 and some rabbits. I must have made quick use of the money as I had no doubt that the Japanese military currency would soon be valueless.

9 July

By then I read of a landing in Balikpapan in Borneo as well as the fall of Okinawa. We had several little parties, mostly at Cecil Wong's house. His parents had stocked up some tinned food and flour. There were slices of genuine cake and even some cocoa to drink in July 1945!

From the middle of July we Cameron Highlanders began to worry, and the rich evacuees from Singapore and Penang made preparations to leave in hurry. The Japanese had begun to dig defensive positions along the hill road and to fortify the highlands. Convoys of 150 to 300 lorries laden with rice began to arrive in Tanah Rata. It was obvious that the Japanese had decided that Cameron Highlands would be a good strategic position to make a last stand though it seemed to me that it would undoubtedly be bypassed by any invading army and mopped up later. Besides, the communist guerrillas as well as Force 136 would harass them. However, this was no consolation to us as the Japanese were certain to wipe out the local population when the action began, as they had done elsewhere. My family had nowhere to go so we decided to stay put and watch developments.

There were rumours of allied landings reminiscent of the days before Singapore fell. Only now there was much more likelihood of their being true. Ducks and chickens were slaughtered to celebrate every rumoured landing and even pork became more easily available as pig farmers panicked when the Japanese announced the registration of pigs! They feared the animals would be confiscated. "The wholesale massacre of livestock is going on all round. Soon there will be nothing left to kill," I noted.

12 August

The most sensational piece of news on 12 August was that the Russians had invaded Manchuria on the 8th after the Potsdam Declaration signed by President Truman, Churchill and Chiang Kai Shek. The Japanese declared that the Russians hadn't signed it. The headline which was an understatement announced the invasion as a "Violation of Borders".

"And so with this momentous event we wonder where Nippon will still insist on battling to the bitter end. One little chap against the world! Courage born of desperation and what fanatical courage! Night after night their cities are razed to the ground by American bombers from Okinawa and Iwo Jima as well as from aircraft carriers. The Pacific coast of Japan is now patrolled by the US Navy and no doubt the inland sea of Japan has more American submarines than fishes. How long can they hold out and go down fighting?

All her glories, triumphs, spoils shrunk to this little measure! From the pinnacle of victory and glory to the depths of defeat. Still she may act in character and choose death with defeat. If so we may die too!"

In the middle of all these I received news that my friend Kwan Sai Kheong had got married. He arrived in Ipoh and came up to see me with his wife Polly for a few brief hours. I think they stayed the night and left by bus the next day. What an adventurous thing to do at such a critical time!

21 August

"Just as suddenly as the Japs began to fortify these hills last month they began to leave it. Strong rumours of Japanese surrender. First it was supposed to have been on the 10th, next the 12th and finally the 15th. It seems Nippon sued for peace on the 10th and an Imperial Rescript ended the war on the 15th. This is the most powerful rumour so far and one most likely to be true because:

(a) The Americans used an 'atomic' bomb on Hiroshima, wiped out the whole city at one stroke. The *Nippon Times* claimed that the whole population, men, women and children, young and old, were snuffed out without a chance of lifting a finger either in defence or defiance. Worse than poison gas, etc. Descending by parachute it exploded in the air with a hitherto unheard of pressure and intense heat.
(b) Russians are advancing rapidly in Manchuria.
(c) Local communities have been holding open meetings in celebration. The Japs have taken no steps to arrest anyone.
(d) All fortifications, tunnellings have ceased and labourers have returned to their homes.
(e) The more important Japs have left Camerons.
(f) Someone from Singapore and others from Kuala Lumpur have arrived with news of the surrender. Apparently some blokes working in the Jap Propaganda Department listening to foreign broadcasts heard of the surrender and were detained in their office

overnight. But I noted that lorries were still bringing up rice though there were only a few of them. Japanese troops were moving about freely — perhaps to keep the peace till the arrival of the British."

We did not yet know for certain that the Japanese had surrendered on the 15th. My good friend Yap Neng Chew and his family left with Lim Boon Keng (later to qualify as a doctor) and Tan See Lai (well-known later as a broadcaster). He left me some chickens and a tremendous present of 150 katis of rice which was unobtainable then although the Japanese had plenty of it. I have not repaid him yet, having forgotten the whole thing! These three whom I taught English to regularly I became very fond of. They gave me the feeling that I was being a useful person. It is such a pleasure to know that all of them have done very well indeed in Singapore.

What with Yap's farewell gifts I organised a party for friends. We missed Yap. We talked. "The question of surrender is uppermost in our minds. Always striving to convince ourselves that it must be true but ever haunted by fears and doubts. The agony of three and a half years is now crowned by this dilemma. If only we could be sure! To doubt is hell. To know the worst would be but little better. I suppose there is no way to be sure till the first British soldier appears!"

I went down to Ringlet. Joy! "A grin on every face; joy abounding, joy resplendent. Happy laughter in the coffee shops and cheerful loud chatter. Happiness on every face except a couple of sad Japs — pictures of dejection and misery. Today I begin to live again after merely existing for three and a half years. Today I feel really happy once more after these many depressing months. Today we all rejoice that we have survived this horrible war without having to endure the holocaust of another Battle of Malaya. Finest piece of luck this is. Met many labourers in the ecstasy of their drunkenness feeling like conquerors about to regain their lost world of unlimited rice meals! What a burden off their shoulders and mine."

22 August

The next day I walked back to Ringlet again to find that the Japanese soldiers had arrested three of their own local informers at the request of the communists or "hilly-billies" as I called them. The hilly-billies were an odd assortment of men, some in jungle-green uniform and some in nondescript shorts and shirts. Armed with a variety of weapons, they were all over the place trying to look impressive. The informers were tried in the open with everyone who knew them giving evidence. It was a Chinese "kangaroo court" which I attended for an hour to hear the denunciations. The atmosphere was almost joyful as the reality of the inevitable death sentences had not been really grasped by the crowd. I left early. My diary reads "looks as if the informers will be beheaded or shot. They are guilty I guess and have probably deserved even the death penalty, but still there should be a proper trial." Apparently many informers have been killed by irate mobs in some of the towns and villages of Malaya as soon as Japanese troops were withdrawn to their barracks. Those of us who knew of the tortures inflicted by the Kempeitai on their victims could have no sympathy for the informers. I never heard one word on their behalf in those days.

I returned home for lunch with Pat Bewsher and "opened my last tin of corned beef to celebrate. How delicious it tasted straight from the tin." I am amazed now that it hadn't gone bad over the years. It had been carefully hidden in the ceiling.

24 August

"Visited Cecil Wong and then on to Ringlet. News that the communist guerrillas had asked the Japs to give up their arms to them and to join them in a common front against the British!" I do not know how far this is true but this was perhaps the reason for the sudden appearance of six lorry-loads of troops guarded by two machine guns fore and aft and with rifles on either side. That was enough to depopulate Ringlet in an instant. All the hilly-billies vanished too. Later in the evening the same lorries descended from Tanah Rata fully loaded with soldiers looking bellicose instead of being crestfallen. I was reading a copy of *The Voice of Malaya*, a communist paper posted on the wall of a shop from behind a small crowd which partially blocked my view. On the appearance of the lorries, I was left alone to read at leisure the obviously distorted communiqués from New Delhi and Moscow along with terms of the Potsdam Declaration and a eulogy of the Soviets. It was all in fairly good English — by an old hand at communist propaganda.

In Ringlet I managed to look at a copy of *Syonan Shimbun* dated 18 August containing the Imperial Rescript ending the war issued on 14 August 1945 and countersigned by the Cabinet. The Son of Heaven (Tenno Heika or Emperor of Japan) after profound thought had decided to take the extraordinary measure of ordering his government to discontinue hostilities because after four years of fighting and in spite of the all-out efforts of the fighting forces and of the civilians, the situation could not be said to be necessarily in Nippon's advantage (surely a masterpiece of understatement). Anyhow from the first Japan had never begun the war for self-aggrandisement but self-preservation! However, now the whole world was against her. Besides, the Americans had commenced using a most cruel bomb unprecedented in atrocity and capable of incalculable damage. To continue the war would mean the final obliteration of Nippon and of human civilisation. Nippon was grateful to the East Asian nations for their cooperation and extremely sorry to let them down. But the Emperor would one day have to account for the slaughter of his dear subjects to the spirits of his hallowed ancestors, and so in the interest of everybody Nippon would have to give up the struggle.

I leave out the caustic comments I made in the diary on this Imperial Rescript.

Meanwhile the Malayan Peoples' Anti-Japanese Army (MPAJA) went on their rounds making enforced collections for their cause. The evacuees from Singapore were worried and very indignant even though the sums yielded up were merely banana dollars. On 25 August, a red flag with three yellow stars — the flag of the MPAJA — was hoisted over Ringlet. A dozen raggedly dressed Chinese stood around the police station rather bewildered as to what to do. Some faced the road and some the police station. They were armed with tommy-guns and rifles. The leader announced that he was there to maintain peace and order till the British arrived and asked for our cooperation. He then proceeded to denounce the British for past ill-treatment of the Asiatics especially the long hours imposed on workers. He claimed that he and his men would fight "a war of words" against the British but said that no "lethal weapons" would be used. He explained the wholesale looting of gunny-bags of rice from the unguarded Japanese stores as a precautionary measure on behalf of the people in case the British refused to distribute rice! Actually they were stocking up arms and food supplies for the inevitable revolutionary struggle which was to break out within four years of the Japanese defeat. In announcements to the people, the Japanese authorities asked for calm and warned against "armed bandits" — an obvious reference to the communist guerrillas — but they did not take any action against them.

In my diary I noted impatiently, "The communists are getting more and more high-handed as the days pass and the British are coming at the usual snail speed. Today several people were arrested including a Dane. Looks as if there may be a bit of a fight after all when the British arrive. Never before did we realise what a nuisance these armed terrorists could be. In our hatred of the Japs we rejoiced to find the bandits ambushing them but the Japs are having the last laugh now. They are lawless, arbitrary and oppressive. Damn the slow British troops who have missed the psychological movement of confusion before these irregulars organise themselves. No sooner does the devil leave us than the deep blue sea engulf us!"

29 August

"Rumours of British troops arriving very strong. But Ringlet is very quiet. Red flag with three yellow stars still fluttering over the police station which is occupied by MPAJA. Today is set for the trial of Hun Cheong whose shop and all its contents, mostly provisions, were 'confiscated' the day before yesterday. People on the way to Ringlet were turned back by the armed bravados while they looted Ng Teong Kiat's shop and the assistant manager's house of everything (Ng owned a large tea estate and the shop supplied his workers). The shop and house were shut and a notice proclaims that they belong to the MPAJA."

Some newspapers arrived with the news of a landing in Tokyo on the 28th by the Americans while the Japanese Emperor ordered demobilisation. Singapore was being prepared for the handing over. There were strong rumours that the Japanese generals had considered defending Singapore and Malaya "to the last man" despite the Emperor's orders. They had been persuaded by Count Terauchi — Commander of the Southern Expeditionary Army Group — to desist. The founder of the Indian National Army, Chandra Bose, was reported to have been killed in an air crash in Formosa. So a very brave patriot who backed the wrong horse came to his end, but without a doubt he had made his contribution to India's freedom from the British. A speech of Chiang Kai Shek's was also reported referring to the ultimate independence for Thailand, Indo-China and Burma; Hong Kong would apparently be returned to the British as a colony. Meanwhile the Russians had cut right across Manchuria into an area north of Peking.

31 August

"Invited to visit a communist camp two miles (three km) in the interior of Bertram Valley — the bait is the offer of some free rice. Saw tents of parachute canvas, a group bathing in the river and another well-armed lot with automatic rifles and grenades in jungle-green but with canvas shoes and some with boots. All look very fit." I was told by some civilians who were there that someone had been shot the previous day after a "fair trial". The accused had been guilty of showing the Japanese military police the way to a farm and as a result the farmer who was arrested never returned. Many friends of the accused gave evidence that he was a good man who had not cooperated with the Japanese. He had been merely foolish and he was not an informer. Nevertheless the captain who judged the case passed the death sentence on the grounds that the accused's action had caused the loss of life so his life was forfeited. An eye for an eye kind of justice! Besides there was no prison and the captain was determined not to let the accused escape scot-free. I think this sort of "trial" was conducted all over Malaya in the interim between the surrender of the Japanese and the reoccupation of the country by the British. There were rumours that the British had already landed in Singapore but as we had no radios there was just no way of knowing anything for sure. I concluded my diary entry for 31 August thus: "End of historic August 1945! The end of the most terrible war; the end of the Fascists and all their tyranny! Long life to reborn Democracy! May there be no more wars! At any rate may I never live to endure another one!"

3 September

"Anniversary of Britain's declaration of war against Germany in 1939. Peace at last. Today the guerrilla Force 136 arrived with a few white soldiers in full uniform! One English officer was bearded and all wore black caps with the sign of the skull and cross-bones, just like pirates. Lots of Chinese soldiers in smart uniforms. Trumpets were sounded for a parade. A few lorries of unarmed Jap soldiers were turned back to Tanah Rata, not being allowed to pass through Ringlet. Couldn't help pitying the forlorn, woebegone devils. How bitterly they must feel their defeat. The proud now humbled in the dust! A large crowd surged around in the village as a couple of white soldiers got out of an old car, accompanied by a Chinese in uniform. They got out, ignored the reception committee (mixed lot) and marched up to the shops. Then they took a look at some downcast Japs; quite obviously both these white men were enjoying themselves, being the cynosure of all eyes but I was not impressed by all this. Neither was Cecil. So we returned home — just as well for soon afterwards heavy rain fell."

5 September

"Celebration day in Ringlet organised by the communists with the agreement of Force 136. Two of the British officers spoke. Captain Grant who gave a brief review of the war said that he had seen action in Italy and France. He had been dropped by parachute in Bidor (near Tapah) on April 28th and had made his way up by jungle tracks to Bertram Valley. He had obtained arms and supplies from the guerrillas. He avoided politics but made a casual reference to the dissimilarity of his politics with that of the communists. The other bloke, a doctor, spoke briefly.

Met an absolutely charming Chinese girl at the meeting. On the way back we were stopped at the police station by the communist guards but the British officers came along and saw us through. Said Captain Grant, 'Tell these fellows that I'm in charge and I'll take responsibility.' First visible clash. Hint of future trouble. There was no need to stop us — just a test or challenge I suppose to see whether the white men would react. They did, quite rightly I think. Spent the night at Cecil's."

17 September and beyond

It was only on 17 September, a little more than a month after the surrender, that the first regular troops arrived — five members of the Berkshire

Yeomanry artillery unit. I chatted with one of them. He told me of the devastation caused in Britain by the V1 and V2 flying bombs or "pilotless" aircraft. He gave a graphic description of the squadrons of planes "darkening the sky" on their way from Britain to bomb Germany. He had landed on the beaches of Port Swettenham and although unopposed, his unit had lost a couple of guns, he confessed. This English soldier was a simple, unpretentious fellow, happy that he had been spared the fighting, and like all honest soldiers, he had no delusions about the heroics of warfare. Perhaps he had read the war poems of Owen, Sassoon and Rosenberg in school. George Bernard Shaw in his delightful play *Arms and the Man* written in the 1890s had wittily debunked "fearless heroes" and the romantic illusions people who have never had any experience of battle, have about war. Along with Bertrand Russell, he had gone to prison for speaking against Britain's involvement in the First World War. Despite war propaganda it would not have been easy for an educated man to charge into battle like the foolish Sergius in *Arms and the Man*. Nevertheless, he would have to go, however reluctantly, to defend his country, his freedom or "democracy" when ordered to do so because history brings forth ambitious conquerors at regular intervals, who cannot resist the lure of power. Almost invariably "greatness" in history books is associated with power so empires have been built in Asia and Europe only to decay and be destroyed by other conquerors after an average of 200 years or so.

Despite such thoughts I was grateful that this soldier had come far from his native land to drive back the Japanese, and hopefully to restore the British Empire to its glory and continue the exploitation of Malaya's resources, but incidentally also to remove the constant threat of imprisonment and death which I had to endure under Nippon. For three-and-a-half years, we had lived in fear — fear of informers, of swoops and searches at 3 a.m., fear of speaking one's mind except to one's closest friends and even then only after furtive glances over the shoulder. For arrest meant medieval tortures by the Kempeitai, perhaps to be stripped and suspended by the thumbs until beaten into unconsciousness, perhaps to have gallons of water forced down one's throat and to be jumped upon or be subjected to a hundred and one other cruelties. Japanese methods of extracting confessions were brutal and usually purely physical unlike the methods used by the communists as described in *Darkness at Noon* by Arthur Koestler. Also, the Japanese did not attempt any genocide as the Nazis did when they destroyed millions of Jews in gas ovens specially constructed for the job. Perhaps the Japanese should be given credit for not exercising the ingenuity of the Nazis in mass slaughter.

One is tempted to speculate what would have happened if the Japanese had been more humane and understanding in the territories they had conquered. The way the Filipinos fought alongside the Americans in Bataan and Corregidor is definite evidence of how the Asian could stand by a colonial master if given a chance in life. But the Japanese had swallowed their own propaganda about the oppression in the colonies by the whites, which was not wholly true of the British certainly, though the Britisher, the Dutchman and the Frenchman had no doubt he was a superior being compared to the "native". The Englishman almost always shied away from physical brutality and his courts of justices were notably impartial.

Japanese culture may have been the cause of much of the ill-treatment of prisoners of war as the Japanese considered surrender dishonourable and preferred to fight to the death. They almost invariably died to the last man in action. They could only regard prisoners with total contempt as cowards. In a brilliant and memorable short story called "A Bar of Shadow", Lauren van der Post who spoke Japanese and understood Nippon culture, makes this point. He was himself captured in Indonesia while commanding a guerrilla unit and only barely escaped execution. When a Japanese soldier charged, bayonet drawn, van der Post addressed him in courteous Japanese. The soldier stopped, taken aback! His character and understanding was so profound that a fellow Australian prisoner, Frank Foster, paid this moving tribute:

> "If Christ ever come back to earth, it will be in the form of Colonel van der Post. He saved our sanity and our lives."

I would like to quote also Colonel W.H.T. Nichols who said of him:

> "Such a man in a P.O.W. camp is the equivalent of a host of angels shedding light and strength upon all sorts and

conditions of men who make up the sad community. Many lives were saved, tragedies averted and souls rescued by his activities and ministrations."

Such a great man would naturally have uncommon and profound insights into the human heart. This is evident in "A Bar of Shadow" which is the first of three stories in his book *The Seed and the Sower*.

Van der Post pleaded on behalf of the Japanese war criminals in the trials in Singapore on the grounds that the atrocities had been the result of Japanese beliefs and that it was as wrong to judge them by Western concepts as they had been in judging Europeans by Japanese conventions. But he got nowhere as the spirit of revenge was overwhelming in 1946. It will be a long time before people brought up in different traditions, customs and beliefs understand and tolerate other races enough to live with them harmoniously. But until such time we will never see peace on earth, I suppose.

I had plenty of time to meditate on the meaning of the war I had been involved in and which had changed my life whether I liked it or not. I had made up my mind not to be a passive sufferer any longer and the rout of the white man by the Japanese had removed the myth of the greatness of the British Empire. But first I had to get to Singapore from the outback as it were, and I was impatient to leave Cameron Highlands. I was anxious to find out what had happened to my father in internment in Singapore. I have recorded in my diary how suddenly the newspapers seemed dull reading without the excitement of the war news even though I was overjoyed it was all over.

More British troops arrived to take control of the area. The communists, who as members of the MPAJA had popular support, began to lose favour rapidly because they began to behave like the Japanese. The use of threats and coercion lost them even the farmers who were once their strongest supporters. Of course there was no open display of displeasure as they were armed. But there was a lot of grumbling till the British took over completely. Meanwhile as everyone began to realise that the Japanese currency was useless, there was nothing on sale. Japanese banana dollars chased invisible goods. Many farmers and even workers were caught with several thousand banana dollars on them. We were the wise ones who merely kept a few notes as souvenirs. We heard that in Singapore prices were being fixed as British currency became available. We were told that sugar was available at 10 cents a kati, rice at 90 cents a gantang (6 katis), pork at 40 cents a kati and eggs at 10 cents each.

On 29 September I received news that my father was alive but very ill from dysentery. I made up my mind to leave for Singapore as soon as I could to see him. I had to get hold of some money so I sold rabbits and eggs. I also exchanged eggs with British soldiers for razor blades and cigarettes which my mother smoked. I received a short letter from my father on 3 October asking me to go down to Singapore. Curiously enough I ran out of ink and the last page of my diary is in pencil. It ends: "Last time I'll write in this book. No more diaries! The ink ran dry just now and there is no more in the bottle. Lasted me till I needed it no longer. Tomorrow to fresh fields and pastures new."

I left on 4 October 1945 with Cecil Wong and his family in the lorry they had hired to take them and their household goods to Singapore. I travelled with the goods in the back with Cecil. The British-built roads had held up well through the years of the Japanese Occupation, but the wooden bridges blown up during the fighting and shoddily repaired often collapsed. We were held up for hours at one while repair work went on. But we were patient. The euphoria of release from fear, the sheer joy of freedom and the hope that we could live our lives and pursue our careers again made the time of waiting gallop. Eventually we reached Singapore — 350 miles (560 km) from Cameron Highlands — late in the night.

My first urgent task was to locate my father in the Sime Road internment camp of attap sheds. There he was emaciated, skeletal. His beard had turned white and his grey hair fell to his shoulders. Above his plank bed was a shelf he had built for his books — his great love. Tattered and well-worn, there were about 20 volumes he had collected in camp from his fellow prisoners. The emotional reunion I need not describe. After a short stay in Camerons he left for Britain. The colonial government arranged for all British prisoners of war to recuperate in England for three months which he spent with his brother and sisters in Surrey.

I spent a few days with Cecil and his kind family to whom I remain deeply grateful, before moving to Amber Mansions in Stamford Road where Cheong Weng Choong, my good friend at Raffles College, was staying with his pretty wife. I landed a job at the Raffles Library which was then housed in the museum within walking distance of Weng Choong's flat. My job was simple. The books dumped in huge piles by the Japanese who wished to discourage the reading of literature in English had to be sorted out and arranged on the shelves according to various categories like fiction, biography and travel. I enjoyed reading and I took my time. At the end of the month I received 110 British Straits dollars which smelt new and crisp. I had earned my first pay! I can still recall the thrill of feeling those crisp red 10 dollar notes.

Singapore was under the British Military Administration (BMA) which had its hands full reorganising the island's services. There was no way that the Queen's Scholarship to England that I had been awarded in 1941 could be attended to. So I looked for a more permanent job as a teacher as the schools began to reopen. I met Mr Richards, the principal of Choon Guan English School (now Presbyterian Boys' School) in Koon Seng Road, Katong, who offered me a job. I moved to Geylang where another Raffles College graduate, Kwan Sai Kheong, lived in a terrace house in Lorong 29 with his wife, his mother and younger sister. I bought a second-hand bicycle and, with my bag of two shirts, two pairs of drill trousers and some underwear, cycled to my new "residence". I had a pair of shoes too.

Sai Kheong had been my closest friend at Raffles College so I felt very welcome in his home. At this time, I really needed good friends as I had received an unexpected missive, which struck me dumb, from my Chinese girlfriend who had fled to India before the Japanese conquest declaring very positively that there was no way she could ever marry me. She could never give up her family for me. She had come to this conclusion living in close relationship with her family in India. I was shattered. Next to the fall of Singapore, this rejection was the biggest shock. It is difficult after all these years to understand that I even contemplated suicide. She followed up her letter with a telegram making it clear that her mind was made up and "persuasion" was "useless". Her decision was irrevocable. I remembered that when I saw her for the last time before she left for India she had said, "Maurice if you let me down I'll never believe in a man again!" We had met in the garden of

Holne Chase, the women's hostel in Grange Road, under a frangipani tree in full bloom. The irony of it — fragrant frangipanis frequently blossom in graveyards! Two good friends at that time stood firmly by me and saw me safely through my unhappiness. Kwan Sai Kheong was working in a bank but he soon resigned to become a teacher because he said he never saw the sun as a banker, returning home at 6 p.m. although the bank closed at 3 p.m. for the public. The other was Harry Lee Kuan Yew who, as everyone knows, was destined to attain the pinnacle of power as Singapore's Prime Minister. I had got to know him in Raffles College where, as a freshman in 1940, he came with a reputation for academic brilliance in school and consequently suffered more ragging than usual. He took it all very well. I never participated in any ragging as I found it distasteful. We got acquainted and I visited him occasionally in his house in Norfolk Road where I enjoyed his mother's wonderful cooking.

During the Japanese invasion of Malaya, Raffles College authorities organised medical auxiliary units to attend to casualties of air raids on Singapore. I was made corporal of a unit of four volunteers. Lee Kuan Yew was in my group. When the Japanese captured Johor and began shelling Singapore, it became dangerous to pick up the victims of Japanese bombing and shelling especially in the Bukit Panjang area. So the principal of Raffles College, Professor Dyer, summoned us to assemble in the lower quadrangle. He explained that henceforth rescue missions would be risky, so only those who volunteered would be allowed to go. I stepped forward, Kuan Yew was next and two others offered themselves. The four of us were the last lot to be sent to the Bukit Panjang area after a severe raid.

There were huge craters in the road and several houses were on fire. We were in a Traction Company bus converted into an ambulance with stretchers to pick up casualties. When the bus could go no further we got out and walked into a rubber estate. I noticed an unexploded bomb with its fins above ground in the distance. Kuan Yew at once walked rapidly to inspect the bomb. He had no sense of danger! I had to call him back. We did attend to a girl who had a broken leg and a severe wound in the groin. He dressed her wound and we took her to the nearest aid station which was still manned. When I think back, I wonder why we had so little fear of death at that time. When you are young you never imagine you can die! That is why Britain found that its best fighter pilots were young men little more than 20 years old. At that age death is something that happens to others. You think you are immortal!

During the wretched years I had kept in touch with both Sai Kheong and Kuan Yew. I was in Cameron Highlands where Kuan Yew at one time thought of joining me but changed his mind to stay back in Singapore. Two or three times a week, Kuan Yew used to pick me up from Geylang, at first on his motorcycle and later in his second-hand car. I wasn't happy as his pillion rider as he tended to speed but the car, a large Ford, was comfortable. We generally went to the Chinese Swimming Club for a drink or two, a game of billiards and a lot of conversation. We usually exchanged views on the harsh Japanese rule and the atrocities. We agreed that the British defeat made it essential that we should work towards independence to ensure that we should learn to protect ourselves in the future. We were hopeful that the Labour government in Britain under Clement Atlee would be more sympathetic to the aspirations of former colonies. We felt inspired by the events in India where Mahatma Gandhi and Pandit Nehru were on their way to gaining independence.

Occasionally, we went to Chinatown where one of the food stalls specialised in roast goose of which Kuan Yew was very fond. Sometimes we adjourned to Bedok where by the sea we used to lie on the grass by a concrete machine gun nest to enjoy the moonlight. Once when we arrived at the Chinese Swimming Club a party was in full swing. We were told that it was for members only so I could not be admitted. I suggested that we should go elsewhere but Kuan Yew decided to check whether the party was indeed exclusive. When he found some white men among the guests he insisted that I should be admitted and I was! He would not tolerate any discrimination. I was often at his Oxley Road home for a meal cooked by his mother and a can of beer with his father. Eddie Barker and Hon Sui Sen were occasional visitors at Oxley Road too.

I remain grateful to Lee Kuan Yew for helping me out of my depression for several months at the end of 1945 and part of 1946 before he left for Britain.

Picture 1: MB with Lee Kuan Yew beside Lee Kuan Yew's second-hand Ford, early 1946.

Choon Guan English School

Teaching at the Choon Guan English School was enjoyable as the staff were friendly and helpful. Having lost four years of schooling during the war, the boys were mostly overaged but eager to learn. So far as I can remember, we had three levels (or "standards", as they were known) — 4, 5 and 6. I taught English language and literature in all the classes and enjoyed it. I do not recall a single disciplinary problem. My trusty old bicycle served me well to take me to school which began at 7.30 a.m. and ended at 1 p.m. There were about 30 pupils in each class, all from the Katong, Geylang and Joo Chiat areas.

Once a thief broke into Kwan Sai Kheong's house. There was little to steal but he did pinch one of my two shirts. When my fellow teachers learnt of this, one young lady bought a comfortable brownish shirt and presented it to me!

When I had to leave the school to go to England — as the British administration finally decided in June or July 1947 to let me take up my Queen's Scholarship — my students showed their affection by presenting me with two large leather bags, a watch (they had noticed I had none) and a dozen handkerchiefs! All these I needed and gratefully accepted. I was given many individual and class photographs too.

Many years later, when I had retired from my diplomatic appointments abroad, several of my students who had themselves retired as teachers gathered together to give me a lunch. It was organised by Tan Boon Seng who was very active in community service. He visited me once in Manila to show me photographs he had taken of Filipino psychic healers in action. He was a man of very wide interests despite his rather poor health. I remember well Boon Seng and Felix Lee among my students at Choon Guan English School.

Voyage to Britain

It was in late July or early August 1947 that 28 of us scholars as well as private students sailed on the *S.S. Scythia*, an old Cunard Line ship which was on her final voyage to be broken up. It was no comfort to learn that we were on a wreck of a ship which was considered unfit because there was a great shortage of ships as a result of the depredations of German and Japanese submarines. We slept on bunks several to a cabin but we were well fed or at least we thought so after the privations of the Japanese Occupation. The food was certainly better than what we were to get in Britain, as we were to discover.

We were a happy crowd on the first long voyage of our lives — the longest before had been from Penang to Singapore. We played deck games and gambled on the average daily speed of the ship which was around 24 knots. There were the usual shipboard friendships and mild romances.

Our first long break was in Bombay which was hot and humid in August. We stayed a week to await the departing British troops who were herded in like cattle on the decks. Indian independence was achieved at last after a long and heroic passive resistance led by Gandhi and Nehru. Some of us felt elated that the end of the British Empire in its most prized possession, India, presaged our own independence one day in the future.

Some of us ventured into the city in gharries drawn by underfed skeletal horses. Our great discovery was to find that "Bombay duck" was a salted fish! We thought it was a species of Indian wild fowl, to the great amusement of the Indian waiter who took our orders in a restaurant.

Oh well, we live and learn. Years later in 1968, I had to pay a courtesy call on the Indian governor of Bombay as well as the chief minister as I was Singapore's first high commissioner to India. I got to know the city better — the contrast between its great wealth and its grinding poverty. The chief minister despaired of ever solving Bombay's problems as he said thousands of rural folk flooded into the city every day in search of work. It was not possible to stop this migration in a democratic country.

We were glad to set sail from the humid Bombay port into the Arabian Sea which remained calm all the way to the Suez Canal. It was a slow glide through the canal with the desert, endless stretches of sand to the left of us and to the right of us. The sunset was unforgettable in its colourful splendour. It would take a poet to celebrate its glory. We have some beautiful sunsets in our part of the world but this was something else. For me the Suez sunset was the most memorable part of the voyage to Britain.

We had but little time in Cairo, certainly no chance to visit the pyramids or the temples, wonders of the Egyptian civilisation. One's reaction to the decadence of Cairo was simply, "How are the mighty fallen!" We knew little of the greatness of Egyptian achievement for thousands of years but more of how Moses led the Jews out of Egypt and the biblical plagues that descended on the country. At least Eu Cheow Chye, who loved Shakespeare, remembered Cleopatra whose beauty "beggar'd all description". She captivated Caesar and ruined Mark Antony. Her beauty was such that in Shakespeare's words,

> "Age cannot wither her, nor custom stale
> Her infinite variety. Other women cloy
> The appetites they feed but she makes hungry
> Where most she satisfies."

How rarely do we encounter such a woman!

The Mediterranean was tranquil till we crossed the strategic Strait of Gibraltar into the turbulent Bay of Biscay which made some of us give up our meals and stay prone in our beds.

Liverpool, our port of disembarkation, was dismal on that dark and drizzly morning. The *S.S. Scythia* had seen us safely to our future though she had none. She had survived German and Japanese submarines but was no longer considered seaworthy by the Cunard White Star owners.[3]

The customs officers showed little interest in our belongings as we could hardly have anything to smuggle but they went through the luggage of Singapore's Governor Sir Shenton Thomas' daughter thoroughly and took so long that she missed the train to London. I mention this as we were impressed that the daughter of so important a person as a Governor was given no special privilege such as she would have in Singapore.

St Pancras in London was a depressing, smog-filled railway station — our first impression of London. We were received by Mr O.T. Dussek and his assistant Inche Baharuddin who had hired a minibus to take us to our first temporary residence in Fulham. It was a huge dilapidated building once used as a poor house. Several windows had broken window panes but the dormitory which held our beds were clean. Bed sheets and blankets were provided. It was not much but it was comfortable and less crowded than on the ship.

We ventured out to look around. There were street hawker stalls for tea and snacks. To our surprise the teaspoons were chained to the stalls! This gave us the impression that Londoners were not very honest, but later we found newspaper vendors who left piles of papers for sale while they were not present. Everyone was expected to drop the right coin into a box for each paper he took. Now this was a tribute to the honesty of Londoners.

The long 30-day voyage and the gloomy weather, the bombed buildings and the general impressions of decay depressed us despite the cheery greetings of the cleaning women who addressed us by invariably enquiring, "How are you, love, this morning?" We were homesick and several wanted to return home within weeks of our arrival! The stronger willed comforted their weaker brothers. It wasn't long before we were dispersed to several student hostels in London while waiting to join universities in the provinces.

---

[3] In 1958, the *S.S. Scythia* was delivered to the shipbreakers at Inverkeithing in Scotland. Apparently she continued to serve as a passenger ship until then.

Chapter 2

University College, Leicester and King's College, University of London
October 1947–August 1952

MOST OF THE STUDENTS from Malaya and Singapore who went to the United Kingdom for higher studies after the war were mature, being in their twenties. The Japanese Occupation from February 1942 to August 1945 had robbed us of about four years and it took the British Military Administration (BMA) which succeeded the Japanese about two years to get things organised, so it was not till the second half of 1947 that those of us on scholarships could sail from Singapore to Britain.

The failure of the Malayan Liaison Office in charge of placing scholarship students in British universities like Oxford and Cambridge as was the custom before the war meant that we had to accept whatever was available. So Mr O.T. Dussek, the officer-in-charge, informed me that, although as a Queen's Scholar I should have been admitted to Trinity College, Cambridge like my predecessors, all he could do for me was to get a place in University College, Leicester which offered *external* London degrees! Furthermore, I had to sit for the Inter-Arts examination in three subjects including Latin. I had no choice but to accept this offer. After the loss of five years, I decided that I could not waste any more time.

I was given £100 and a ration book to equip myself with some woollen underwear, a brown Donegal tweed jacket, a mackintosh and a heavy, dark grey overcoat for the onset of my first winter. It was already October 1947, a very pleasant autumnal month with the trees dressed in beauty which presaged a bleak and icy November according to those who had experience of the notorious English weather. Food and clothes were rationed as a result of the war during which Britain had suffered devastating bombings by German planes and much of her merchant fleet had been sunk by enemy submarines. Although we had meat only once a week and could buy only an egg a week, at least we were able to purchase enough warm clothes to survive a winter to which we were wholly unaccustomed, coming from sunny tropical Malaya. As we had endured the Japanese Occupation with its food shortages, the rationing of food did not worry us. We were young and resilient enough. We appreciated that the people of Britain had undergone years of privation during the war as indeed we had under the Japanese. Privations were a part of our lives.

But what surprised me was that I found accommodation on the outskirts of the midland town of Leicester, in a place called Anstey Grange — a grange being a farm with a dwelling house and outbuildings — which had been converted into a boarding house. I was allocated a small but comfortable room. I had to take two buses to reach the university college. This proved a strain in November when bone-chilling winds blasted me on the way to the first of my bus stops. I made up my mind to find more suitable accommodation nearer the college as soon as possible. This I did soon when I got acquainted with two Sudanese students who had found better rooms in the town itself.

Two things I remember about Anstey Grange. One of the boarders was an old English gentleman more than 80 years of age who was seated by the fireside in the common room every night. On one occasion I found him pushing a heavy armchair nearer to the fire, so I got up to help. He smiled and said, "Thank you, young man but I like to do this myself. It keeps me in touch with life. I can feel that I'm still alive!" I began to chat with him and learnt that he had several children settled in different parts of England but he preferred to be independent. He said that he didn't want to be a burden to them. I found this attitude of his interesting as in Asia parents not only expect but consider it a duty of children to look after their parents. I certainly learnt something new.

The other thing was the splendour of the cold morning after a night of heavy snowfall. All the green fields were dressed in one glorious white; the trees stood decorated with endless icicles. It was a scene of beauty — a joy forever. Snow is radiant, glistening in the morning light in the countryside, but it is nothing but mush under your feet in a city like London, though to watch the falling snowflakes through your window blown hither and thither dancing in the wind is a memorable sight. Seated by the radiator glowing with warmth, I witnessed many a scene of dancing snowflakes from a hostel window in Gloucester Road in London. The beauty of an English winter is best appreciated through the windows of a warm and well-lit room! To be caught in the street on foggy winter evenings is sheer misery.

Leicester's University College itself, as I recall it, was pleasantly situated amidst many mature trees. The buildings were unpretentious, being basically functional in 1947. No doubt having achieved full university status later it has expanded significantly over the years. I chose English, history and the compulsory Latin as my "Inter-Arts" subjects. I had to concentrate on Latin which I had wholly forgotten since studying it for my matriculation examinations in 1938. I wrote to Wolsey Hall, a famous Oxford tutorial college, for its short courses in the subject and woke up at five every morning to work at the lessons. Leicester's professor of Latin told me frankly that it was not possible to pass the subject within the academic year of about eight or nine months. However, I managed to get a "B" in the examination, to his amazement, simply because I had no problem with English and history as I had covered the syllabus in these subjects at Raffles College. In fact, I topped the list in history and also scored a first class in English in the first-term examinations.

The professor of history, Dr Jack Simmons, thought I should read history for my honours, as Professor Dyer of Raffles College had also advised me years before. But my heart was set on English literature because of my love for Shakespeare. I got to know Professor Arthur R. Humphreys, the young head of the English Department who was an inspiring teacher. Many years later, when I was head of the Department of English at the University of Singapore from 1972 to 1977, I invited Professor Humphreys to be our external examiner for three years. Later when I was sent abroad as Ambassador to the Philippines he visited me in Manila. My successor, Professor Edwin Thumboo, invited him again to Singapore as visiting professor. He was a brilliant and well-loved teacher.

Sadly, he died of cancer in Leicester in 1992 leaving behind his devoted wife, Jean.

I made friends with an ex-naval officer named Ian Jackson who was older than the average undergraduate. We used to go down to the local pub between lectures on cold wintry days for a tot of rum to warm ourselves up. He was kind enough to invite me to meet his family, with whom I shared the only Christmas I spent in Leicester. It was a very foggy evening, so at times Jackson had to get out of the car his brother was driving, to walk along the pavement with a powerful torch in hand to guide the car. It was quite an experience. Fogs in the later 1940s were common in winter, especially in London where we had to endure them as well as the bitter chill. Later, the use of coke for the heating of homes was banned, so London and other English cities no longer suffer from smog and their buildings are no longer coated with soot. It was so bad at times that the soot penetrated one's nostrils and throat. Shirt collars turned black with dust in a single day. A graphic description of a fog is that of Charles Dickens in the opening chapter of *Bleak House*:

> "Fog everywhere. Fog up the river, where it flows among green aits and meadows; fog down the river, where it rolls defiled among the tiers of shipping and the waterside pollutions of a great (and dirty) city. Fog on the Essex marshes, fog on the Kentish heights. Fog creeping into the cabooses of collier-brigs; fog lying out on the yards, and hovering in the rigging of great ships; fog drooping on the gunwales of barges and small boats. Fog in the eyes and throats of ancient Greenwich pensioners, wheezing by the firesides of their wards; fog in the stem and bow of the afternoon pipe of the wrathful skipper, down in his close cabin; fog cruelly pinching the toes and fingers of his shivering little 'prentice boy on deck. Chance people on the bridges peeping over the parapets into a nether sky of fog, with fog all around them …"

Dickens, who placed the law courts where the fog was densest, made the fog a symbol of the workings of the Chancery Court in the novel. Caught in London on a winter day in the middle of the 20th century,

I appreciated that great writer's experience of a London fog a hundred years before.

My friend Jackson and I decided on a week's holiday in Switzerland during vacation time. This was in 1947. We were allowed only £25 each for our holiday abroad but the fares could be paid in England. We crossed the English Channel by ferry from Dover and went by train to Lucerne. From there we took a bus to Wolfenchiessen, a mountain village. Switzerland had remained neutral throughout the Second World War, so there were no food shortages. We were happy to eat delicious three-course meals and we certainly ate our fill. We walked a good deal and travelled by bus to Lucerne, a beautiful city beside a lake. Everything was so clean, fresh and invigorating. We were so happy that we miscalculated the date of our departure and missed the bus which served the village only on alternate days. We had no more money for our meals but the landlord said, "You are from England. Do not worry. I can trust you. Send the money when you get back!" What a relief! What a compliment to the English. But when we returned to Leicester we had a problem obtaining government approval to send money to Switzerland. So we concocted a story that I had had a fall, sprained my ankle and hence we were delayed. We related the hotel proprietor's faith in the English. Soon we were granted the £10 we needed and gladly sent it off to Switzerland! Incidentally, before we left London we were told that the Swiss were so honest that if you left your bag in the railway station it would remain there safely till you came back for it even a day later. This is no longer true. At Zurich airport you are warned not to leave your baggage unattended!

Once the Inter-Arts examinations were over, I discovered to my surprise that Professor L.F. Casson, who had been the head of the English Department at Raffles College, was teaching at King's College, University of London. He had been fortunate to have left Singapore before the Japanese onslaught, unlike his colleague and the only other member of staff of the English Department, Graham Hough, who had to suffer internment for three-and-a-half years. I called on Professor Casson who was anxious to know what had happened to all his students during the Japanese Occupation. He himself was not much changed from the frail, slightly hunched, friendly chain-smoking scholar whom we all liked and admired. He had just returned from a local holiday visiting cathedrals and old churches to make brass rubbings which he had spread out on the floor of his office for my benefit. He promised to speak to the dean of the Faculty of Arts on my behalf to get me admitted to King's College and sure enough, I was interviewed by the dean and admitted to read English language and literature in October 1948.

King's College, University of London

While looking for a cheap room or "digs" in London, I stayed in a foreign students' hostel called Nutford House where a few Malayans, but mostly African students, resided. Two close Raffles College friends of mine stayed there so I was quite at home. Every Saturday night there was a dance which was far from being the tame conventional social affair we were accustomed to at Raffles College. More often than not, it ended as a "dance of the sheets". Nutford House acquired a notorious reputation as being more of a brothel than a students' hostel. As the authorities could not put an end to the sexual activities of the undergraduates from the British Commonwealth, the hostel was eventually closed down. The women who frequented Nutford House on Saturday nights were invariably white — English or Irish who in earlier times might have gone out to the colonies of the British Empire and lorded it over the "natives". They would have been the "memsahibs", but in London they mixed and mingled with coloured students as equals. At least one girl married an African prince and settled happily in his country. A few African young men looked upon their sexual "conquests" of white girls as a sort of revenge for the humiliations their parents or relatives had suffered at the hands of their colonial masters. A few fell genuinely in love with the girls and married them. Some brought prostitutes into the hostel and wasted no time in getting down to business. Many white women walked the streets in those difficult years soon after the war which ruined Britain. Everything was in short supply and conditions were at times as bad as in Malaya during the Japanese Occupation.

After some weeks, I found suitable lodgings in the Earls Court area which was popular with foreign students. I moved into a small, narrow room at 39 Bramham Gardens. There was enough space for a bed, an armchair, a table with shelves for some books and a fireplace with a gas ring for boiling water. The gas fire for cold winter evenings had to be fed a shilling (about 40 cents) at a time. The heater lasted for about an hour, long enough to warm myself before hopping into bed with a hot water bottle to take the chill off the bedsheets. A window overlooked an enclosed garden graced by some mature trees. The quiet street, lined with the three-storied terrace houses on one side opposite the garden, was uncluttered. Not a single car was parked there — indeed cars were few in war-torn London in 1948. When I visited Bramham Gardens again in 1962 on sabbatical leave from the University of Singapore, cars were parked bumper to bumper along the street! In the five years I spent in Britain, mostly in London, there were no traffic jams so far as I can remember. Buses ran on time as did the underground trains. Transport was cheap and efficient. I never felt the need for a car at any time.

Like other students from the Commonwealth I followed a regular routine. Up at 6.30 or 7 a.m., I had the usual breakfast of cornflakes in cold Jersey cow's milk, rich and creamy. The milk in half-pint and pint bottles was delivered from horse-drawn vehicles very early in the morning. The Jersey brand which I favoured had a gold foil top and it was a little more expensive than milk in silver foil-topped bottles and it tasted better. I rarely had tea or coffee in the morning before setting out on a brisk 10-minute walk to the underground station.

I usually got off at Holborn Station and took another walk down Holborn to the Strand where King's College was situated. I attended all lectures faithfully although we had one eccentric lecturer built on Falstaffian lines who, in his very first lecture, warned us that it would be a waste of time attending his classes! He told us to employ ourselves better in the library. I was assigned to him for a tutorial on one occasion. His office was cluttered with books and across the room on a string hung his socks and underwear to dry! I wonder whether he actually lived in his office! When vacation began I saw this ungainly figure with a knapsack on his back trudging off down the Strand. In Britain there is a great tolerance for eccentrics and people who prefer not to conform to the normal social pattern. The rest of the King's College staff did not exhibit any eccentricities. The English Department was well run under the headship of an eminent scholar, Professor Geoffrey Bullough.

All of us ate subsidised lunches provided by the college. We bought lunch coupons for under two shillings (80 cents) and formed long queues to the refectory. The odour of boiled cabbage and brussel sprouts wafted down the queue. We were served lashings of potatoes and over-boiled cabbage. There was only rabbit available by way of meat. The alternative was whale meat which tasted neither like meat nor fish. A pudding of some sort was always available and welcome. The cold weather improved one's appetite and the potatoes certainly supplied the necessary carbohydrates for us to survive the dismal chills of winter. At least, so far as the quantity of food was concerned, we had no complaints. I was surprised to find how much more I could eat, and in fact needed to eat, what with the cold weather and the long walks. As King's College did not serve dinner we had to find cheap restaurants. There was one in Earls Court where one could buy a reasonable meal for three shillings and sixpence — the slices of meat were so paper thin as to be almost transparent! Once a week I visited an Indian eating place in Earls Court with fellow Malayans for some spicy food. But as this cost five shillings, we could only afford it once a week. We found another Indian Muslim restaurant near the Warren Street Underground station where a generous portion of beef in curry was available at five shillings. Some months later we read in the newspaper that this restaurant was prosecuted for selling horse meat as beef! We stopped patronising the place when it reopened. We had never eaten horse flesh and had the same distaste for it as the English. In France, however, horse meat was, and probably still is, popular. Sometimes one of my Indian friends, Sockanathan, used to receive a food parcel of curry powder from his parents in Kuala Lumpur. This came in useful for a rice-and-curry meal on Sundays when we put together all our meagre meat rations for a week and enjoyed a delicious meal cooked by Sockanathan.

Talking of meals reminds me that when in London I became friendly with a petite English girl, Patricia, whom I took to the only Chinese restaurant in Leicester Square. It was called "Freddie Mills" and belonged to a well-known boxer of that name. I imagined she would be thrilled by Oriental flavours. London in the late 1940s had not been invaded by Chinese culinary experts and the English palate remained conservative. I ordered a couple of "Chinese" dishes but Patricia clearly found them strange and unappetising. So I asked her what she would really like to eat. Her shy response was "fish and chips"! English taste has undergone such a revolutionary change that Chinese and Indian restaurants are now full of English men and women tucking into Peking duck and tandoori chicken with relish! Chinese and Indian food in packets are displayed in supermarkets. Marks and Spencer, popularly called "Marks and Sparks", have a fantastic range of Oriental foods all cooked, needing only to be heated. It is true of course that Indians and Pakistanis have settled in large numbers in London and other industrial cities such as Leeds and Birmingham to work in the factories but the proliferation of Chinese restaurants and "take-aways" can only be attributed to the popularity of Chinese cooking among the British.

The taste for exotic food was not a factor among my classmates at King's College, although many of them had been in the armed forces in North Africa, in Italy and even in India. Apart from the girls and two or three young men, the undergraduates were mature, being in their mid-20s or older. Their experience of war, the experience of being in danger of a violent death at any moment from bombs, shells and other weapons of war made them realise how fragile, how brittle life can be. I had had the same experience during the battle for Singapore and afterwards during the Japanese Occupation. Shared dangers made comrades of us all. We studied together, shared notes and discussed topics at our own seminars. There was never the competitiveness or rivalry so common in the universities in Singapore which one hears about so often. We worked together and cooperated to get the better of the examiners instead of competing against each other. More importantly, there was the sheer joy of discovering the delights of literature. My closest friend was Brice Bending from Ottery-St. Mary in Devon which was the birthplace of Samuel Taylor Coleridge. I spent two vacations in Devon with Brice and his family, walking in the lovely countryside, eating fish and chips wrapped in old newspapers. Every season in Britain displays its beauty in different colours unlike the tropics with its unchanging green nature — there it's rain or sunshine all the time. Spring and autumn with its mellow fruitfulness are perhaps the most colourful and beautiful seasons in Europe. English poetry and drama are so full of imagery and references to spring, summer, autumn and winter that experiencing the seasons makes English literature much more meaningful.

The honours course in English at King's College covered the whole history of English literature beginning with the classic epic poem *Beowulf* in Anglo-Saxon which to me was literally a new language — albeit a dead language — through Middle English to Geoffrey Chaucer, who, like Shakespeare, was a great observer of human frailties and blessed with a wonderful sense of humour. Shakespeare, England's and perhaps the world's greatest dramatist and poet, was the most enjoyable genius whose works were a pleasure to read, and was accorded one-eighth of the whole course. The rest of the English literature course was divided into historical periods right up to the "moderns" like Christopher Fry, who was all the rage in my time but is now forgotten except for his play *The Lady's Not for Burning*, and T.S. Eliot. We undergraduates had the advantage of seeing many of the plays performed by professionals on the stage in London's many theatres — modern dramas like T.S. Eliot's *Murder in the Cathedral*, *The Family Reunion* and *The Cocktail Party* — as well as European dramas like Anton Chekov's *Three Sisters* and *The Cherry Orchard* and Henrik Ibsen's masterpieces. We enjoyed the wit and humour of Bernard Shaw's *Man and Superman* and spent a fortnight in Stratford-on-Avon where I was fortunate enough to witness a memorable performance by John Gielgud in *King Lear*, which had most of the audience in tears. Although Stratford-on-Avon was commercialised, it was still a thrill to visit Shakespeare's birthplace and watch the graceful swans on the River Avon.

On two or three evenings a week a group of us visited the pubs for a drink or two and a lot of conversation. This I did with my fellow undergraduates and more often with fellow students from Malaya and Singapore like Eu Cheow Chye and Goh Keng Swee who enjoyed his pint of beer. The pub is a very British institution where in smoky rooms people meet to enjoy the pleasure of conversation and each other's company. Whereas with my King's College friends literature and British politics were the topics of discussion, with my countrymen invariably the urgent need for independence and how to free ourselves from British rule occupied us.

London was the scene of much activity among foreign students from the Commonwealth who had waited for the end of World War II to continue their studies. Malayans and Singaporeans met in Malaya Hall at 44 Bryanstan Square, conveniently near the Marble Arch Underground station. This was close to Tyburn where in earlier centuries public hangings, which attracted vast crowds of the curious and the morbid, took place. In the late 1940s and early 1950s on Sunday evenings, soapbox orators held forth in Hyde Park Corner on any subject under the sun including communism. We students made a point of attending these open-air sessions to enjoy the jokes and the repartee as some members of the audience invariably heckled the speakers. One joke I remember was the one about the American soldiers who "invaded" Britain before the allied invasion of France. The speaker asserted that in a future war the United States did not need to send soldiers but only uniforms as they had fathered an army of children in Britain! There was total freedom of speech and a spirit of give and take which astonished us who had come from British colonies. Frankly, as I write this, I can say that nowhere in Southeast Asia, and certainly not in Singapore, will total free speech be tolerated in a multiracial society with so many sensitivities, racial and religious. Every political theory was eloquently propounded and equally passionately attacked; government policies and ministers were criticised without fear of arrest.

The British did not show the same tolerance in Singapore or Malaya, as I was to discover when I returned in late 1952, having obtained my honours degree in English and a certificate in education from the Institute of Education in London. While on board the *S.S. Carthage* in Cairo, I received a handwritten letter from the Malayan Director of Education, a Mr Holgate, informing me that my services would not be required in Malaya because of my political views. I had, as president of the Malayan Students' Union, been critical of the British colonial administration and had, along with Abdul Razak Hussein (later to be prime minister of Malaysia) and Dr Goh Keng Swee (later to be finance minister and deputy prime minister of Singapore), organised The Malayan Forum which called for independence for Malaya and Singapore. I was the editor of *Suara Merdeka*, a newssheet which proclaimed our views. As Malaya was closed to me, I hoped to be employed in Singapore, but here again I was told there was no vacancy for teachers when in fact there was a desperate shortage of teachers! This was the British way of punishing critics and pro-independence colonials! Had there been any evidence that I had communist leanings, no doubt I would have been arrested as there was a full-scale battle on with the communist guerrillas in Malaya from 1948.

But to get back to my London days and nights. While at Leicester University College, when I was attending a history lecture, I happened to sit next to an attractive English girl. We got talking to each other before the lecture and went for a cup of tea in the canteen afterwards. Our friendship grew and later, when I left for London, she used to visit me on weekends. We frequented the theatre and attended concerts. We enjoyed each other's company for a year or so. Though we were intimate there was never any suggestion of marriage. English girls were generous in granting their favours and never assumed that mutual affection would necessarily lead to matrimony — quite unlike Asian girls, in those days anyway. In fact, Malayan boys used to complain that Asian girls seemed to assume that a show of friendliness indicated serious intentions; so most of them preferred the company of English, Irish or au-pair girls from the Continent who came to the United Kingdom to improve their English. I found English girls were more widely read and more interesting to talk to than my contemporaries in Raffles College in the late 1930s. Unlike the memsahibs in India and elsewhere in the British colonies, the English women did not appear to be colour-prejudiced except for some landladies who refused to rent rooms to African students. I never came across any racial discrimination among university undergraduates. But over the years, with West Indian and Asian immigrants arriving in large numbers, racial prejudice grew to be widespread, especially in the industrial cities. But this is a controversial subject which I have no wish to discuss, except to point out that racialism has gathered strength in other European countries too, especially France and Germany which had liberal immigration policies at a time of economic prosperity. We students were in the United Kingdom soon after the war sharing privations with the local population who had seen soldiers in uniform from India and elsewhere in the Commonwealth. Shared dangers in war time and the communist threat of death made comrades of us.

Travels to France and Switzerland, and Behind the Iron Curtain to Hungary, 1948–1949

During the 1948 summer holidays, four of us Malayans decided to visit Paris which we had been told was the cultural capital of Europe, a great city of cathedrals and monuments which had escaped being devastated by German bombs as it was declared an open city. The German army had marched triumphantly into Paris with no opposition. When the allied army approached Paris in August 1944, Hitler ordered the German General von Choltitz to destroy Paris but fortunately he disobeyed Hitler and surrendered to the allies. So Paris, unlike London or Berlin, was twice spared destruction.

We had to take the train to Dover to catch one of the channel boats to cross over to Calais. I recall it was a rough crossing and some of us were sick. Once in France we had to take a train to Paris. Though none of us spoke any French we managed to find a reasonably cheap hotel as we had only £25 spending money each — the limit imposed on travellers leaving the United Kingdom by the Labour government of the time. We were equipped with a little pocket book of French phrases and sentences for travellers. We knew items on the menu, the word *combien* (how much), the phrase *l'addition si vous plais* (the bill, please) and not much more. We visited the famous Notre Dame Cathedral and Napoleon's tomb, walked down the grand Champs Élysées and bought replicas of the Eiffel Tower. We made a trip to see the fabulous palace of Versailles and its wonderful gardens. All these sights were impressive, but it was the night life of Paris that enthralled us. We were often in the Place Pigalle sipping wine and watching life go by.

We enjoyed a couple of splendid shows of almost nude beauties with gorgeous colourful headgear dancing and prancing on the stage. This was at the Folies Bergère and another theatre whose name I have long forgotten. I must confess that the girls who walked the streets by night were so attractive that I can't bring myself to call them prostitutes, though no doubt they were. They were charming and elegant. It was said that they were earning their dowries in Paris before going back to their village or small towns to settle down and raise a family! We were young and they were irresistible. One of my friends sold his new shirt for an hour of pleasure before returning to London. He never regretted it. I have to admit I yielded to temptation more than once and never regretted it either. Only the shortage of cash brought too early an end to our delight in what Paris had to offer. So back to foggy London we returned, poorer in the pocket but richer in experience. It was in Paris that we found that hotel rooms were equipped with mirrors on the walls as well as the ceiling. You can't beat the French for sexual refinements!

A trip of a totally different kind took place in 1949, when a representative of the Moral Re-Armament (MRA) organisation invited four of us Malayan students to visit their headquarters and training centre in Caux, near Montreaux, Switzerland. The MRA was a non-denominational religious movement founded by American churchman Frank Buchman who hoped to improve the moral and spiritual life of people. The idea was that each person should change his life through practising the four moral absolutes: purity, unselfishness, honesty and love. These absolutes were called the four pillars of Moral Re-Armament. The movement was Christian but members of all religions were welcome at the conferences. Buchman and his followers believed that cooperation among people who experienced moral and spiritual awakening could lead to the avoidance of war such as the world had suffered with millions of deaths between 1939 and 1945. The MRA was anti-communist. We were given the principles of the movement in a couple of lectures. We were told that the trip and a fortnight's stay in a huge hotel in the mountain resort of Caux would cost us nothing, but all the work including the cleaning of rooms, the cooking, the washing of dishes, etc. would be done by us. Wholehearted cooperation would be encouraged. We would be divided into work teams.

We were flown into Switzerland in a small aircraft, probably a Skymaster. We took a special train up the mountain from Montreaux to Caux. We were given comfortable old-fashioned rooms in a large old-fashioned hotel which was owned by the MRA. The movement clearly had rich backers who had bought the hotel and other training centres in the United States and at least one hotel in Japan.

It was fun doing everything ourselves in enthusiastic teams. I was one of the kitchen helpers, cutting up vegetables, peeling potatoes, slicing onions and so forth. The meals were good and certainly better than what we had in the university refectories in London. Every morning, we were

Picture 2: Sockanathan, Ghazali Shafie, MB and Aziz Ali at Caux, Switzerland during a visit to the Moral Re-Armament (MRA) headquarters and training centre, 1949.

required to gather together in small groups of eight to ten for meditation and confession. What with purity and honesty being two of the four MRA absolutes, the confessions could be embarrassing as all sexual thoughts had to be disclosed. If one had felt a sexual urge looking at a pretty girl one had to admit such a sinful thought and cleanse one's mind. But alas! The cleansing never lasted long as there were many attractive girls around. Perhaps the females had similar problems in their group sessions too. The confessions were meant to bring about a change in one's life.

It was all well-meant but I do not know how successful the MRA philosophy was in bringing about a moral and spiritual awakening in individuals. It certainly did not succeed with any of us Malayans, although we liked the idea that if people were honest with themselves and led lives guided by love there might never again be world wars. But we knew in our hearts that the MRA absolutes were unattainable given human lust, greed and the urge to exercise power. Every evening, all participants were encouraged to go on stage to state how our experience in Caux was changing or had changed our lives. There were many who did but no one in our group mounted the stage. All the same, we were impressed by the cooperation and sincerity of people of so many different religions and races living together for a fortnight. It was a period of touching friendship and hopes that the world could be made a more peaceful place.

I read somewhere that the Moral Re-Armament movement lost its impetus and declined after the death of Frank Buchman in 1961.

We Malayan students learned that the National Union of Students of Britain was organising a cheap tour to Budapest, the Hungarian capital, later in the 1949 summer holidays. What some of us did not know was that Budapest was to be the gathering place for young communists and fellow travellers to celebrate the triumph of communism in Eastern Europe. It was the Second World Festival of Youth and Students. The tour must have been subsidised by the communists for it extended from 9th August, when we left London for Paris, to 29th August, when we left Budapest by train on our return journey. It included two days in Paris on the way out by train through France, Switzerland and Austria.

The Malayan group included Goh Keng Swee and his wife, Alice, Lee Kip Lin who was studying architecture, Eu Cheow Chye, a civil servant, Fred Arulanandom, a welfare officer who also studied law, Un Hon Kun and Dennis Lee, a law student. There were a few others whose names I have forgotten. Lee Kip Lin kept a diary of our journey which has helped me immensely in recalling details which I would otherwise have forgotten.

We crossed the English Channel to Dieppe and then boarded an overcrowded train for Paris in uncomfortably hot weather. The organisers of the tour, after some confusion, identified us and brought us to a hostel at Marcel Sembat, a long way from the railway station. We were very tired but at least the hostel was quite comfortable. We were too exhausted to appreciate the beauty of historic Paris. We had to leave sightseeing to the next day. A group of us visited the Place de la Concorde and the Rue de Rivoli, and hired a carriage to take us around the Champ Élysées and the Arc de Triomphe. When evening fell we made our way on the Métro to the Place Pigalle where we saw an exciting floor show at the Bal Tabaria, a nightclub.

The next day, 11 August, three of us went to the Hungarian Legation to get our visas. I was lucky to get mine but Kip Lin and Fred were unsuccessful. However, all were told to get into the train at the Gare de l'Est station that night even without visas. We were told that those without visas would get theirs in Vienna. There was no explanation as to why only some of us were granted visas in Paris. All ten of us from Malaya caught the train that night. There were no sleeping berths so we had to doze off while seated. We passed through Switzerland the next day and reached Austria early in the evening of 12 August. The scenery was beautiful and the Tyrol mountains were magnificent. We reached Innsbruck by about 4.30 p.m., the famous city of Salzburg by 10 p.m. and Vienna at 1.30 a.m.!

In Vienna, those without visas got a shock. They were ordered to leave the train. As we were in the Russian zone, we feared that they would be sent back or even imprisoned! In fact, they were told that they would have to wait while visas were obtained from the Communist Youth League in Vienna. Lee Kip Lin said later that he was deeply depressed especially as it was cold and the rain poured down in torrents. But an Austrian who was fluent in English took the group by tram to the communist office which was in a highly decorated but war-damaged baroque building full of propaganda posters. He was kept waiting, along with Fred Arulanandom and a dozen others till nightfall. They had spent a whole day waiting, having arrived in the morning. To make things worse someone said that he had had to wait a whole week before getting a visa! Meanwhile, a couple of reporters arrived, one of them female, to interview them about conditions in Malaya. They bluffed their way by saying that as they were students in London their letters from home were censored so they knew nothing about events in Malaya. When asked for his name the quick-witted Fred introduced himself as Nathan from Singapore!

Having had nothing to eat since breakfast, all of them were famished so although told not to leave the office as they could be arrested, not having received official permission to stay in Vienna, they took the risk of looking for a restaurant. They found a posh one with the waiters dressed in formal clothes! But the price for a large dish of meat and vegetables was reasonable at six shillings (40 shillings = £1).

On returning to the office building, they were surprised to be invited to a party nearby to pass the time as their visas would not be ready till 11 p.m.! They were conducted to a large room decorated with four large portraits of Stalin, Lenin, Marx and the Austrian communist leader whose name was not known to them. A three-piece band provided some lively jive music — a bourgeois surprise in a communist area. The female reporter who had interviewed Fred seemed to be fascinated by his handsome presence so Kip Lin had to remind him that he was "Nathan" from Singapore. Everyone was quite friendly though on the whole it was a rough-and-ready crowd. The women looked a hardened lot perhaps because of their war experiences. None looked particularly attractive or appealing. The party ended at 11 p.m. with everyone standing to attention singing the "Internationale". On returning to the office by midnight they found their visas ready. So they continued their train journey and arrived at Budapest by 9 a.m. on Saturday, 14 August.

Budapest was a battered city where the Russians had fought the German army. Of the seven bridges across the Danube only one was left. Bomb-damaged buildings were visible everywhere as in London. Walls were marked with bullet holes. The city wore its battle scars, a testimony to the suffering of its inhabitants.

When we got off the train we were met by interpreters and even porters for our luggage. We were amazed to find two rows of young people who resembled scouts and girl guides lined up to cheer and greet us, clapping their hands welcoming us! We smiled and waved as we climbed aboard the bus which was to take us to our lodgings in what appeared to be an old castle. We were given a dormitory for 12. We were treated to an excellent lunch at the Hosok Tere, a large Romanesque castle where waiters served us. Coming from Britain where we had to endure strict rationing, we ate to our heart's content. Throughout our stay in Budapest we were truly well-fed. There was no shortage of meat and vegetables, much to the surprise of all of us from London.

We were conveyed in buses to the stadium which was decorated in Olympic style for the grand occasion. We were by this time fully aware that this gathering of youths was communist, and organised for propaganda purposes. Naturally we were nervous that the authorities back home would strongly disapprove of our presence in Budapest, but there was no way we could avoid participating in the ceremony which involved a march past by the contingents from different countries. We assembled at the entrance to the stadium in different groups. We Malayans were a motley crowd compared to the other delegations who were in smart uniforms or national dress carrying large banners. The Central Asians — the Mongolians and the Turkestan delegation — looked splendid. We were just in our trousers and shirts waiting anxiously for our banners which we hoped would not be too belligerent. Fortunately we were given a banner which read "Malaya — For Freedom, Peace and Progress". Goh Keng Swee carried this and I was given a red banner which I bore with as much dignity as I could muster. As we marched past, tremendous cheers greeted us for we were mistaken for the guerrilla fighters in the Malayan jungles! We were unwilling frauds, feeling rather embarrassed and self-conscious but we had no choice in the matter. Many cameras clicked away and we guessed that the Malayan government would, through its agents, learn of our part in this ceremony. Indeed, stern official letters admonishing us awaited on our return to London. Scholarship students were threatened that their stipends would be withdrawn if they slipped up again!

The rest of the ceremonial opening of the Second World Festival of Youth and Students consisted of long boring speeches which we could not understand except for those of the British and American delegates. Perhaps the most impressive items at the opening ceremony was the appearance of the Russian delegation carrying a huge portrait of Joseph Stalin (7 ft by 5 ft (2.1 m by 1.5 m)). The whole crowd went berserk, cheering and hand clapping in rhythm. Little did we know what a murderous tyrant Stalin was. It is estimated that he was responsible for the deaths of up to 40 million people. The Nobel laureate Aleksandr Solzhenitsyn, whose *The Gulag Archipelago* and *One Day in the Life of Ivan Denisovich* reveal the horrible truth, estimates that Stalin's victims numbered 60 million!

The rest of our holiday in Budapest was spent in exploring the city, signing autographs for young people who were excited seeing foreigners from many different countries especially the darker skinned ones. Fred Arulanandom had an unusual experience in the street when a girl rubbed her fingers on his arm and looked to see whether the colour had come off on her fingers! Africans emerging from the underground trains had their heads touched! Hungarians had never colonised any country so they were just curious about coloured folk whom many of them had never seen before.

At times we could sense the tension in the city between those who supported the communists and the older folk who resented the new regime. The rebellion was to break out in 1956 when the Russian tanks moved into Budapest to ruthlessly suppress the outbreak. What surprised us was the existence of nightclubs and prostitutes loitering under the street lamps waiting for customers. There was even one nightclub decorated with pornographic pictures on its walls! We had expected the communists to be like the Puritans who, under Cromwell, closed all the theatres in London once they took over the country after executing King Charles I in 1649. Most forms of entertainment were considered sinful.

After the closing ceremony we left Budapest on the evening of 29 August which was a Sunday. Whenever the train stopped at stations in Hungary there were crowds on the platforms to bid us farewell. At the border town there were two brass bands to say goodbye in musical style! So ended our excursion behind the Iron Curtain where we had a warm welcome from friendly people.

The end of the summer holidays saw the beginning of the academic year in the first week of October, usually a very pleasant autumnal month before the first signs of winter in November. It was my second year at King's College and I was well settled in. The previous year I had been summoned to appear before a lady in the Colonial Office in charge of Commonwealth scholars to explain why I had left University College, Leicester without permission and joined King's College. It was true that I had not informed the Leicester College authorities that I was leaving and had, with the help of Professor Casson who had taught me in Raffles College, gained admission to King's which conferred internal degrees. In a confident mood with the blue and red King's College scarf prominently wrapped around my neck, I explained to the official that I had not come thousands of miles to suffer the privations of rations in food and clothing to do an external BA honours degree which I could have obtained in Singapore. I argued that I should be congratulated on my enterprise in improving my educational prospects instead of being reprimanded. I had done better than the Colonial Office! As the Queen's Scholarship was an open one, with no restrictions except for good behaviour and good examination results, it could not be withdrawn. But I did apologise for not informing Professor Humphreys and Professor Simmons that I was leaving. They

Picture 3: Stadium in Budapest, Hungary, where the parade was held during the Second World Festival of Youth and Students, August 1949.

had been so kind and encouraging that I just could not bring myself to inform them that I was leaving Leicester. It may be an Asian trait, this reluctance to hurt the feelings of someone who has been kind to you although it might not be of much importance to one's superior. The Colonial Office representative accepted my arguments and I had no further problems with her. Even after the trip to Budapest, I was left alone, although several scholarship holders were reprimanded and threatened that their scholarships might be terminated if they visited a communist country again. But of course reports of our activities in Budapest, together with photographs, were sent back to the colonial governments in Singapore and Kuala Lumpur. We were informed about this by Kenny Byrne, a local Eurasian who was in the civil service and who later became a minister in the first People's Action Party (PAP) government. He was a useful source of information on the thinking of the British colonial administrators for the PAP when it was first formed.

Picture 4: Marching in the parade at the Second World Festival of Youth and Students in Budapest, August 1949. From left: Un Hon Kun, Lee Kip Lin, Fred Arulanandom, Goh Keng Swee (carrying placard), Alice Goh, Eu Cheow Chye and MB (carrying banner).

Picture 5: Un Hon Kun, Goh Keng Swee, Eu Cheow Chye and MB with student participants at the Second World Festival of Youth and Students, Budapest, August 1949.

Picture 6: MB at the dormitory in Budapest where the Malayan group stayed during the Second World Festival of Youth and Students in August 1949. Top from left: Un Hon Kun, Eu Cheow Chye, Lee Kip Lin. Bottom from left: Fred Arulanandom, Alice Goh, Dennis Lee, MB.

The Malayan Student Organisations, Including the Malayan Forum

Many of us from the colonies were scattered in provincial universities but about 340 out of a total of 540 Malayan students were in London, mostly at the University of London and the Inns of Court. As Malaya Hall was at 44 Bryanstan Square in the Marble Arch area it was naturally a meeting place for all of us in London and for all the others from the provinces during the vacations. There were two Malayan student organisations in Britain in 1947. One was the Malay Society of Great Britain which had been founded by Tunku Abdul Rahman. Its membership was confined to Malays. The second organisation was the Malayan Students' Union (MSU) founded by a group of students. Its membership was open to all races from Malaya as well as Penang and Singapore, which were British colonies directly under the control of the Colonial Office, unlike the Federated and Unfederated Malay States which were ruled by the

Sultans advised by British Residents. We students considered ourselves Malayans no matter which state or colony we came from. I was myself from Perak, having gone to the Anglo-Chinese School in Ipoh.

I was elected president of the MSU in 1948. All the Malay students, encouraged by Abdul Razak who succeeded Tunku Abdul Rahman as president of the Malay Society of Great Britain, were members of MSU. He persuaded them not to isolate themselves as they had tended to do at Raffles College but to participate fully in MSU's activities. Abdul Razak, who was from Pahang, and I knew each other from Raffles College days where he was two years my junior. He was a star footballer and a keen and serious student who was respected by all his contemporaries. I felt strongly that the two organisations should be united under Razak's leadership but he explained to me that the Malay students had to be organised to work together, to be more responsible and self-reliant. He did not think forming a single student organisation was feasible at that time and declined my offer to step down as president of MSU. He wanted every Malay undergraduate to be as industrious as himself. He certainly set a good example but others tended to take life easy. They were altogether more relaxed about life — *kampung* style. He wanted the Malays to be more progressive, more competitive, to strive to reach the top in whatever they set out to do. This was always his driving ambition but he did not, unfortunately, live long enough to see his dream fulfilled. It was not till the 1980s and 1990s under Dr Mahathir's leadership, that the Malays became extremely successful businessmen and industrialists. Even Dr Mahathir had his doubts about the capabilities of the Malays, as he revealed in his book *The Malay Dilemma* published in 1970. However, under his leadership and with special bumiputera policies and the emphasis on education, he asserted in 1997 that his pessimism had been proved wrong. "But now I reverse my stand," he said, "I no longer believe what I wrote in *The Malay Dilemma* but there is a lot to be done before we can stand tall with other progressive races in the world".[1] He pointed out that whereas the Malays had only one per cent of the country's economic cake in 1970, they held 20 per cent in 1997.

---

[1] *The Straits Times*, 12 May 1997.

The colonial government was against the two societies discussing politics although many of us were politically minded after the shock we suffered at the disastrous defeat of the British forces in 70 days by the Japanese. Our bitter experience under the brutal Japanese regime made us feel that we could no longer trust the British to defend us. We had to have a say in our future. The Malay scholars, led by Abdul Razak, were strongly influenced by Dato' Onn bin Jaafar's efforts to defeat the new constitutional arrangements of the MacMichael mission[2] which had persuaded and even intimidated the Sultans to agree, under the Malayan Union proposals, to transfer their sovereignty to the Crown and to grant citizenship to the Chinese and Indians who had settled in Malaya.[3] The Malay reaction was vigorous. They feared the ascendancy of the Chinese would be the doom of the Malays in their own country. The United Malays National Organisation (UMNO) under Dato' Onn came out openly against the Malayan Union and exerted great pressure on the Sultans to repudiate the MacMichael agreements. Faced by this determined opposition at a time when the Malayan Communist Party (MCP) was disrupting law and order by organising numerous labour strikes, and the absence of firm support from the Chinese who wanted to retain their separate nationality and enjoy Malayan Union citizenship at the same time, the British government gave way.

Although the Malays and Chinese had clashed in several areas in the interregnum between the surrender of the Japanese and the return of the British, I did not sense any ill feeling among our students of different races in Britain. Even after the outbreak of the communist terrorist revolt in 1948, which was almost wholly organised by the Chinese, we got on well together. The communist outbreak was a serious blow to our hopes of independence in the near future. My own political consciousness had been sharpened by the Malayan Democratic Union (MDU), a left-wing organisation in Singapore which had its office in North Bridge Road. It occupied the upstairs floor of an old two-storey house which at night

---

[2] Harper, T.N. (1998). *The End of Empire and the Making of Malaya*. New York: Cambridge University Press, p. 84.
[3] Gullick, John (1981). *Malaysia: Economic Expansion and National Unity*. London: Ernest Benn, p. 83.

became a dance hall called the Liberty Cabaret. The movement was led by Eu Chooi Yip and P.V. Sarma who had been at Raffles College, Lim Kean Chye, a Cambridge-educated lawyer from Penang, and John Eber. I was merely on the periphery of the organisation working with Sarma to lay the basis for a teachers' union. I was asked by Chooi Yip to tutor three young members of the MCP whose headquarters were in Queen Street. I gave the lessons in English twice a week.

When the terrorist campaign began in 1948, several leading members of the MDU were arrested. The MDU dissolved itself. I did not know that it had strong links with the MCP so some of us in London called a meeting of the students to protest against the arrests. Goh Keng Swee, Ali Hassan and I were elected to call on the colonial secretary, Mr Griffiths, to demand an explanation for the arrests. Goh Keng Swee was reading economics at the London School of Economics and Ali Hassan was a law student at the Inns of Court. We were received by Griffiths who explained the seriousness of the situation in Malaya. He promised that if there was no evidence that those arrested were communists they would be released after proper investigation.

Both Goh Keng Swee and I were surprised and somewhat disappointed at the lukewarm support of our fellow students on this occasion. Most of them were too busy with their studies. A few were too busy skirt chasing! We decided that something should be done to make them more politically conscious so as to prepare for ultimate independence. We approached Abdul Razak and it was in Razak's flat in Cromwell Road that the idea of The Malayan Forum was born. Razak and I made Keng Swee the chairman, although he was reluctant as he preferred to remain in the background. We decided that we should co-opt Mohd Sopiee Ibrahim, an energetic personality who was studying social science, as the secretary. We invited two more individuals who were politically minded to join us. They were Fred Arulanandom and Philip Hoalim Junior, who were both studying law.

We were a multiracial group consisting of two Malays, two Chinese, an Indian and a Eurasian. We were all socialists in the sense that we supported the Labour Party which we knew would be more sympathetic to our aspirations for independence than the Conservatives. We were aware that the great Winston Churchill was opposed to Indian independence and had contemptuously referred to Mahatma Gandhi as a "naked fakir" and made clear his determination not to preside over the break-up of the British Empire. We envisaged The Malayan Forum as a debating society for all Malayans, whatever their ethnic origin or social background, to discuss the question of independence and the problems of political development. We hoped to attain independence by constitutional means and not by rebellion like the one launched by the MCP in 1948 with a campaign of terror. None of us who founded The Malayan Forum was a communist. We had not studied communism or even read Karl Marx's *Das Kapital*, but we knew *The Communist Manifesto* drafted by Engels and Marx. I had also read Bernard Shaw's *Intelligent Women's Guide to Socialism, Capitalism, and Fascism* and attended lectures by Harold Laski, the guru of the Labour Party at the London School of Economics. Although our ideas of socialism were vague, we did believe in the Labour Party's nationalisation scheme and admired its national health service scheme which enabled those who could not afford it to receive medical attention. We were idealistic, hoping to eliminate the huge gap between the rich and the poor by state control of the means of production.

How were we to make our fellow Malayans more politically conscious and keen on attaining independence? We decided on inviting speakers from the British Parliament, including from the Conservative Party, although MPs who came were mostly from the Labour Party like Fenner Brockway and Woodrow Wyatt. Brockway was our favourite as he was left-wing and sympathetic to us. We also seized every opportunity to get eminent Malayans like Dato' Onn to address us when they came to Britain. We questioned, debated and argued with our guest speakers as well as among ourselves. We even had Sir Henry Gurney, British high commissioner to Malaya, address us shortly before he was assassinated in Fraser's Hill by the communist terrorists who ambushed his convoy. Whitehall officials such as John Higham were invited to address The Malayan Forum. We held debates and discussions on politics. We produced a bulletin daringly entitled *Suara Merdeka* (Voice of Freedom) of which I was the editor and also author of several articles under pseudonyms like "El Hakim" and "Eciruam". The articles stressed the need for early independence, democratic elections and Malayanisation of the civil service.

Much to our surprise, the Colonial Office appeared to tolerate the activities of our Forum although my landlord told me that my "digs" at

39 Bramham Gardens had been searched by intelligence officers once. He had been instructed to keep the matter secret but Mr Barcham revealed it to me as we were good friends. We did have a problem with the chairman of the Board of Governors of Malaya Hall, a Mr Ward, an ex-planter who was a typical "old guard" colonialist who was used to giving orders to Asians and who could never treat us as equals. We clashed with him over our invitation to Gerald de Cruz to address the Forum as Gerald, the headmaster of a school for the handicapped, was an ex-communist who had been very active in the MDU in Singapore. We threatened to demonstrate in Trafalgar Square. Mr Ward gave way. He reported me to the director of colonial scholars as a "tiresome bounder", according to Associate Professor Yeo Kim Wah of the National University of Singapore who did research in London on the attempt of the communists to convert English-educated Malayans in the United Kingdom to their way of thinking. The director, Mr J.L. Keith, who investigated the matter, came to the conclusion that "Baker is a pleasant fellow who is much liked by all Malayan students who have appointed him President of the Students' Union"! It was well-known that there was a communist group in England led by Lim Hong Bee who published a journal called the *Malayan Monitor*. He made no headway in Malaya Hall as all three student organisations based there were firmly anti-communist. Mr Keith, in a minute quoted by Associate Professor Yeo, wrote that "Malaya Hall is one of the bulwarks against Communism". It was this enlightened view that ensured the tolerance of The Malayan Forum by the British authorities. We were free to invite any speaker we wanted. We were free to debate any topic we wished. We were free to criticise the British administration. We could write as we pleased in our *Suara Merdeka*.

We invited Lee Kuan Yew from Cambridge to address us. He had been too busy with his studies to take part in the formation of The Malayan Forum but we knew he was with us in spirit. Had he been with us, he would have been one of its founder members. His speech to the Forum examined the difficulties that stood in the way of gaining independence. The racial composition of Malaya with a near balance between the Malays and the Chinese meant that a society had to develop which was not Malay, Chinese or Indian but Malayan, based on racial harmony and cooperation.

The danger of communalism was a threat to independence, which would benefit the communists who believed in armed struggle. John Drysdale in his book *Struggle for Success* discusses this speech and makes the point that it "brought into relief two issues which were to be the rock-bed of his future political philosophy: the imperative of communal equality and the threatening reality of communism".

Social Life

But to get back to student activities. Those of us in London met every Saturday regularly for dances to which English girlfriends were invited, but the majority of the females were Malayan. All social activities such as Saturday night dances and dinners were held jointly by the two student organisations and in our own hall although the annual dinner and dance took place in a hotel restaurant. During the vacations, all those

Picture 7: Goh Keng Swee, MB and Mohd Sopiee Ibrahim in front of Malaya Hall, 44 Bryanstan Square, London, 1948.

Picture 8: MB with Lee Kuan Yew in London, 1948.

Picture 9: MB on a train back to London after attending a Labour Party meeting in Wales, 1948.

in provincial universities such as Nottingham and Leeds as well as the universities in Wales returned to London. We were not limited to social activities only. We had a good hockey team led by Cecil Wong from Cambridge and Raja Azlan Shah (later Lord President of Malaysia (1982 to 1984), Sultan of Perak and Yang di-Pertuan Agong) from Nottingham which toured the southern counties playing matches with some success.

It was in Malaya Hall that I first noticed a pretty Eurasian girl from Singapore who had been schooling in England after the war. She was lively with a captivating personality and an infectious smile. Her bright dark eyes intrigued me. She was very popular, a good dancer, warm, friendly and unaffected. I was attracted but having loved and lost once, I moved with caution. Two of my friends, Ong Swee Keng and Fred Arulanandom, thought her the right girl for me! They knew her well, having sailed in the same ship with her in 1946. Swee Keng took me to visit her in the Cromwell Road flat which she shared with her sister and two brothers. Barbara Edwina Balhetchet was then just about 20 years of age when we were introduced in 1948. I learnt that her father was a well-known doctor in government service in Singapore. The family was Roman Catholic. I was a Methodist, having been baptised at the age of 14 in Ipoh. I was already 29 when I found myself attracted by her. I decided to be rational and resist but I had as much chance as a nail next to a magnet. It's the same old story — she grew on me. I couldn't take my eyes off her at parties and dances and felt a pang of jealousy when she danced with others. She was quite unaware, innocent of the effect she was having on me for some time. My close friends realised what was happening. Ong Swee Keng, a law student, once told me that Barbara's father had asked him, as an old family friend, to keep an eye on his pretty daughter. Swee Keng replied, "Keep an eye on her? I can't take my eyes off her!" That, he added, must have worried the old doctor even more! Swee Keng encouraged me as he considered her ideal for me. He gave me no reasons nor did I ask for any. Abdul Razak, who liked her, was of Swee Keng's view also. Who was I to go against the opinion of so many good friends? But clearly I needed no pushing — I was fast sliding that way on my own!

Everything went smoothly despite Shakespeare's warning that the course of true love never did run smooth. It was not till years later that the truth of that observation hit me hard. I was then at the University of

London's Institute of Education in Russell Square undergoing training to be a teacher. The course consisted of theoretical lectures in the principles of education as well as practical teaching in a school to qualify for a certificate in education. On completion of the course and after the examinations, the Institute organised trips to Czechoslovakia and Yugoslavia for groups of students. I chose to go to Yugoslavia. I had to register with Professor Laureys, who was in charge of those who chose to visit Yugoslavia. Outside his door stood a very pretty English girl. She smiled and asked, "You going to Yugoslavia too?" We introduced ourselves; her name was Rachel. We chatted for a while, met the professor and parted. As I said, she was very pretty, simply dressed and without any make-up. I am susceptible to feminine beauty, I'll admit.

There were about 25 of us in the tour group, a mixed lot of men and women, almost all British except for four of us Africans and Malayans. All the girls were English except for one American. We got on very well together — all keen to see the country which had had a troubled history and which so recently had resisted the Nazis with its partisan underground led by Tito. The Balkans had been the battleground of Europe. The countryside, bare and barren, shows the effects of its past history of warfare. The assassination of the Austrian Archduke Franz Ferdinand had triggered off the terrible First World War in 1914. It was altogether an unfortunate country with its different religions and races. But when we visited Yugoslavia it was at peace under a strong dictatorial ruler. Authoritarian rule is perhaps justifiable in a plural society with the potential for trouble. But the only trouble we had was the rather cold end of March weather when there was even the occasional snowfall. The people were warm and friendly wherever we went. I think this is true of most countries that people are hospitable.

We returned to London at the end of two weeks. I was invited by Rachel to the end of the academic year dance which celebrated our gaining the certificate in education and entitled us to be qualified teachers. She was radiant in her pink evening dress. With her delightful personality and her sense of humour she was always a joy to be with. That evening she was more than pretty, she was beautiful. I was dazzled. She must have sensed that I admired her. We danced. And we danced.

"Let's go outside for a while," she said. We walked out into the balcony. Then she looked at me. "Maurice," she said "don't you realise that I'm in love with you?" It was stunning. We had talked, joked and laughed together but I never for a moment imagined that she could fall in love with me. "Oh, my God Rachel," I exclaimed, "I'm engaged to a girl from Singapore. We are going to be married in a few months!" She looked downcast. We walked down to Russell Square gardens close by. Seated on a bench I told her about my engagement. "You are beautiful, Rachel, and I admire you. But I am committed to someone else. I am sorry." I was sad and strangely moved by her gentle presence. I walked her slowly back to her hostel, kissed her goodnight and made my way to Russell Street Underground station.

I was depressed. It began to dawn upon me that I was in love with two girls! I had never thought such a thing possible but there it was! I was enchanted, enraptured by the gentle sweetness, the soulfulness of Rachel but also much in love with my spirited vivacious fiancée Barbara to whom I got engaged in 1951. On the horns of a dilemma, I was not then wise to the ways of the world. Years later, I came to know an intelligent woman who was in love with and made love to two men happily for years. She clearly had no sense of guilt whatsoever.

As it was the end of the academic year, Rachel invited six of us down to her house in Milford, opposite the Isle of Wight. My good friend Kenneth Parkinson was one of the party. We were introduced to her mother, but her father had gone off to Belgium in the family yacht. Every day we set sail in a borrowed boat to the Isle of Wight with Rachel at the tiller. She was experienced and we felt safe even in bad weather, but on our third trip we nearly met with disaster on the way back as we encountered a howling gale. Rachel was great but all the same I thought I was going to be drowned. We made it to Lymington where we pulled up at the jetty drenched, soaked to the skin. It was only Rachel's skill that had saved us. Clambering out of the boat to the jetty, I dropped my spectacles into the sea! We got back home by bus. I resigned myself to the loss of the spectacles and hoped to get a new pair in London. Imagine my surprise when Rachel handed me my lost glasses which she had recovered from the mud by the jetty after an hour's digging in the slush at low tide! She had set out early on her quest without letting me know as she had doubts about recovering the lost specs from the sea. What a relief it was for me. I was really grateful.

The next day, after a picnic lunch by the sea we said our farewells. She swam far out into the sea in her sadness and I worried for her but she swam back, a sea nymph in her beauty. We parted in tears. It was forever.

> "How many times do I love again?
> Tell me how many beads there are
> In a silver chain
> Of evening rain,
> Unravelled from the tumbling main
> And threading the eye of a yellow star
> So many times do I love again."
>
> Thomas Lovell Beddoes

It was so beautiful and so sad. I remember her whenever I am by the sea.

The days went by, the weeks and months. I had to visit a Catholic priest for counselling as I had been baptised a Methodist. The first priest I saw was a middle-aged ultra-conservative Irishman who decided to lecture me on religion. I suspected he thought I was barely educated, so I decided to give him a bit of a shock. I told him that I had read Darwin's *Origin of the Species* and that I believed in evolution. I added that I was an admirer of Bertrand Russell and Bernard Shaw. When I went for my next session the Irish priest was no longer there. A young Englishman had taken over. We had some interesting discussions after which all I had to do was to agree to bring up any children as Catholics.

I married Barbara on 2 August 1952 with Ken Parkinson as my best man. Sheila, Barbara's sister, was her bridesmaid. Her parents and brothers attended the ceremony. My family was represented by my father's sister Mrs Girling, a charming lady. Our honeymoon was spent in the little village of Mousehole in Cornwall. We have been happily married for more than 60 years. I had made the right choice.

Abdul Razak had left London on the sudden death of his father in Pahang in May 1950. He succeeded his father as Orang Kaya Indira Shahbandar. Goh Keng Swee had left in 1951. I left in September 1952 with my wife for Singapore on the *S.S. Carthage*. Toh Chin Chye took over The Malayan Forum but when he left, Lim Hong Bee and John Eber seized control of it. But they did not remain in control for long as Goh Keng Swee went back to Britain to read for his doctorate in economics. He organised the students and regained control of the leadership. But the exciting days for The Malayan Forum were over. Perhaps it had done its job in playing a part in the move for Malaya's independence from colonialism by making the students politically conscious.

Chapter 3

Return to Singapore
September 1952–June 1967

SOMETIME IN SEPTEMBER 1952 my wife and I embarked on the S.S. *Carthage*, on our way home. It was a relaxing, enjoyable voyage as the sea remained calm. We made several friends on board ship including a Ceylonese who was a lecturer in English literature at the University of Malaya in Singapore. The only shock I had was a letter of rejection from the British director of education in Malaya, which I received in Cairo. I had not even applied for a job! It was the British way of punishing me for my political activities in England. I had organised and urged the Malayan students to work for independence and edited the *Suara Merdeka*. Whereas British tradition had tolerated this in England, it was a different story in the colonies.

I was not too upset by the letter as I had every qualification for a teaching job including a certificate in education from the London Institute of Education as well as an honours degree from the University of London. I had had two years teaching experience in 1946 and 1947 before taking up my Queen's Scholarship. I had a Raffles College diploma as well as a year's study for an education diploma although the Japanese attack on 8 December 1941 had prevented the examination from taking place. In any case, as my wife was a Singaporean whose family had settled in the colony after the war, I preferred to work in Singapore. But I had another surprise awaiting me at the Singapore Department of Education.

I was told that there were no vacancies! It was a big lie. Fortunately, my wife, who was fully qualified, found employment at her old school, the Convent of the Holy Infant Jesus, so there was no danger of us starving. I soon found a temporary teaching job at the Kuo Chuan Girls' School, headed by the friendly Miss Sirkett. I had the pleasure of teaching a class of intelligent and industrious teenage girls for several months.

The opening of a new secondary school in Bartley Road led to the Department of Education offering me a temporary job as education officer at $720 a month. There was an acute shortage of teachers so the director of education had little choice in the matter. I was fortunate that, at the same time, a Raffles College contemporary of mine, Ahmad Dzafir, who was a close friend, was also teaching at the same school. He had a car, so he picked me up at about 6.30 a.m. or so from my flat in River Valley Road. Bartley Secondary School was in what was then a rural area surrounded by vegetable and pig farms. There were some excellent experienced teachers at the school, but there were others who were mainly interested in discussing horse racing in the staff common room. One of them even collected bets to be placed with illegal bookies! In the early 1950s, horse racing was staged on Wednesdays as well as weekends. This was unfortunate as the mid-week racing distracted not only teachers but many civil servants as well.

Some of the classes were co-educational, but most of the pupils were boys, many of whom were overaged as a result of the Japanese Occupation. A few of these boys used the recess for a quiet smoke in the *lalang* (coarse weedy grass) patches which grew profusely behind the school. One could see the smoke rising from the *lalang*! But the boys were well-behaved and so there was never a disciplinary problem. They excelled at games, especially football. The girls outshone the boys in their studies and one, Chia Siow Yue, went on eventually to become an associate professor in economics at the National University of Singapore. One of the boys, Chandra Das, became a People's Action Party (PAP) member of Parliament and chairman of the National Trade Union Congress (NTUC) Fairprice shops. Out of a group of Chinese-educated students who were transferred to the English stream, several excelled in mathematics and were reasonably proficient in English. One, James Fu, with his bilingual qualifications, rose to be the press secretary in the Prime Minister's Office. No doubt many others have done well in life.

As the new Bartley Secondary School had no library, I volunteered to spend a vacation to buy the books to set up one. I was helped by one of the younger teachers, Bobby Kway. The British director of education who visited the school was very pleased with the library.

My colleagues were friendly and helpful. I especially remember Francis Baruch and Ian Hope who emigrated to Australia. He often read the news on our radio programmes with an impeccable English accent. Both were outstanding teachers along with Ahmad Dzafir, who rose to a high post in the Ministry of Education after Singapore became independent.

I was a little more than a year at Bartley before I was transferred to the much older and more established Victoria School. I had visited this school in 1937 when I came down from Ipoh for the matriculation examinations which were held at this centre. I was told that the Victoria School principal was a martinet, but I found Michael Campbell fair-minded, though a strict disciplinarian who ran the school very well. The pupils were certainly terrified of him. I was put in charge of Senior "A" — a school certificate class which, along with the other two classes, prepared the students for the Cambridge examinations. One of these classes had science students with the well-known teacher Jesudason, who was later to become the principal of Raffles Institution. While one of the pupils in his class was destined one day to be a cabinet minister, one of mine was destined to be convicted of murder and hanged! There's a destiny that shapes our ends.

My class of about 35 boys was a keen one which it was a pleasure to teach. They enjoyed *Macbeth* best of three literature texts — the others being a selection of long poems and *Gallion's Reach*. We often acted different roles in class, which the students did with enthusiasm. I myself as a school boy in Ipoh had enjoyed *Julius Caesar* with its conspiracy and murder, its ghost and battle scenes, the great speech of Mark Antony over the body of Caesar and the sympathetic character of the idealistic and gentle Brutus. I think these two Shakespearean plays are the most enjoyable for teenage school children. It is possible that school girls might prefer *Romeo and Juliet*. I believe Shakespeare's insight into human motives, his perception of human character and the rich imagery of his poetry make a study of his plays something of immeasurable value. It is a great pity that in a highly competitive setting many schools have dropped literature simply because it is very difficult to score such high marks as in mathematics or scientific subjects. Literature deals with life — the joy and sorrow of love, the virtues and vices of men. But all this seems of little account in Singapore today. Every year Singapore schools are graded on their examination results. The newspapers publish a list in order of merit of the schools with the most students who obtained distinctions. The consequence is that every school struggles to improve its position on the list. One way of doing this is to drop subjects such as literature which are considered "difficult" and hard to get a distinction in. It is also true that arts subjects like history and literature are not regarded as "useful" subjects in Singapore, so the schools tend to neglect them. But this was not so during the British colonial period. When I was a school teacher in the early 1950s, all subjects, whether arts or science, were given equal attention in our schools. I do not wish to discuss the pros and cons of educational policies which are tailored to meet the needs of our society. Years later, one of the senior ministers giving a talk to the National University of Singapore's undergraduates was shocked to discover that they knew nothing of the merger with Malaysia and the separation in 1965. History then became respectable and the schools began to teach history again!

But to get back to my class at Victoria School. Several of the boys went on to become lawyers, businessmen, civil servants and teachers. But one, Sunny Ang paid the ultimate penalty. He was intelligent, above average in his studies. I recall him seated in the back row at the extreme end on my right, quiet and sometimes lost in thought. He had an enigmatic smile as if to say, "You can never guess my thoughts." Sunny, who came from a middle-class family, was knowledgeable about aircraft. On one occasion I took him along with me to a lower class when I had to conduct a lesson that had something to do with aeroplanes. I got him to answer questions on planes. He did it competently. His ambition was to be a commercial pilot. He certainly had an adventurous spirit.[1]

---

[1] "In 1957, [Sunny Ang] left his teacher-in-training course to train as a pilot under a government scholarship scheme, but his brash behaviour during training, including flouting safety regulations, cost him his chances of becoming a commercial pilot. He entered the 1961 Grand Prix in Singapore but shortly after was fined for killing a pedestrian through negligent driving. He was again arrested in 1962 during an attempted burglary, after which he was put on probation. He then began studying law part-time and wanted to go to England for a law degree. However, he was made a bankrupt sometime in 1962." (*Source*: Infopedia. The Sunny Ang murder case, p. 3)

In May 1965, Sunny Ang was found guilty by the jury of murdering his girlfriend Jenny Cheok, a former barmaid who went diving with him in dangerous waters between the Sisters' Islands in August 1963. She disappeared on her second dive and her body was never found. He had insured her heavily for S$400,000.[2] There was no doubt about his guilt though her body was never recovered. The evidence was circumstantial but the jury's verdict was unanimous.[3]

Justice Buttrose said,

> "Ang you have been convicted by the unanimous verdict of the jury of a terrible crime. You killed this young girl Jenny whose only fault apparently was that she had the misfortune to fall in love with you, and to give you everything she possessed — her all. You killed her for personal gain. It is a crime cunningly contrived to give the appearance of an accident, and it was carried out with consummate coolness and nerve. At long last the time has come for you to pay the penalty for your dreadful deed."

It was reported that he went bravely to the scaffold. Nothing in his life became him like the leaving it. May he rest in peace. Most countries, especially in Europe, have abolished capital punishment. Statistics prove that there has been no increase in murder in Europe, so the belief that murderers would have a field day is no longer tenable. But it will be a while yet before Asian countries abolish state executions. In fact, there

---

[2] "At the time of [Jenny Cheok's] disappearance, one of the policies had expired the day before, but Ang extended it for five days just three hours before the diving trip." (*Source*: Infopedia. The Sunny Ang murder case, p. 3)

[3] "The Sunny Ang murder case was one of the most high-profile crimes in 1960s Singapore ... The case was unusual in that the victim's body was never found and the prosecution's case was based solely on circumstantial evidence and the connections between the evidence ... Ang never entered the water to look for Cheok that day and did not seem anxious when she failed to resurface or display any urgency in getting help from nearby St John's Island. Yet less than 24 hours after the incident, he notified the insurance companies of Cheok's mishap and sought to make full claims. Ang was tried in the High Court before a seven-man jury between 26 April and 18 May 1965. Justice Buttrose was the presiding judge while Senior Crown Counsel Francis T. Seow led the prosecution. Ang was defended by Punch Coomaraswamy. (*Source*: Infopedia. The Sunny Ang murder case, p. 4)

are more crimes for which hanging is imposed — drug trafficking for instance. Those who believe in the need for the death penalty should read *De Profundis* by Oscar Wilde, England's wittiest dramatist who himself spent a couple of years in prison.

Victoria School, like all schools in Singapore, began the daily routine at 7.30 a.m. Each lesson lasted 50 minutes. There was a recess at 10.30 for half an hour and school ended at 1 p.m. There were games in the afternoon. I usually had a free period a day to mark essays and precis pieces. The students had to write an essay a week and do a precis too in addition to written responses to the longer poems and *Macbeth*. I organised extra classes in literature for the weaker pupils on Saturday mornings for a couple of hours. Many who had no need to attend these classes came along too! We, all of us, had a good time.

Senior "A" of which I was the form master was well-behaved. There was only one mischievous and high-spirited Indian lad I had to send out of the class once. He is now a successful lawyer in Singapore. He will no doubt recognise himself if he ever reads this book! The years 1954 and 1955 were happy ones for me in Victoria School despite the heavy marking of exercise books every week. It was a delight to see the improvement made by every pupil especially in written English.

One day, quite unexpectedly, Professor Roy Morrell, head of the Department of English at the University of Malaya in Singapore, visited me in the school. He said that a member of his staff had suddenly packed his bags and vanished, leaving the undergraduates stranded. These were final-year students, about 20 of them, who needed tutoring. He wanted me to take afternoon classes twice a week. As the school principal agreed, I was glad to undertake teaching literature at a higher level. The following year — 1955 — Professor Morrell offered me a lectureship. As I was merely a temporary employee, I gave a month's notice to the director of education and prepared myself for a change in career.

Some of the staff at the University I already knew from my Raffles College days. The dean of arts was Professor Dobbie, who had been a lecturer in geography before the war and one of the hostel wardens who enjoyed ambushing those of us who returned late to the hostel after a night out and fining us $3! I was the first non-expatriate to join the

Department of English, which was staffed wholly by expatriates including the Ceylonese de Chickera whom I had met on the ship on the way back to Singapore from London in 1952. There were only six of us in the Department of English. We got on very well, especially as Professor Morrell was a warm, friendly and relaxed head of department. Apart from his love of literature, he was a keen collector of butterflies. This hobby took him to the outskirts of the island into nature areas still unspoilt or undeveloped. There were fewer golf courses in the 1950s as many of the local elite had not taken to golfing for relaxation. Golfing has since become a craze and nature has had to give way to this game which has swallowed up huge areas of land-scarce Singapore. Professor Morrell donated his entire collection of butterflies to the Singapore Museum when he left Singapore in 1957. He published a book on his hobby entitled *Common Malayan Butterflies*. It was entirely due to Professor Morrell that I joined the University. I never even thought of applying for a job at the University, and I got the job without even applying for it! All because a lecturer acted irresponsibly and left the country suddenly. So, indeed, there is a destiny that shapes our ends, rough-hew them how we will. And a few years later this was to happen again to me.

So, there I was in 1955 back in the Bukit Timah campus where I had enjoyed four happy years in Raffles College from 1938 to 1942 when the Japanese invaded Malaya. By a curious coincidence, I was also back in "C" block in the Eu Tong Sen building which was now the Department of English. The same block also housed the Department of History and Malay Studies and Chinese Studies downstairs in what was known in my college days as "A" block. The main solid and well-designed structures around two quadrangles — upper and lower — were the same as in the 1930s. The Japanese had added another block of the same design on the lower quadrangle. The Oei Tiong Ham block was transferred to house a larger administration with increased staff as well as a much bigger library. On one side of the upper quadrangle, a new building of the same pattern occupied what had been tennis courts in Raffles College days. This building housed the Physics and Zoology departments. The expansion was necessary to accommodate the rapid increase in the intake of students.

When the University of Malaya was officially established in 1949, the first batch of students enrolled was as follows:

    Arts   168
    Science   82
    Medicine   310 [includes students from Year I to Year VI]
    Dentistry   85 [includes students from Year I to Year V]
    [Note: The numbers for medicine and dentistry include all students from the former King Edward VII College of Medicine, established earlier in 1905.]

By the time I joined the University in 1955, the numbers were as follows:

    Arts   426
    Science   184
    Engineering 50
    Medicine   438
    Dentistry   99
    Pharmacy   23

By 1956, the figure for arts had jumped to 725 but science had increased by only 18 and medicine by 21. The total number of students was 1,574. This total comprised both Malayan and Singaporean students. (Note: Student statistics from University's annual reports, 1949, 1955 and 1956.)

New departments were established. In 1956, Indian Studies came into being to complete three departments in Oriental Studies which recognised the multiculturism of Malaya. More utilitarian subjects like law, engineering and pharmacy were also created in the 1957 to 1958 session. All these expansions meant more lecture rooms, laboratories, hostels, staff and staff quarters. There was the suggestion of the Carr-Saunders Commission that a new university be established in Johor but the vice-chancellor pointed out that the cost, estimated at $145 million, was prohibitive. A joint committee of the Federation and Singapore governments recommended that the University should develop both in Kuala Lumpur and Singapore. This was accepted and acted upon. By 1962, the University of Malaya was established in Pantai Valley, Kuala Lumpur and the University of Singapore remained in Bukit Timah and the King Edward VII College site. The Federation of Malaya had become independent in 1957 and it was natural that an independent university should be established in Kuala Lumpur to meet her needs and fulfil her ideas of university education. This was the reason for the big increase in the intake of arts students. Malaysia wanted to educate its civil servants. Bright young Malays were awarded scholarships to the university. All were compelled to undergo courses in the English language. I was put in charge of organising courses for them. Part-time teachers had to be recruited to cope with the demand. Tutorial groups of four to five students were given weekly classes apart from lectures. Many of these students went on to distinguish themselves in their civil service careers, becoming secretary-generals in various ministries.

Years later when I was appointed high commissioner to Malaysia, these students of mine were very helpful. Asians as a whole, and I think Malays in particular, respect their "gurus" for a lifetime. It was certainly a great advantage for me during my diplomatic assignments to Malaysia. Only one of the scholars, Musa Hitam, became a politician and rose to be deputy prime minister before giving up politics altogether after some disagreement with the Prime Minister Dr Mahathir.

Academic Freedom and University Autonomy

The 1960s witnessed a collision between the University and the newly formed PAP government on the interpretation of the terms "academic freedom" and "university autonomy". The University was of course heavily subsidised by the government as is usual with education at all levels all over the world. The authorities at the University believed in academic freedom as practised in the United Kingdom and enshrined in the Robbins Report commissioned by the British government and published in 1963. English universities have enjoyed a long history of freedom — indeed freedom, both individual and institutional, is deeply rooted in the history of the country. This is not true of developing countries, even in the former colonies of Britain.

The first test on this issue of academic freedom happened in 1960. D.J. Enright, an eminent poet and critic who was professor of English, delivered his inaugural lecture on "Robert Graves and the Doctrine of Modernism". In his introductory remarks he criticised Singapore's Ministry of Culture's efforts to attack "yellow culture" and to create a Singaporean culture. It promoted, for instance, dances combining Chinese, Malay and Indian features. It banned juke-boxes. The government wished to promote racial harmony by actively promoting cultural reforms. Professor Enright believed that a people's culture must come from the people themselves and not be imposed from above. He termed such a culture "sarong culture". The daily newspaper *The Straits Times*, which was at the time independent and critical of the PAP government, came out with large headlines, declaring a "Hands off" challenge to "culture vultures". The Minister for Culture Mr Rajaratnam, an ex-journalist, saw red. He attacked Professor Enright as an alien who had no right to interfere in local politics. He released the following letter to the press which was rude and pompous. It referred to Enright as a "mendicant and beatnik" professor. It was signed by Acting Minister for Labour and Law Ahmad bin Ibrahim, who was dying of cancer.

> "Dear Sir
>
> In January this year you were granted a professional visit pass to take up appointment as professor of English at the University of Malaya. Your duties were to supervise the teaching of English at the University.
>
> Since then, it would appear, you have arrogated to yourself functions and duties which are reserved only for citizens of this country and not visitors, including mendicant professors.
>
> On two occasions you have used the facilities afforded you as professor of English to involve yourself in political affairs which are the concern of local people. The Government has made clear before and after the elections that it will not tolerate any alien like you who misuses our hospitality by entering the political arena.
>
> Whether the Government is right or wrong in banning juke-boxes or whether it should or should not try to foster a Malayan culture is a matter for the citizens of this country to decide. We have no time for asinine sneers by passing aliens about the futility of "sarong culture complete with pantun

competitions" particularly when it comes from beatnik professors.

This is to inform you that should you again wander from the bounds of your work for which you were granted entry into the country, then your professional visit pass will be cancelled as in all such cases. You are being paid handsomely to do the job which you are presumably qualified to do, and not to enter the field of local politics which you were unqualified to participate in. You would do well to leave such matters to local citizens. It is their business to solve these problems as they think fit. They have to live and die in this country. You will be packing your bags and seeking green pastures elsewhere if your gratuitous advice on these matters should land us in a mess.

The days are gone when birds of passage from Europe or elsewhere used to make it a habit of participating from their superman heights of European civilisation.

If you bear this in mind your stay in this country may be mutually profitable."

The newspaper report did not even mention the topic of the inaugural lecture on Robert Graves. The report was provocative and certainly succeeded in rousing the wrath of the minister. His vulgar letter in turn roused the normally apathetic students who decided that the warning to Professor Enright was an attack on academic freedom. Much to the surprise of the government, they held a massive demonstration to support the professor's right to express his views freely. I went to see Prime Minister Lee Kuan Yew whom I had known since our Raffles College days. I explained that Professor Enright was not the imperialist-colonial type at all but that he was a famous poet and outstanding teacher. Preliminary remarks on his lecture on Robert Graves had been used by *The Straits Times* to attack government policies on culture without even mentioning the title of the lecture and omitting four-fifths of the text! The prime minister said that his minister for culture had "got out of the wrong side of his bed that morning" and sent off his reprimand to the newspaper. The outcome of all this was that the prime minister set the boundaries of academic freedom. Expatriate teachers should steer clear of local politics and confine themselves to their specialties. An expatriate who is an authority on Greek literature should leave alone the question of whether or not Malay should be the only official language for instance.

It must be remembered that it was only in 1959 that the PAP came into power with the support of the communist elements. All the politicians and the people supporting them had but recently emerged from colonial rule dominated by white men. They were in no mood to put up with an English professor, no matter how well-meaning, criticising a national cultural policy. However, the prime minister made it clear that expatriates would be needed in the University to "liven up the minds of our students". The editor of *The Straits Times* was severely reprimanded by the prime minister for his distorted account of Enright's lecture. One outcome of the fracas was that D.J. Enright wrote his memoirs, entitling them *The Memoirs of a Mendicant Professor*, an entertaining book which was not banned but was nevertheless not available in Singapore. Bookshops indulged in self-censorship for fear of government reaction. It was never necessary for the authorities to ban any book — the booksellers did it themselves. However, copies of the book were easily available across the Causeway in Johor Bahru. Years later, Professor Enright gave a comic account of how he approached a Singapore bookseller who did not recognise him for a copy of his book. The man looked nervously around him, reached out under the counter and produced a wrapped-up copy! Enright did not resign but perhaps pleased with the response of the undergraduates who rose to his defence, stayed on.

The second conflict between the University and the government took place in 1963 over the admission of Chinese language stream students. The vice-chancellor was a well-known and highly respected doctor, Dr Sreenivasan, who believed sincerely that the University, and only the University, should decide who should be admitted. All persons of either sex and of whatever religion, nationality or class, provided they had the requisite examination results, would be admitted. The government decided that Chinese language stream students from schools or Nanyang University who qualified should be accepted provided the Ministry of Education approved their application. The government feared that since the Chinese language stream schools had been penetrated by the communists, who had established cells in them and in Nanyang University, communist students would influence and disrupt the English stream undergraduates. The PAP government which had come into power with the collaboration of the communists was faced with the breakaway of the latter to form a new party, the Barisan Socialis. This group had the support of the Chinese middle schools and the Chinese-medium Nanyang University students who were militant. They had disturbed public order, organised strikes and barricaded themselves in their schools defying the police. They were idealistic students manipulated by the communists. They were well-trained and dedicated to the communist cause.

The government wanted the Chinese language stream students applying to join the English-medium University to produce a certificate of suitability issued by the Education Ministry. By an Act of Parliament in 1964, the requirement was also imposed on Nanyang University, the Singapore Polytechnic and Ngee Ann College. So the government had the power to bar students from institutions of higher learning on security or political grounds.

Dr Sreenivasan refused to accept the imposition of a suitability certificate. The Council of the University sent a delegation of four to meet the prime minister. I was a member of the delegation. I had been elected by the staff to represent them on the Council. We were shown into the conference room adjoining the PM's office in the old City Council building. There was a long table stacked at one end with more than a dozen files which probably contained evidence of communist student activities. The files were no doubt meant to impress us. We didn't carry a single file to support our case in defence of Dr Sreenivasan's position. Dr Goh Keng Swee emerged from the PM's office first and seated himself after a perfunctory greeting. Of course, I knew him well from our London days. After another five minutes the prime minister strode in and began to lecture us for the next 45 minutes on the unrealistic attitude of the vice-chancellor despite his efforts to make him understand the danger of exposing the undergraduates to the communist Chinese students. None of the delegation had a chance to argue. We were dismissed after his lecture. Dr Sreenivasan resigned. Every candidate for admission had to obtain a certificate of suitability from the Education Ministry. Professor Lim Tay Boh, the mild-mannered professor of economics, was appointed acting vice-chancellor. He was in no position to continue Dr Sreenivasan's challenge to the government. It was now clear that admission to the University was to be based not only on academic merit but also on political purity. No candidate who had a record of being tainted by communism had a chance to undertake tertiary education in Singapore, but he could go abroad of course if he could afford it. As Singapore had merged with Malaysia, it was in the Malaysian Parliament that the Internal Security (Amendments) Act was enacted whereby students wishing to enrol in institutions of higher learning had to obtain their suitability certificate.

Forming the Local Staff Association — the Kesatuan Akademis Universiti Singapura (KAUS)

Singaporean and Malaysian academic staff in the University of Singapore had for sometime felt unhappy with the expatriate domination of the Senate which decided academic policy. It was natural for the expatriates, who were mostly British or Asians trained in Britain, to think that the local university should be western-oriented. What we desired was to have our University be a truly national institution serving the community. Some of the local staff thought that the expatriates who held the highest positions as professors and deans had influenced Dr Sreenivasan unduly in his refusal to acknowledge the dangers of admitting dedicated communist students to the university. Twenty-three out of 34 professors and heads of departments (67.6 per cent) were expatriates. While in medical, dentistry and pharmacy there were eight local professors and an equal number of local heads of departments, there were some local lecturers — 27 as against 17 expats. However, expats dominated the Arts Faculty. There were seven professors and heads of departments who were expatriates and only one local person. There were four expat senior lecturers as against two locals, 23 expat lecturers as against 10 locals. So 78 per cent of the senior staff were expatriates in the arts faculty. In the Science Faculty, 63 per cent of the senior staff were expats. The figures quoted are from the University calendar of 1964/1965. While on the whole the numbers of expat and local staff were about equal, the power lay with the upper echelon, which was predominantly expat.

I had thought for some time about the situation and discussed it with colleagues like Wong Lin Ken (history), Arthur Rajaratnam (physics) and Sharom Ahmat (history). It was at a Senate meeting to elect a representative to the University Council that I made up my mind. We had put up an eminent local medical professor as our candidate against an expatriate professor. Some of the expats who were farsighted voted for the local man so there was a tie — 24 against 24. The acting dean of arts, who was an expat from Sri Lanka, gave his casting vote to the expat. I then made a dramatic announcement that the Malaysian and Singaporean staff would break away from the Academic Staff Association to form their own association. We would of course split from the original staff association and go our own way in order to ensure that the policies of the University would serve the people and not some abstract ideals imposed on us by our former colonial masters. There was shock all around and later on some of the expatriates who knew me well tried to dissuade me from taking steps to start a separate association, but I went ahead and called for a meeting of the locals.

The inaugural meeting of the Malaysian Staff Association of the University of Singapore (or Kesatuan Akademis Universiti Singapura as it was known in Malay) took place on 27 September 1964 at New Lecture Theatre 2 in the Bukit Timah campus. There were more than 70 people present at the meeting. I addressed the meeting on the necessity for the direction of university policy by nationals. A memorandum on the founding of the association was presented to the general body. This memorandum was approved. The meeting had also been called to approve the aims and objects of the proposed constitution. There were a few among those present who questioned the need for a new association to achieve the objectives outlined in the proposed constitution. This was put to the vote and the view was rejected by a decisive majority. The constitution as a whole was adopted in principle subject to amendments from some members. It was agreed to discuss such amendments at an adjourned meeting of the association.

The election of the office bearers resulted in the following returns. I was elected president, Professor Monterio vice-president, Dr Rajaratnam honorary secretary, Mr Hon Yun Sen honorary treasurer. Committee members included Professor T.H. Elliott, an expatriate but a strong supporter of the local association and a socialist. Professor Lim Kok Ann, Professor Jansen, Lee Yong Leng and Donald Wyatt were the other committee members. A subcommittee was also appointed under Professor Elliott as chairman to look into the revision of salaries, another subcommittee was appointed to look into the question of staff housing loans and a third subcommittee for scholarships and training schemes under Dr Rajaratnam was also appointed. There was also a publicity subcommittee under Lee Yong Leng with Sharom Ahmat as honorary secretary. The association was called the Malaysian Staff Association because we were at the time still a part of Malaysia.

One factor that may have led to my election as president was the belief that because I had been a contemporary at Raffles College and later in Britain of a few leading government ministers, I might be a useful linkman between the government and the University. The PAP government was then exerting great pressure on the University by withholding money so that at one time there was even the possibility that the staff could not be paid.

Over the next four to five years, our journal *Suara Universiti* published a number of articles, mostly of academic interest but sometimes controversial ones too when the expatriates attacked the Malaysian Staff Association. I myself made it very clear time and again that while the expatriates were most welcome and in fact necessary to liven up the thinking in the University, they should leave policy making to the local staff.

There was a fear that the expatriates might resign, but this did not take place apart from the usual retirements and the occasional resignations of people who wanted to move on to better jobs elsewhere. Recruitment in fact increased and now, at last, there were more locals recruited at the lectureship and assistant lectureship levels, which had in certain departments, been blocked by the expatriate professors in the past.

As a result of the activities of the Kesatuan, the terms of employment of expatriates were revised. New expatriates were no longer given permanent tenure. Instead, they were offered a gratuity payment of two months salary for every year of service. Such expatriate staff as the University wished to retain after the three-year contract were given six months' leave on full pay and the gratuity. Naturally there were no complaints about this. The really able professors had their contracts renewed time and again without any difficulty. An example was the outstanding Indian professor of botany, Professor A.N. Rao. The aim of the Kesatuan Akademis Universiti Singapura (KAUS) to ensure an increase in the recruitment of qualified local personnel to the staff of the University received an impetus. It was never the intention of the Kesatuan to have 100 per cent of the staff made up of Malaysians and Singaporeans. It emphasised that there had to be vacancies for gifted expatriate teachers and researchers in the University.

Dr Toh Chin Chye, who succeeded Professor Lim Tay Boh who died suddenly in late 1967, cancelled the generous terms of six months' leave with gratuity to three months' leave without gratuity.

Department of Extra-Mural Studies

Extra-mural departments provided courses for working adults who had not enjoyed the benefit of higher education. The University's Department of Extra-Mural Studies aimed to forge a major link between the public and the University through the provision of evening courses on a variety of topics. This was in line with the thinking of the Kesatuan Akademis Universiti Singapura which had urged a closer link with the public. In the early 1950s, the establishment of such a department had been discussed but it had never materialised because it was felt that there would be no demand for such courses and because of inter-faculty rivalries. However, with the appointment of the farsighted but ill-fated Dr Sreenivasan as Vice-Chancellor, the idea was revived, and under his less controversial successor Professor Lim Tay Boh, an expert in adult education or "extension learning" as it was sometimes called, was invited from Britain. Dr John Lowe was to find out whether there would be any response in Singapore to evening classes taught by the University staff (for extra payment, of course). Dr Lowe was received with the scepticism normally accorded by all established university departments to any professor of a new branch of knowledge.

Most members of staff regarded the new arrival with indifference, and some with contempt, as an expert on a subject which could well be considered inappropriate to the University. He was subjected to a good deal of pressure from both locals and the expatriate staff who resented the starting of a new department which would compete for the same funds to which they felt they were entitled. However, these petty jealousies had to give way to the greater good of the community. Despite these difficulties, Dr Lowe did well, except when he was bitten by the conference bug — a malady most common to academics. No sooner had he arrived, when he was away abroad at the expense of well-intentioned foundations and organisations whose funds have to be spent on worthy causes. Despite his peregrinations, Dr Lowe soon proved that there was in Singapore as insatiable an appetite for learning as there is for any other profitable activity. All courses which in any way promised to increase one's income would be well supported provided that certificates were awarded at the end of each series of lectures.

On this discovery was laid the foundation of the Department of Extra-Mural Studies, a department which has gone from strength to strength, from gain to greater gain, until it built up the largest reserves of any department in the University. From time to time, lip service may be paid to the ideals of extension education as any respectable educational outfit is expected to do, but the survival of the Department of Extra-Mural Studies in Singapore is dependent on the fact that it makes money. Otherwise it might have suffered the fate of the University's School of Education which was closed down in 1971.

When Dr Lowe's pilot project proved successful, the University authorities decided that it was time to get rid of him and appoint a local person at a cheaper rate. It so happened that I had gained some notoriety among the expatriate community of the university by setting up a separate staff association for the local academic staff. As I was the only non-expatriate in the Department of English at that time, the vice-chancellor might have thought it diplomatic to move me out. So I was asked to take over the Department of Extra-Mural Studies with the promise of a promotion. I had no qualifications in adult education but the eminent D.J. Enright, the professor of English, was kind enough to give me a one-sentence testimonial which stated that not only was I the right man but, as far as he knew, the only one in the University for the job! He was probably right, as I doubt whether anyone else wanted it!

In 1965, I took over the department. Though I had accepted the job with reluctance, I was to find the work challenging. Devising courses, persuading members of the University staff and some well-qualified professional men from among the public to lecture, as well as ensuring that more mundane details such as making sure that the lights were functioning in lecture rooms, kept me busy till past 9.30 p.m. on most nights when the lecture-discussion sessions ended. The recruitment of Mr J.F. Conceicao, a former teacher at St Patrick's School, as a lecturer (later he went on to become a distinguished Member of Parliament and diplomat) and an exceptionally efficient and dedicated secretary, Miss Goh Pin Hoon, helped in the running of the department. Their presence made it possible for me to go abroad during the University's long vacation on a study tour of extra-mural studies departments at leading British universities and attend a course in Denmark, culminating with an international Adult Education Conference in Krogerup near Copenhagen — an ancient city of architectural beauty, well-known for Hans Christian Andersen, The Little Mermaid and modern sex fairs. I visited Hull and Cambridge after the conference. I was fortunate to meet the great modern poet Philip Larkin in Hull. On his office table he had a picture of a gorilla! I learnt a great deal from this tour.

A year passed after my return from Britain during which Mr J.F. Conceicao went to Manchester University for a postgraduate course in adult education and I was given another assistant who was also very helpful. This enabled me to involve myself in some public service as chairman of the National Theatre, as a member and later acting chairman of the Adult Education Board, as a member of the Film Censorship Appeals Board, and as one of the governors of the Youth Leadership Training Centre at Buona Vista Road under the chairmanship of Dr Goh Keng Swee. The Training Centre was under the stringent control of a 6' 2" (1.88 m) Israeli ex-commando whose intellectual toughness matched his physique. His pet off-duty topic of conversation was the quickest way to kill an enemy. He was eloquent on hand-to-hand combat to strangulate, stab or otherwise dispose of the foe. One could almost hear the skin snap at the point of the bayonet as he spoke. His conversation gave me gooseflesh but I admired his dedication and efficiency. The military discipline he imposed on the student leaders certainly helped us to turn out a rugged lot of graduates from the school to man the community centres. He had been chosen by Dr Goh who had an unerring instinct to select the right man for a job. Characteristically, however, he nominated more liberal persons to the Board of Governors to keep the commandant in check.

Part 2

Chapter 4
High Commissioner to India
July 1967–August 1969

97

Chapter 5
High Commissioner to Malaysia and Return to Academia
August 1969–August 1971 and 1972–June 1977

151

Chapter 6
Ambassador to the Republic of the Philippines
June 1977–August 1980

201

Chapter 7
Return to Malaysia
September 1980–April 1988

231

Chapter 8
Retirement in Singapore
1988–present

277

Chapter 4

High Commissioner to India
July 1967–August 1969

MY PUBLIC SERVICE activities may have brought me to the attention of the minister for foreign affairs, Mr S. Rajaratnam, whom I did not know personally. Early in February of 1966 I was suddenly summoned to the Ministry of Foreign Affairs to be asked to represent Singapore at an Asian Cultural Conference in New Delhi within a week or so. I was also to present a paper to the conference on the cultural situation in Singapore and the problems we faced. At the conference which was attended by learned representatives from many countries, I was happy to meet R.K. Narayan, the well-known Indian novelist. He made a scathing speech on the final day of the conference suggesting that whatever cultural gains had been made at the conference, the English language had emerged bruised and battered by the participants and by the Indian professors in particular. Other eminent authors present as observers were Mulk Raj Anand and Syed Hussein Alatas who was later to become a professor at the University of Singapore. Most memorable was the tea party given by the scholarly vice-president of India, Zakir Husain, in his garden of roses. He was one of the best known rose-growers in India and a respected man of learning as well.

The minister's last-minute request to me to attend the conference might have been intended to test my reactions to India but it is more than likely that he was unable to find someone reasonably suitable. The conference was well-organised, the February weather cool and pleasant, and our hosts very hospitable, especially the secretary of the Indian Council of Cultural Relations, Mr Rehman, a man of considerable charm and learning.

I had a pleasant impression of New Delhi in winter and the hospitality of its people. However, through a mix-up in timetables, I missed my plane in Delhi and had to take the next one which disgorged me in Calcutta (now Kolkata) where I suffered overnight at the Great Eastern Hotel. One night of Calcutta is more than enough to haunt one for a lifetime. Only the strong in mind, inured to suffering, should ever descend into this sinkhole of human poverty and degradation. For me, it was a living hell. I made sure that I caught the plane to Singapore the next day.

One evening in August 1966, the minister for foreign affairs telephoned to ask me to call on him the next day. He did not say why, but for some months rumours had swept the campus that I was one of the two marked for appointments abroad as ambassadors. The prime minister had informed the University Council in characteristic style that it was time the staff of the University stepped out of their ivory tower and joined in the hustle and bustle of the workaday world. He argued that staff sent abroad in Singapore's service would benefit from their experience and return better equipped both to teach and administer university departments. The University Council and the vice-chancellor had long given up the habit of arguing with the prime minister — they rarely do so in developing countries — and in any case it was flattering that the University which had been in considerable disfavour, was now considered fit enough to meet the needs of Singapore by partially staffing our foreign missions.

The minister for foreign affairs asked whether I would agree to go to India as high commissioner. As the Indian government had been the first to recognise independent Singapore, he felt that we should establish a mission in New Delhi without too much delay as we had already sent a high commissioner to London and an ambassador to Washington. Singapore, along with Malaysia, had supported India verbally in her disastrous border war with China in 1962 when more powerful nations had stood aloof. (Soon we developed sufficient political astuteness not to take sides in the 1965 Indo-Pakistan clash.) Apparently some well-known

Singapore businessmen of ethnic Indian origin had offered their services free of charge but the minister had politely declined such offers.

I had to make a difficult decision on whether to accept the government's invitation to serve as Singapore's first high commissioner to India. On the one hand, I had two children in the primary classes in the Anglo-Chinese School. My elder boy had topped his class in the final examinations and the other was in the top ten in his class. Was it not risky to disrupt their education? This problem is a perennial one which foreign ministry staff sent abroad always have to face. My wife, who was an education officer teaching in the convent, was not happy about going abroad although she would be on no-pay leave for the term of my appointment. I was myself happy in my job at the university and the thought of being a diplomat about whose duties I knew nothing of was no inducement. But it was an honour to be invited to serve Singapore. Another reason which led me to agree to go to India was the shortage of mature men to accept the responsibility of being heads of missions. I was acquainted with several of the People's Action Party (PAP) cabinet ministers and decided I should not let them down. The pay offer was the same basic salary of $1,770.00 which I received in the university, with the same variable allowance. There was a 10 per cent overseas allowance of about $200. Singapore's economy had not taken off yet and the Ministry of Finance was tight-fisted. It knew next to nothing about the financial needs of ambassadors. Wisely the government had appointed two millionaires as high commissioner and ambassador to Malaysia and Thailand respectively (without pay) who did not need any pay. All together what was offered was about the same as the combined incomes of my wife and me. But at that time money was not the important factor in making my decision. In contrast, in the 1980s and 1990s, attitudes had changed a great deal as civil servants and ministers had to be paid huge sums to prevent them from quitting public service for the prosperous private sector.

I accepted after a week, but made it clear that I could not leave the Department of Extra-Mural Studies for some months until the new courses planned for the first half of 1967 were launched. The Indian government raised no objection to my appointment and a simultaneous announcement was made in Singapore and New Delhi one night in November 1966. The first appointees of the Singapore mission were despatched early in 1967 to do some house hunting, for we had neither office nor residence in New Delhi. The first secretary, Anwar Ibrahim, made herculean efforts but he was given little scope for initiative as our Ministry of Foreign Affairs was shackled by the Ministry of Finance which had no clue as to the costs of establishing an overseas mission. Even worse, it had in fact suffered a setback by making a bad investment on a house in London. It laid down conditions impossible to fulfil. Apparently certain junior officials in the Ministry of Finance looked on the idea of establishing missions abroad as an unnecessary luxury. Their scepticism, aggravated by their ignorance, made the task of our envoys doubly difficult.

Time and energy were unnecessarily wasted in exchanges of increasingly acrimonious letters. This was the common experience of all of us who went abroad in the early years. In fact, Dr Wong Lin Ken, our ambassador to Washington, who also had to represent Singapore in the United Nations, confessed to me that all he could afford were hamburger lunches at drugstore counters. He suspected, probably quite rightly, that janitors in American hotels were paid more than Singapore's ambassador! An example of a Ministry of Finance official's obtuseness was when the first secretary in New Delhi wrote that both air-conditioners and heaters had to be purchased for the residence. The Ministry of Finance official was flabbergasted by such a strange request and would not yield till he was given geographical information about the latitude of New Delhi and facts about Indian winters and summers which, of course, he could himself have found out with a little initiative.

The Indian summer from April to June is the season of sunstrokes. I believe it must have been the British administrators' memories of Indian summers which made them recommend cork helmets for school children of all races in Malaya. Station masters and civil servants including high commissioners and governors in ceremonial uniform were invariably equipped with splendidly shaped white helmets, sometimes with a cockade atop! I remember having to use a cork hat or "topee" daily to school in Ipoh. Fortunately, it was light and passably airy. Nowadays it is a rare sight. Cork is wedded firmly to bottles these days. Even in India cork helmets are no longer worn despite the searing heat which sometimes exceeds 45°C. It was partly the thought of such scorching days in the sun that delayed my departure from Singapore even after I had arranged the extra-mural programme for 1967. The Indian high commissioner in Singapore was kind enough to warn me privately that I should avoid the summer months and arrive no earlier than September in New Delhi, if possible. Summer in Delhi normally sees the exodus of ministers, top military brass, ambassadors and anyone else who has the means, to the Indian hill resorts or preferably to temperate lands on state visits. Under the British Raj the whole seat of government had migrated annually from Delhi to Simla from April to September.

I would have succeeded in staying in Singapore till September but for the arrival of the then Indian foreign minister, the eminent lawyer Shri Chagla, on a state visit in May 1967. Inevitably, as high commissioner-designate, I was invited to meet him. At the first official dinner at Sri Temasek, our minister for foreign affairs, Mr S. Rajaratnam, could not resist introducing me to the distinguished visitor as one who was "likely to retire before he takes up his appointment" (announced more than six months previously). The laughter arrowed on me and jangled my nerves. Mr Chagla said with a sigh that I was establishing a record in the time interval between the announcement and my appearance and asked when I would actually arrive in New Delhi. "Next month," I said promptly, hoping he would think that I had planned it that way all along. On the last day of June after eating the last of many farewell dinners and equipped with my first ever formal dinner jacket, and loaded with the blessings of various sections of the Indian community in Singapore (who were barely on speaking terms with each other), I set off ahead of my family. I was in the first-class cabin of the BOAC aircraft and for the next two years always travelled first-class — by order of the government and at the taxpayers' expense! I was entering first-class into the world of diplomacy in a country of vast complexities and violent contrasts.

Settling In

1.30 a.m. Delhi time, 1 July 1967. Temperature 86°F (23°C). The deputy protocol chief of India (and ever afterwards my good friend), Dennis Pereira, was with the Australian deputy high commissioner, Mr Nutter, on the tarmac to receive me. "Welcome to India Your Excellency," said Mr Pereira. I looked back over my shoulder instinctively for the VIP he was addressing. It was me! I was expected to excel! But where was Singapore's first secretary? At first I mistook Dennis Pereira for the first secretary for never before had a high commissioner not been met on arrival by his own staff! The first secretary, Anwar Ibrahim, whose car had run out of petrol, caught up with me later at 3 a.m. at the Ashoka Hotel full of apologies. The five-star hotel was to be my home for seven months until a suitable house was found miles from the city centre at a rental acceptable to the Ministry of Finance. The inadequacies of the hotel, despite its panoply of stars, was made up for by the courtesy and kindness of the staff in spite of the inevitable monthly strike and passive demonstration by one section or another of the workers. The North Indian food was greasy but tasty. The western cuisine was perhaps more in the stodgy English tradition but the resident band with its array of Indian instruments made the food more palatable.

The first surprise had been the absence of the first secretary at the airport. The second was that President Zakir Husain was away on a state visit to Canada and was not expected back for about three weeks. This meant that I could not present my credentials and officially I had no diplomatic existence.

However, this need for formality did not prevent me from calling privately on the Malaysian high commissioner, Zaitun Ibrahim, who had been a fellow student in Britain in 1949. Protocol insists that every new high commissioner or ambassador has to call first on the dean of the diplomatic corps (the most senior diplomat accredited to the country in terms of years of residence) and all the others as and when they are ready to receive you for about half an hour. This is more than a "get to know you" meeting as the heads of missions often give the newcomer their own impressions of the country as well as advice on what to do and what to avoid doing. However, all this could be done only after the presentation of one's credentials – the formal handing over of a letter of appointment from the president of Singapore to the president of India. I had been given the letter of appointment by Singapore's President Yusof Ishak at a little gathering in the Istana at which my wife and I were presented formally to him and Puan Noor Aishah, our beautiful and gracious first lady.

For three weeks, I went sightseeing in Delhi in the first secretary's Mercedes (mine had not arrived) and worked in his sitting room, which was our makeshift office, while the new building rented on Ring Road was being completed and gradually furnished. Anwar Ibrahim's home was not only the Singapore High Commission office but frequently also the staff mess. He managed to provide us food with a Singapore flavour deliciously cooked by his mother. This and the friendship of his many children and musically gifted wife boosted my morale. Living alone in a massive 700-room hotel away from my family was a lonely experience.

Delhi, redolent with history, is a city of tombs, monuments and historical ruins. Ancient forts, temples and tombs of Mughal emperors stand in silent testimony to its eventful past. But New Delhi, like most capital cities of the world, is not really representative of life in India. The long tree-lined avenues, the large bungalows with spacious lawns which were the homes of top civil servants, the monumental red government buildings were all inherited from the days of British imperialistic splendour when the ruling race had to hold themselves aloof from the natives they ruled. The diplomatic enclave in Chanyakapuri (named after the famed Indian philosopher of the third century BC) displayed the rival architecture of many wealthy and not-so-wealthy nations, where a minimum of four acres (1.6 ha) was considered necessary to support diplomatic dignity. The enclave was not without its touch of humour as the choicest central area of Chanyakapuri of more than 30 acres (12 ha) was granted to the Chinese in the early Bandung days (after the Asian-African conference held in Bandung, Indonesia in 1955) of "all Chinese-and-Indians-are-brothers" which was shattered by the Sino-Indian border war of 1962. One of the roads in the enclave was named Panchsheel Road after the Panchsheel Treaty (from the Sanskrit *panch* (five) and *sheel* (virtues)), or the Five Principles of Peaceful Coexistence signed in Peking in 1954 between China and India. The five principles were subsequently incorporated in modified form in the statement of ten principles at the Bandung Conference.[1] A formidable wall, second only perhaps to the wall surrounding the Soviet embassy, isolated the Chinese diplomats from the outside world but the tallest of flagpoles flew the Chinese flag and Chairman Mao was wished a long life in huge bold

---

[1] *Five Principles of Peaceful Coexistence.* (*Source*: Wikipedia)

letters in both English and Chinese characters from the highest reaches of the embassy building. When I drove by outside the gates, I noticed an Indian army detachment which stood guard day and night to keep an eye on the "Chinese brothers". In fact, a tent was pitched right there.

Chanyakapuri was certainly a tourist scenic high spot. I must say that as cows and bullock carts were not allowed and no slum huts were permitted, and the area was away from the shopping centre and major trunk roads, Chanyakapuri was ideal for early morning and evening walks. As the Ashoka Hotel, India's largest five-star government hotel in 1967, was located there and as I conducted some of Singapore's diplomatic business from this hotel for the first seven months of my stay in India, the quiet lawns and lanes of the diplomatic enclave were my haven. Morning and evening the birds sang in the many trees carefully cultivated by the successive diplomats who lived and worked in the enclave. The variety of the birds and their comparative fearlessness of man were among the most pleasant aspects of this part of Delhi. At the Ashoka Hotel itself, innumerable pigeons squabbled over bits of food and mated incessantly, not to be outdone by the inhabitants! I suppose the restaurants solved the pigeon population explosion. Birds show remarkable initiative in their search for food. I once saw a crow unpick the strings of a cardboard box full of cakes, lift the top with its beak and fly off with a bun! Later I saw this most intelligent of birds actually burying a small bone in a pile of dry grass for future use. I am convinced of the truth of the fable which I read as a boy, of the crow that dropped stones into a narrow-necked jug of water so that the water would rise to a drinkable level.

Far more impressive in appearance than the crows were the pariah kites, a pair of which I got to know well. These attractive brown birds deserve a better name. They glide gracefully on air currents, surveying the ground below for food. These kites are common in cities as they have adapted themselves to living in proximity to human beings and to some extent depend on them for food. This pair at the Ashoka Hotel certainly got to know me. Every evening, they would wait on the roof top and swoop down for the bits of bread I flung out from the seventh floor of the hotel. Swooping, diving and gliding with grace and speed, these birds learnt to take bread from my hand and carry it in their talons across to the other end of the roof. The kites lightened many lonely hours of my diplomatic days. For the life of a diplomat is often a variation of routine boredom and exhilarating crises.

The journey from New Delhi to Old Delhi was a drive into a suffocating nightmare. Masses of people resembled ants pouring out of a disturbed nest. Gaunt horses drawing gharries, skeletal men dragging overladen carts, foul open drains, squatting vendors, innumerable beggars — suddenly we were in another century, another world. Some tourists find Old Delhi picturesque, which it is, I suppose, if you are just passing through. But to live in its squalor and poverty would be to be never out of torment even though it is the city of Shah Jehan, the greatest builder among the Mughal rulers, the creator of the Taj Mahal, the Red Fort and mosques of great beauty. I suppose to the citizens, the mind proved to be its own place, making a heaven of hell.

During this period, the commandant of the Military College, Lieutenant General Khanna, called upon me and invited me to give a talk to top military brass on Singapore's relations with its neighbours, especially Malaysia and Indonesia. The lecture was part of a course attended by selected officers, the least of whom was a captain. After failing to convince the general that as an unaccredited diplomat I should not make speeches, I prepared the lecture carefully. It was well received. The question period lasted much longer than the hour's lecture and the main concern of the audience was the position of Indonesia vis-à-vis Singapore and Malaysia. My years of university teaching experience made me feel quite at home with the audience and I was accorded the honour of being invited annually by Lieutenant General Khanna and his successor. The general, a distinguished soldier, and his wife, became our friends while we were in Delhi.

The Accreditation Ceremony

When at last President Zakir Husain returned from Canada, the day was set. Nervously, all three of us (myself, the first secretary and my personal assistant) who represented the Republic of Singapore in India awaited the formalities of accreditation. My speech was thoroughly rehearsed and ready, and I had been given the details of the ceremony, which I had read many a time and tried to visualise. But the event beggared expectation.

The open Cadillac, though of ancient vintage, was impressive enough in a procession of black limousines which drove through the city. If only I had remembered to carry a small comb, I should have looked less dishevelled on arrival at the Rashtrapati Bhavan.

At the gates of this presidential palace, 24 turbaned horsemen, splendidly uniformed, split into two groups, a dozen before and a dozen behind the car, and escorted us into the palace grounds. Ready to receive me with drawn sword was a bearded Major-General Gill resplendent with medals, backed by a guard-of-honour drawn up for my inspection. Fortunately, I had a little experience of this duty as I had once inspected a guard-of-honour at our Youth Leadership Training Centre in Buona Vista Road. I hoped I was able to put on a bold face to conceal my nervousness as I paced down the line with self-conscious dignity after both national anthems had been played. I was strangely moved by the impressive rendering of "Majulah Singapura" — it is perhaps only in a foreign country that one's national anthem makes such an enormous impact. The next time I heard the version recorded by the London Symphony Orchestra at our National Day celebrations at the Ashoka Hotel, I was even more moved! It was perhaps the sense of loneliness far away from home sharpened by the emotive power of Zubir Said's inspired composition.

But to come back to the ceremony in the courtyard of the president's palace. Fully escorted and accompanied by the distinguished Shri T.N. Kaul (former Indian ambassador to Moscow and India's foreign minister, and later ambassador to Washington) and followed by Singapore's first secretary and my diminutive personal assistant (perhaps all of five feet in height), I strode up the interminable steps to the Great Hall. At every landing and turn of the staircase three trumpeters blew a fanfare as we approached. After what seemed an age, we arrived at the closed doors of the reception hall and paused for breath after the arduous climb. No diplomat with a weak heart could have made it! All of us relaxed for five minutes before proceeding in a line with as much dignity as we could muster to pause before the President of India. I took one step forward from the line to read the carefully worded speech which I already knew by heart. The President replied in his soft but firm voice. My letter, signed by Singapore's President Yusof Ishak, was placed on a silver tray mounted on a red cushion and taken away. I shook hands with the president and instantly became "His Excellency, the Republic of Singapore's first High Commissioner to the Republic of India".

Ten minutes with the president in his library followed. I asked him how the orchids were getting on, the orchids we had presented to him when he visited Singapore as vice-president early in 1966. He had then lectured at the University in his role as one of India's leading educationists. As director of Extra-Mural Studies, I had made all the arrangements. Flowers, especially roses, were perhaps closer to President Zakir Husain's heart than even education. Being president, he said sadly, left him but little time for roses. On another occasion, a year later, when I called to present him his honorary degree of doctor of laws conferred by the University of Singapore, we had a longer chat in a reception room overlooking the beautiful palace gardens. His informality was always fringed by shyness but the gentle soul of the man shone through. One sensed his kindly nature and sensitive consideration for others. He discoursed on India's almost insoluble problems and the depths of her poverty while I listened sympathetically. We came round to the food problem and I asked why

Picture 10: MB marching under escort up the steps of the Presidential Palace, India, to present credentials, July 1967.

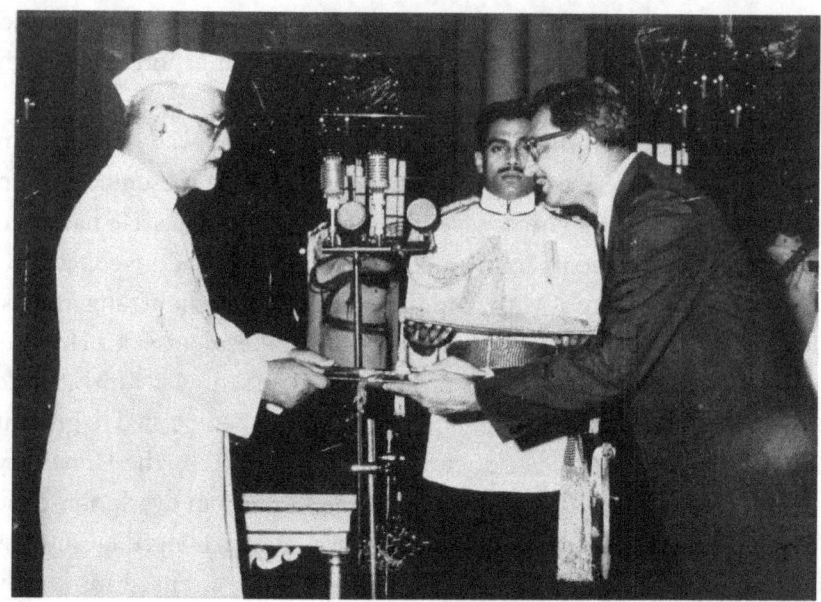

Picture 11: MB presenting credentials to Zakir Husain, President of India, at Rashtrapati Bhavan, July 1967.

no effort was made to export the great variety of fruits, especially mangoes grown in India. He thought for a moment. "Last month," he said, "I received a package of two dozen peaches from Europe carefully wrapped up and in perfect condition. A week later, I received also peaches from Kashmir, badly packed and mostly damaged en route. We Indians have a great deal to learn. We slip up on the details."

Courtesy Calls

The speed with which one gets used to being addressed "Excellency" without looking over one's shoulder for someone else will surprise the less cynical. In India, the title is magic — shopkeepers bow lower and charge more, the simple seem awestruck, the shrewd cadge whisky. Diplomat after diplomat on whom I called talked of beauty and poverty, the splendour of the past, the misery of the present, the endless problems with solutions nowhere in sight. Mr Chester Bowles, the great American ambassador on his second tour of duty in India, was the exception. He saw hope where others despaired. His faith in India was born of his great love for the country and his compassion for its peoples. He had been governor of Connecticut, President Kennedy's undersecretary of state, and he had written a number of books. Bowles was incredibly unassuming for an American, and an American of such distinction. Though in poor health, he repaid my courtesy call very quickly. His Republican successor simply sent word that he hoped we, heads of missions of the smaller countries, would not mind if he did not call on us! After Chester Bowles, this diplomatic discourtesy at least spared me the anti-climax of meeting with his successor. A year or so after I had left India, I read that this new ambassador had offended the prime minister, Mrs Gandhi, by forgetting to be at the airport to see her off on her visit to the United States. An unforgivable act of discourtesy!

All my courtesy calls went off well with one exception. The Egyptian ambassador, hurt by the disastrous Six-Day War in 1967, was ruffled by Singapore's neutrality at the United Nations. But when I explained our position, he calmed down. We parted amicably. The Indian foreign minister was equally critical of our stand. India's posture in the Middle East conflict was dictated by her need for Muslim friends in the Middle East to counter Pakistani moves in the Islamic world. So the Indian government was very vocal in supporting the Arabs. I myself came to feel sympathy for the Arabs after listening to the Arab ambassadors, some of whom put forward their views passionately, even with tears in their eyes. I was given details of the ruthlessness of Israel, especially the slaughter of every man, woman and child in the village of Deir Yassin. I was reminded of the Israeli underground activities in the late 1940s and early 1950s by the terrorist Irgun Zvai Leumi and the Stern Gang who assassinated the Swedish peacemaker Count Bernadotte, blew up the King David Hotel and kidnapped and murdered British soldiers in Palestine. These facts are rarely remembered in our part of the world. One ambassador argued that the Palestinian struggle for their lost homeland would be pursued with the same ruthless terrorist tactics once adopted by the Israelis themselves and the struggle would never end till Israel ceased to exist!

Outside of such understandably tense political moments, the Arab diplomats were men of remarkable courtesy and friendliness who were sometimes given to embarrassing hospitality. Not all observed the strict Muslim injunction about alcohol. Those who did, like the Saudi Arabian ambassador, saw to it that guests were feasted in Arabian Nights' style with whole sheep stuffed with yellow rice and an array of dishes reminiscent of the days of Harun al'Rashid. The ambassador himself, a Falstaffian figure always in Arab dress, was a widower who understood English though he rarely spoke it. Some ambassadors do this possibly as a matter of national pride but also to give themselves time to think before replying to awkward questions. The interpreter's presence is a useful gambit in the diplomatic game. On one occasion, I heard the Indonesian foreign minister, Adam Malik, stop to correct his interpreter in the middle of his speech, improving on his English phraseology! All of us at the dinner table burst into laughter in which the minister joined spontaneously before he went on with his speech in Bahasa Indonesia. The Saudi ambassador in oriental fashion made the rounds to see that his guests' plates were full and rarely ate anything himself at the dinners he hosted.

Mohammed Shubaili of Saudi Arabia was a very friendly and generous man. When after seven months in Ashoka Hotel I moved into his neighbourhood in Maharani Bagh, I returned home one evening to find a large basket of fruits on my dining table. My son dashed down the stairs shouting, "The ambassador brought a goat, a big, big goat! It's at the back!" There indeed was a large black goat tethered to a pole, looking very disconsolate. I walked immediately to the ambassador's residence to thank him and determined to return the lonely animal separated from the herd but to no avail.

Not only did he gently refuse; he left me in no doubt that any attempt to do so would be considered rude. It was, he said, the customary Saudi welcome to a good neighbour. "If you had become my neighbour in Arabia," he said, "I would have given you a camel!" That ended my protests. For now I had merely a goat to dispose of, not a huge recalcitrant camel. It was not possible to eat a creature whose sad eyes I had looked into, so I sent it away to join my first secretary's chauffeur's herd. As I did not inform our Ministry of Finance of this gift, I was not asked to pay the price of the goat to the Treasury!

The best attended all-night parties were thrown by another Arab ambassador, the representative of an oil-rich country. When his wife gave birth to a son, after a monotonous sequence of five daughters, the overjoyed father gave a party with fireworks that rivalled the Indian National Day celebrations! A keen hunter, the ambassador shot a couple of "blue bulls" or Nilgai antelope to feed the guests, and for entertainment he flew out film stars from Bombay. The ambassador's one great ambition was to shoot a tiger before leaving India. This he did and had the animal stuffed, mounted and placed at the entrance to his residence for all to admire. Some sceptical diplomats hinted that the impressive tiger had been bought but I prefer to give the ambassador the benefit of the doubt. Alas, he was transferred to another Middle East country where he said, he could only shoot sparrows! When I admired one of his many cars, a Jaguar, he actually offered it to me as a gift. Naturally I refused. The Arabs are so generous that one has to be careful not to admire too much some object in an Arab house as one is likely to be offered it as a gift.

Tigers, which are among the most beautiful of animals, are becoming rare in India, having dwindled to fewer than 3,000 from an estimated 60,000 only 30 years ago. They are now an endangered species as there are fewer than 1,500 left. Perhaps one day they will survive in zoos and be remembered from James Corbett's many stories, especially his *Man Eaters of Kumaon,* and from William Blake's poem:

The Tiger

> Tiger, tiger burning bright
> In the forests of the night
> What immortal hand or eye
> Could frame thy fearful symmetry?

This is only the first four lines of William Blake's great poem. The magnificent tiger is unfortunate in that the Chinese fervently believe that its bones make excellent medicine and its penis is a powerful aphrodisiac. As they pay large sums of money for tiger parts, poaching in Nepal, Bangladesh, Thailand and even India is fast driving this splendid creature to the verge of extinction. Even the majestic Siberian tiger is on the endangered list since the disintegration of the USSR. The beautiful skin and the bones are smuggled into China with the connivance of the border guards. Although in India strict control is exercised in protecting tigers and leopards, poachers still menace the diminishing tiger population as the profits to be made from the Chinese are enormous. It would be a pity if Chinese medical traditions should be responsible for the impending extinction of the rhinoceros and the tiger.

A pet story that made the diplomatic rounds was that on the Duke of Edinburgh's visit to India in 1961, a tiger hunt was organised. Since a tiger was difficult to come by in the wild, in order to save the duke from disappointment, a captured tiger travelled in the rear of the same train as the duke. It was apparently drugged and released at a suitable time and place for the duke to bag his trophy! It is good that the duke is now a leader in protecting wildlife. There were keen hunters among the diplomatic corps who shot wild ducks on annual migration from Siberia and numerous other beasts and birds.

Indiscriminate hunting and poaching have reduced other species of wildlife to near extinction and it is sad to record that some like the Indian cheetah have disappeared totally, the last being shot in the late 1940s. The famous Emperor Akbar in the 16th century is said to have kept a thousand cheetahs for hunting deer. Yet not one cheetah is left in India today! It is a pity that the sleek, beautiful cheetah, the fastest animal on earth, has not been sighted in India since after the last war and it is only in Africa that this animal still survives in the wild.

So-called "sportsmen" use the lights of jeeps at night to dazzle wild animals and butcher them. I was told that American officers and soldiers stationed in India during the war went out at night in their jeeps with machine-guns to slaughter animals merely to satisfy their blood lust. At least the Indian poachers kill for food or in the case of the rhinoceros for its horn, which the Chinese believe is an effective aphrodisiac for which they will pay its weight in gold. Though some Britishers like Corbett and E.P. Gee have done a great deal to encourage wildlife preservation, there are others whose slaughtering skill is recorded on a huge stone monument near Bharatpur at what is now the most famous bird sanctuary in India, the Keoladeo Ghana National Park. I spent several days in the Forest Rest House at this bird sanctuary, formerly the hunting preserve of the Maharaja of Bharatpur, which he has now donated to the nation. By the largest lake in the sanctuary stands the record of British kills, the most disgraceful of which I quote below:

> Lord Hardinge with 49 guns killed 4062 birds
> in December 1914
> Lord Chelmsford with 50 guns killed 4206 birds
> in November 1916
> Lord Linlithgow with 41 guns killed 4273 birds
> in November 1938

At least one Malay sultan took part in a later shoot but the above slaughter was not equalled. Most of the victims were migratory ducks and geese.

The Indians are becoming more conscious of the need for wildlife conservation and the government has set up a number of sanctuaries where birds and animals may be photographed but not shot. The Keoladeo Ghana National Park in Rajasthan is one of the most fascinating of these sanctuaries where a warden and his forest guards protect the birds and animals from poachers. These excellent men are dedicated to the saving of wildlife — no easy task in a vast overpopulated country of underfed people. However, the peafowl which is the national bird and the sarus crane famous for lifelong fidelity between male and female, are safe at all times.

The sarus crane is among the tallest of flying birds at about 1.6 m in height. As it pairs for life and is almost always seen together with its mate, it can thrive in many areas of northern and central India living in harmony with the human population. It feeds on grains, frogs, insects and small reptiles. Its courting ritual is fascinating as the birds circle each other, dancing with outspread wings and trumpeting in unison.

Another famous crane which is a winter visitor to the Bharatpur sanctuary is the Siberian white crane which migrates 6,000 km from the tundra regions of Siberia across Pakistan, Afghanistan and Iran to Bharatpur in India for the winter. Sadly, from more than 200 birds in the mid-1960s the numbers shrank to just 10 birds in the 1990s. When I visited India in December 1994 to see my son Bernard, who was then a Singapore diplomat in our High Commission in New Delhi, he reported that no Siberian crane had arrived in India that year. Unfortunately these beautiful birds are trapped in Pakistan and kept as pets. In Afghanistan uncontrolled shooting has decimated this migratory bird. An article in *National Geographic* showed a picture of a dead crane in an Afghanistan market for sale as food. International action has been taken to protect the Siberian crane, one group of which winters in Southern China, but I fear for the survival of this beautiful bird.

I stayed at the Bharatpur Bird Sanctuary, as it was then called, in 1968 for some nights and had the pleasure of seeing large numbers of migratory ducks and geese from Siberia as well as resident water-fowl, darters or "snake birds" with their long shapely necks, egrets, cormorants and breeding "painted" storks, moorhen and coot in the large expanses of water. Birds are among the most colourful creatures on earth (excluding vultures, of course) and Singapore has produced at least one world-famous photographer of birds, Loke Wan Tho, to record their beauty. He is remembered in the bird sanctuaries of India. In E.P. Gee's well-known book *The Wild Life of India*, Loke Wan Tho is mentioned for his patience and skill in photographing birds. Accompanied by the most famous of Indian ornithologists, Salim Ali, Loke Wan Tho is said to have sometimes waited patiently three whole mornings and afternoons at his hideout before taking the perfect picture he wanted. "Every feather! Every feather!" he is quoted by E.P. Gee as saying in his attempts to capture every detail accurately.

A member of the Singapore High Commission in New Delhi who bought a gun limited himself to hunting sparrows and the occasional stray tame pigeon. Knowing that I disapproved of hunting, he claimed that he went shooting only for his food! Once he narrowly missed my gardener's small son. After this incident, he gave up hunting. Fishing was not as popular among the diplomats as hunting but the best known fisherman amongst us was Sir Arthur Tange, the Australian high commissioner, who tempted the trout in the snow-fed mountain streams of Kashmir. He used to remark wittily that every summer his diplomatic efforts were conducted at the highest levels.

Among the more scholarly ambassadors was Prince Prem Purachatra of Thailand, a professor well-known in Asian academic circles as an authority on education. He was a popular speaker and was frequently a guest lecturer at leading Indian universities, while his wife was a tireless social worker who organised the ladies of the diplomatic circle to do more than their rounds of coffee, cocktail and dinner parties. The prince was also a gourmet, an expert on wines, cheese and cigars. In true princely style he nominated a few of us as chairmen of his exclusive "clubs" which met in his residence, and I was the "cheese chairman" despite a conspicuous lack of qualifications. But at least I ate cheese (the less smelly varieties) whereas being a non-smoker I couldn't be chairman of the "cigar club" to which the prince was keen to appoint me as the best cigars could be imported from the famous old shop Robinsons of Singapore. I did import good cigars from Robinsons for his after-dinner sessions. The prince had undoubted influence on Thai Airways for the Orchid flights were invariably laden with varieties of cheese for the prince's tables. His good lady used to complain that whenever she returned from trips to Paris she had to stagger down the gangway with a basket of choice cheese in each hand. It was a privilege to have known this warm-hearted, happy couple.

Another of our good friends was the intellectual Polish ambassador whose wife, a fervent Catholic, disliked the communists. She was close to my wife who is a Catholic too. They had two grown up children, a boy who was a brilliant pianist and a beautiful daughter. Sadly, the boy fell in love with an Indian university undergraduate and because of parental opposition from her conservative parents the boy committed suicide. The whole diplomatic community was shocked by the event. Years later the ambassador was posted to Washington where he defected to the Americans and was sentenced to death in absentia by the then Polish government. I expect he is all right now that the communist states have collapsed with the disintegration of the USSR. Both husband and wife visited us in Kuala Lumpur when I was high commissioner there the first time from 1969 to 1971. The Soviet ambassador in Kuala Lumpur was not too happy that the head of mission of a Soviet satellite had preferred to stay with a non-communist friend rather than with him!

It was to be expected, of course, that amongst a large diplomatic establishment of over 100 missions, there would be a sprinkling of the snooty and the sullen, the lecher and the black marketeer. I fear that the representatives of some of the developing countries whose ministers and civil servants were corrupt were true reflections of their home government. Whisky was much in demand in partly prohibitionist

India as it was in the United States during the prohibition era. Every bottle commanded five times its diplomatic tax-free price. One head of mission, who was reputed to have made a round-the-world tour on his profits, said that he planned to retire after another world trip. There was naturally a scandal and the regulations were tightened up for the issue of alcohol to diplomats; more forms had to be signed and greater delay was experienced. However, these deterrents did not really hinder the determined. The Indian government caught one of the culprits when an Indian middleman was arrested with 70 cases of whisky, but diplomatic immunity prevented any prosecution.

Among junior diplomats there was reputed to be a business arrangement with certain importers who had the monopoly of supplying tax-free goods to foreign missions. All the diplomat had to do was to get the approval to order the goods by producing the requisite forms signed by the Ministry of External Affairs and his own head of mission and hand these forms to the importer. The goods thus ordered were disposed of on the black market by the importing firm and the diplomat received his cut. I was told that at one time, certain diplomats used to import a car annually to resell to private individuals at 300–400 per cent profit. This was possible because no imports of cars and luxury vehicles were allowed in India and the only model made in India was the sturdy "Ambassador" which closely resembled the 1948 Morris Oxford. The government of India broke the car resale racket by ruling that diplomats could dispose of their cars only to the State Trading Corporation at an agreed price. The car was then auctioned to private buyers at three or four times that price, the profits now going, quite rightly, to the Indian government rather than into private pockets. This car resale racket was also prevalent in Indonesia among the more unscrupulous diplomats who were a disgrace to the countries they represented.

The dean of the diplomatic corps in India was a famous Mexican poet, Octavio Paz, a collector of Indian art and antiques and an incarnation of the romantic idea of what a poet should look like. Though he did not speak English fluently, he carefully wrote down and read out the many speeches a dean has to make to say farewell to colleagues leaving the country. Although this happened at least once or twice a month, our poetic dean always said something worth listening to. His sense of humour and his rare imagery were as startling and lively as the dresses of his young wife who was petite, pretty and French. Octavio Paz resigned after more than 20 years in the Mexican diplomatic service when the Mexican police killed a number of students in the riots before the Olympiad of 1968. He wrote a poem of protest, and left for Paris where he hoped to obtain a job as a university teacher. As Muhammad Ali might have said of himself, "He is the greatest." Octavio Paz was awarded the Nobel Prize for Literature in 1990.

Another poet colleague of ours was from the Middle East, fair-skinned and tall, with a Byronic presence. He had been told to stay away from his country because of a poem he had written which his government disapproved of. He was allowed no nearer to his home than Beirut. Poetry can make exiles of good men even if it is much less widely read than fiction. It is a rare politician in authority who will tolerate criticism if he has the power to strike back, no matter what lip service he pays to democratic ideals and freedom of speech. The politician has to put up with these ideals in countries like Britain and the United States where he is forced to by tradition, but in most of the developing and all the totalitarian countries, writers from the humblest newspaper reporter to the most gifted novelist and poet will continue to suffer for their views. India is the exception as the press is free and often critical of government leaders. The cartoonist Laxman was famous for debunking pompous politicians in the leading Indian daily *The Times of India*.

Potential political rivals are, more understandably perhaps, disposed of one way or another. One of the African ambassadors to India was an army officer whose classmate, a corporal, had eventually taken over the country. I read an article in a reputable British journal which mentioned that the ambassador was the best educated and most competent general who had enough support in his country to succeed the present ruler. I mentioned the article to the ambassador who had a good sense of humour. He laughed as he recounted how he had been summoned into the presence of the ruler of the state. "Thomas" he was told, "You are a nuisance to me but I don't want to liquidate you. We have been boys together. We have played together. So I am sending you away, as far away as possible. You will be our envoy to India." So Thomas arrived in India with his wife and seven children. In a little more than a year, he was transferred to Japan with his wife and eight children. Perhaps his chief of state had looked up an atlas and discovered that India was not far away enough after all!

More Courtesy Calls

Courtesy calls on ministers and top government officials were interspersed with calls on diplomatic colleagues. The latter was a never-ending duty as continually friends left and strangers arrived. Coffee, biscuits and cigarettes were the customary offerings at these half-hour getting-to-know-you sessions except for the Arabs who served a variety of sweetmeats and sandwiches too in case the visitors did not take to oriental delicacies. Ministers offered nothing more than coffee and cashew nuts so as not to encourage the visitor to linger too long. A Nepalese minister pointedly left a large alarm clock right on the coffee table to make matters even more obvious. However, some like the then Minister of Defence Shri Swaran Singh (later to be foreign minister), were friendly and genuinely interested in Singapore while others obviously knew little and cared less about our very existence. The prime minister, Mrs Gandhi herself, was always courteous and seemed to listen intently while doodling away incessantly in her office. It was disconcerting for the visitor but I'm sure it was not meant to be so. One amusing incident was when one of our Malay ministers of state, Haji Ya'acob bin Mohamed, visited India and had to be formally introduced to her. She was kind enough to invite us to her home. She was at that time distracted by a thumping defeat the Congress Party had suffered at the hands of the opposition parties in West Bengal. She explained how all her experts had misled her by assuring her of victory. In the course of the conversation, she suddenly asked our Malay visitor, "And how is the Tunku? We think very highly of him over here." I could see the Indian officials squirming in their seats, embarrassed, but not daring to interrupt. The rest of the meeting went off well over coffee and biscuits after I had explained that our visitor was from Singapore. I added that I was myself a great admirer of the Tunku who was then prime minister of Malaysia.

Mr Morarji Desai, deputy prime minister and finance minister, was a strict vegetarian and a teetotaller notable for his abstemiousness and his youthful appearance despite his 70 years. I was impressed by his alertness and informality. Shrewd and experienced in politics, a devoted follower of Gandhi, he practised the simple virtues of self-denial and never even drank tea or coffee. He would rarely appear at cocktail parties or dinners and then only if no alcohol was served. This was a blow to the majority of the diplomats who could not endure cocktail parties without alcohol. His unswerving insistence on this is reminiscent of our own Prime Minister Lee Kuan Yew's refusal to tolerate cigarette smoking at any of his dinners. A man like Morarji Desai roused strong likes and dislikes, so he probably had more enemies in the political arena than any other politician because of his uncompromising attitudes. He refused invitations to go abroad on state visits unless he was exempted from innoculation and vaccination and he told me that he had turned down an offer to visit the United States for this reason. Like the great George Bernard Shaw who was equally adamant about these compulsory medical requirements, Morarji Desai was a spare and neat figure (but unlike Shaw, clean shaven). He was a striking contrast to the obese and obviously self-indulgent hedonists on the Indian political scene. During my courtesy call, he showed interest in Singapore which he had never visited, so I was able to arrange for him to stay in Singapore as our official guest on his way to Australia for the Commonwealth Finance Ministers' Conference. I was aware that this move was not popular among some of his cabinet colleagues, but I admired the man for what he was and thought some of our ministers should get to know him. The only problem was to find a nanny goat to provide milk for his breakfast! His daily diet was milk, honey, steamed carrots, coconut water, bitter gourd and cottage cheese. He claimed that he drank his own urine as a cure for illness!

Morarji Desai fell from power before I left India. I called on him to say farewell although some colleagues of mine did not think it wise. All the carpets in his government house had been rolled up; everything was packed and stacked up against the wall. The usual crowd of hundreds of visitors and supplicants who gathered daily at his doorstep had vanished. I found him in a small back room in his Gandhi dhoti serenely spinning cloth as his master used to do. This, he said, helped him to think. We talked of many things. He was not one to mince his words about some of his former colleagues including the lady he had helped to make prime minister who had now cast him aside. He was convinced that she was a communist but perhaps he spoke in bitterness. The fall of Desai removed the last Gandhian, after the death of Nehru's successor Shastri, from the active political arena. Subsequently, Morarji Desai became prime minister when Mrs Gandhi lost an election in 1977. He formed a coalition government which remained in power till 1980 when it fell apart after bitter squabbles among the coalition partners. Desai retired from politics. He died in 1995 at the age of 99, according to the BBC though some claimed he was 100 years old.

One of my most enjoyable calls was on the then chief justice of India who was later to act as president when Zakir Husain died suddenly. In India, many senior judges have a chance to attain the highest honour as the term of office of the chief justice is limited to five years and every judge has to retire at the age of 65. Chief Justice Mohammad Hidayatullah had obtained his first degree in English literature at Cambridge but because lecturers were so poorly paid (about 200 rupees a month), he was advised by relatives to return to England to read law. Being a man of great ability, he had distinguished himself rapidly as a lawyer in a nation of lawyers and had been eventually appointed a judge. But English literature remained his first love and to keep up with the subject, he spent part of his spare time tutoring a friend's undergraduate children. "There are finer things in life than the law," he used to say. He surprised me with his up-to-date knowledge of modern authors and even critics, and the normal 30-minute call went on for an unprecedented hour-and-a-half while we discussed T.S. Eliot. As my chief interest in life is literature and certainly not diplomacy, we met several times after this in mutual enjoyment of a subject we shared in common. My wife and I got to know the CJ and his equally charming and cultured wife well. Though she was a Hindu who did not convert to Islam, this was acceptable in a tolerant secular India. The learning and wide terms of reference so obvious in the conversation of leading Indian civil servants were as impressive as those of their counterparts in England. I knew a socialist member of Parliament, the late Nath Pai, remarkably well-read in history and literature, who could quote Shakespeare at will in Parliament, an assembly noted for its oratory in Hindi and English. Our own administrators may perhaps be more efficient but most of them are dreadfully dull to talk to because of their limited reading. They have little time "to stand and stare" in their relentless drive for progress and self-advancement. The time of gracious living, the time to pause and think, is not yet in Singapore. Perhaps the best is yet to be.

One last courtesy call I must mention was my visit to Vice-President Shri V.V. Giri who later became president from 1969 to 1974. A portly and voluble man in his 70s, I found him energetic and active; he had been sent to Dublin to read law as a boy but because of the First World War, his parents had wanted him to return. Eventually he did so, via Singapore, risking possible sinking by the German cruiser *Emden*, a guerrilla at sea, which after many exploits was eventually run aground by her captain to avoid sinking after severe damage at the Battle of Cocos on 9 November 1914. An astrologer, Shri Giri said, had prophesied that he would one day be President of India. I recall this because Shri Giri saw the prophecy fulfilled under unusual circumstances after the death of President Zakir Husain. Shri Giri failed to be nominated as the official Congress presidential candidate, so he took the unexpected decision of standing as an independent candidate, thus splitting the Congress party. The president of India is elected by the central and state parliaments and there is no general popular vote as in the United States. No one at first gave Shri Giri a chance against Sanjiva Reddy, the witty and capable Speaker of Parliament and a veteran Congress politician. However, at this time Mrs Gandhi saw that the election of the official Congress candidate who belonged to the old guard would circumscribe her power. So she moved shrewdly and swiftly, and threw her support behind Shri Giri. In a closely contested election, he won by the narrowest majority in Indian history. One up for astrology!

Astrology is a highly respected art (some claim it is a science) of predicting the future in India. During Nehru's premiership of a professedly secular state, ministers were said to use the back way to astrologers' apartments, but after his death they were more open about such consultations.

Astrology, which originated in Mesopotamia and spread over the Egyptian and Greek civilisations, had reached India perhaps in the first millennium. It has taken firm root in the lives of Indians and even western-educated Indians cannot shake off altogether the belief that the stars and the planets exercise a personal and unique influence on every individual.

Whereas most of us in Singapore treat astrology as a joke, limiting our interest in it to the Sunday newspaper predictions, Indian businessmen and industrialists consult their astrologers for auspicious days to sign a contract, politicians and ministers seek the advice of the stars before taking a crucial decision and marriage arrangements usually demand the horoscopes of male and female applicants. Only if horoscopes match and the required dowry is forthcoming can the usual "decent" marriage take place between the inevitable "fair slim girl and the graduate with good salary" of the right caste. The well-known Indian novelist R.K. Narayan enjoys a quiet smile at astrologers and horoscopes in *The Financial Expert* where the newly rich father Margaya having selected a suitable bride for his son from numerous applicants, then selects the most obliging of astrologers to make the right predictions. To Margaya "it seemed necessary as a first step to dictate to the planets what they should do. Margaya had made up his mind that he was going to take no nonsense from the planets."

Observations

Ronald Segal in his controversial and fascinating book *The Crisis of India* argues that because Hinduism is pessimistic, distrustful of the real world and concentrates upon the personal relationship of man with God, it has led to a "self-centred view of life" which disregards the physical and emotional sensitivity of others. He claims that even that great and good man Mahatma Gandhi who at the age of 16 had been appalled by his own passion when he lay with his wife as his father was dying and who, at the age of 37 gave up sexual relations altogether, was unintentionally cruel to the women with whom he tested himself to ensure that he had attained *bramacharya*. Segal seems to imply from his observations in India that the Hindu is, more than most of mankind, indifferent and inattentive to the needs of others and he quotes from psychologists and sociologists to support his point of view. While I suspect that sociological studies of most Asian societies and perhaps even European societies would prove the same (one may exempt tribal societies as in Africa from this), the common indifference among Indians to the indescribable poverty of their fellow citizens gives grounds for agreeing with Ronald Segal's observations. Segal argues that the Indian's self-centred view of life leads to a firm belief in astrology and it is natural for each man to conclude that the stars and the planets should influence his life.

The importance of astrology in matchmaking brings me to the subject of arranged marriages. Many Indians are as obsessed as the Chinese about fair complexions of girls. Indeed it might be believed from marriage advertisements that a girl with dark skin stands little chance of finding a husband unless her father is very rich. This love of fair skin is observable also among the Chinese, Indians and Eurasians in Malaysia and Singapore. I recall with amusement how the fair-skinned Eurasians who had to line up with the rest of the community on the Singapore *padang* (field) in front of the Singapore Recreation Club a few days after the fall of the "fortress" on 15 February 1942 were mocked by the others — "I say! How come there are Europeans among us today?" For once the fair-skinned ones must have regretted their snobbery in the past. That good Japanese, Mamoru Shinozaki, who had lived for years in Singapore, must have saved many of them, for Japanese passes were issued by him to almost all the Eurasians whatever the shade of their skins.

Chinese female workers on rubber estates and on building sites wrap themselves almost completely so as to expose as little of their skin as possible to the sun. The paler the skin, the more marketable the girl. However, I find the colour of honey the Malays call *hitam manis* more attractive. In New Delhi at a dinner party, I recall drawing the attention of an Indian lady to the classic beauty of the Ethiopian charge d'affairs' wife, perhaps the best-looking lady in the diplomatic circle at that time in India. The fair Indian woman exclaimed in surprise, "But she is so dark!" It was only the complexion that mattered, not the features. African students in India are sometimes discriminated against both because of their colour and because they are considered to come from a primitive civilisation.

Colour also contributes perhaps to the attitude of contempt the northerners, who are of Aryan stock, show for the Dravidian descendants of the South like Tamil Nadu and Kerala. The other factor is that physically the wheat eaters of the North are so much bigger than the rice eaters of the South. The dislike is reciprocated and sometimes it was not easy to believe that fair and dark, tall and short, all belong to one nation. I once mentioned to a Sikh businessman the fact that drivers of vehicles in Madras seemed to obey traffic rules much better than drivers in

New Delhi where even buses and lorries are frequently driven the wrong way up one-way streets. He explained that the Madrassis were a timid race who had no guts! Lorries in the north are almost invariably driven by the Sikhs, notable as warriors; and a trip on any major trunk road would prove that these drivers treat the trucks as battle tanks and consider it a point of honour to overtake every other vehicle on the road and also to play "chicken" with approaching vehicles. The wrecks on the road are evidence of this. Some of Singapore's "hell-drivers" would turn pale with fright on an Indian trunk road. I know of one diplomat who drew his vehicle aside on the grass to let a truck pass but despite this, the truck in rushing by scraped his car. The enraged envoy drew his revolver and fired several shots at the speeding truck but failed to hit it, fortunately for all concerned.

One member of my staff, a Chinese bachelor, fell in love with our attractive young Indian telephone operator cum receptionist, an Indian university graduate. The romance proceeded apace despite the cautionary advice of our first secretary who took a paternal interest in both parties and anticipated the inevitable reaction of the girl's parents. I stumbled onto the romance when I found the young lady in tears one morning, nervously tearing up bits of paper which were strewn all around her. Her parents were horrified at their daughter wanting to marry a Chinese. It did not matter to them that he was a Singapore citizen. A Chinaman was a Chinaman. I suppose one must remember the humiliating defeat the Chinese Army had inflicted on India in 1962, the threat of invasion of Bengal and the subsequent strained relations between the two countries. Even without this political factor, I doubt whether the romantic path of our pair of star-crossed lovers would have run smooth. My only objection to the romance was that my staff member, who was upstairs, was so often on the phone to the young lady at the reception desk downstairs that I had difficulty in getting the phone for my own use! Anyway, one morning, we had difficulty in rousing the young man from his sleep. It turned out that he had taken a heavy dose of sleeping pills; so I decided it was best to send him home to his family in Singapore. This I did and within three months, the young lady was married to a young man selected by her parents, very happily too. They have since had two children.

Winter and Summer

Winter is the kindest season in New Delhi. November is pleasant but February is the friendliest month without the mist and frost of English winters. Cool all day in the sun, with the temperature in the seventies (low to mid-20s °C) with never a threat of rain, most nights are cold enough to need a heater. The best time for work, the time of roses. After the summer monsoon has drenched the earth in August, the parched soil sprouts luxuriant green. The swift change of scene is incredible to a stranger and the weedy rose bushes which wilt all summer shoot forth leaves and buds. By November, hundreds of varieties — all shades of red, pink, yellow and blue even — bloom in a riot of colours and of a size only matched in Cameron Highlands or Fraser's Hill in Malaysia. I bought 80 plants for my garden, a happy investment.

The rose-grower, aptly named Mr Arora, who supplied me the plants could have stepped out of the *Readers' Digest* "The Most Unforgettable Character I Have Met" series. Stocky and Pickwickian in appearance, the greying Mr Arora had given up his law practice for rose growing and he thought it was the wisest decision of his life. He waxed poetic on roses especially after a couple of pegs of whisky, his second love. He had won many trophies at the annual rose exhibitions in Delhi and elsewhere in India and he was the supplier of blooms and cuttings to many diplomats. Roses, he said, had brought him more friends in the highest social circles than law had ever done, especially friends with genuine imported whisky. He thought the local Indian blends putrid despite their highfalutin names such as Black Knight and White Castle. He loved to sit cross-legged and shoeless on my carpeted floor (he disliked chairs) and discourse lengthily on Indian philosophy while the content of the bottle on the table fell steadily inch by inch. The more he drank, the more he apologised for drinking. I refilled and listened. Eventually he rattled off in his antiquated vehicle, which had brought roses for the evening's entertainment, neither car nor driver any too steady but enviably happy. Like his beloved roses dehydrating in the summer drought, Shri Arora thirsted through the hot dry months, short of money and dreaming perhaps of the Scottish glens. Only the thought of winter with its roses and genuine Scotch saw him through the harsh summer.

Mr Arora took away empty bottles of Black Label to be filled with local blends for his parties. He claimed that his friends were very impressed that he could afford expensive imported brands of whisky!

A Day in the Office

Winter or summer, I was usually first in the office as a result of a habit acquired in Horley Hall, the boarding house attached to the Anglo-Chinese School, Ipoh. I was the bell-ringer up at six in the morning to get all the other lads out of bed. It was the first of a prefect's daily chores. As a college undergraduate, I kept up the habit and as a schoolmaster I had no choice. My early arrival at office meant that the rest of the staff arrived on time. An African ambassador told me that he had been in the habit of getting to work about 10.30 a.m. although his office was scheduled to open at 9 a.m. One day he arrived at 9.30 and found no one else! His staff trickled in between 9.30 and 10.00 and got the surprise of their lives from his irate Excellency! Our summer hours were from 7.30 a.m. to 2 p.m. During the rest of the afternoon, very few would venture out of their houses into the 110°F (43°C) heat.

My first task was to read through the five or six English daily newspapers published in New Delhi, Calcutta, Bombay and Madras. As the press was genuinely free in India until 1975, the reader was able to get a representative view of what was thought and said by the small ruling elite, the English-speaking group in India. There are hundreds of vernacular papers, a few of which we subscribed to. Any item of importance in them was translated for us by one of our locally recruited staff. No one from Singapore was able to do this, nor was any Indian employed or paid specifically to do this job. This was obviously something to be remedied but who could convince Singapore's Ministry of Finance? However, the English press reflected most political views, from the communist *Patriot* (pro-Russian) to the capitalist *Hindustan Times* (pro-American). In between were *The Times of India* and *The Indian Express* (edited by the famous Frank Moraes). These three papers were and perhaps still are owned by some of the richest industrialists. *The Statesman* and *The Hindu* (Madras) were perhaps the most informative of all the papers. There were a couple of papers we took from Bombay along with several weeklies including the communist *Blitz* and its opposite number *The Current*. No individual from the prime minister downwards and no institution (except the Presidential Office) was spared criticism. Though some of these papers were at times rabid and hysterical, they usually maintained a moderate tone and kept a critical eye on government policies. The standard of journalism was high and far less space was devoted to advertisements and sensational headlines about rapes and robberies than in our part of the world. This is not because these things do not happen in India, but simply that these items were not played up by the press. Perhaps the English-educated reading public is more discriminating and better educated in India than it is in Singapore. Further evidence of this is the fact that bookshops were more numerous and better stocked in any major Indian city than in Singapore in the 1960s. Booksellers sold at reasonable prices and when the government thought of imposing a tax on imported books, they were vigorous in their protests. As a result, no tax was imposed. Politics was and perhaps will always be the prime subject of interest in India, and the editorials were almost invariably fearless political comments. The world coverage of news was impressive and articles of interest by British and US journalists appeared frequently. The quality of political cartoons recalled the best of David Law and a single cartoon by Laxman of *The Times of India* often summed up the chief topic of the day brilliantly and was worth the whole paper. If one's appointment book happened to be full for the day, it was best to glance at the cartoons first so as to be up-to-date with the hottest topic of the day.

At least once a week, political reports had to be sent off to Singapore. These were assessments of the situation — political, economic, industrial, agricultural and military — with some comments on the rivalry of the USSR and the USA with their huge diplomatic representation of hundreds — a good number of whom naturally belonged to the intelligence service. Subsequently, both reduced the size of their missions perhaps for reasons of economy.

In the beginning, I had no help from my staff as the first secretary was wholly immersed in administrative duties. Besides, he avoided attending parties which he detested, preferring to spend his evenings at home with his wife and children. Later, Harry Crabbe was sent to join me as second secretary. As he was young, energetic and outgoing, he proved invaluable in his political reporting. He got to know journalists and politicians very quickly, and the only limit to his activities was his inability to pay for entertainment as he was given a miserly allowance for this purpose. His attractive wife was no cook, so he hired a cook who was also his chauffeur. However, as most Indian journalists regard whisky as the elixir of life, Mr Crabbe managed, despite all handicaps, in presenting stimulating reports often written in a fine frenzy. I had merely to sober them down a little for Singapore.

Commonwealth heads of missions (with their many sources of information denied to tiny missions like ours) and sometimes their number two men were very helpful in one's assessment of the situation. Mr John Freeman, the famous editor of the *New Statesman* who was the British high commissioner to India, Sir Arthur Tange of Australia and his deputy Mr Cunningham, and Mr Chester Bowles, the American ambassador, were particularly helpful. Mr Bowles in a fortnightly journal *The American Recorder* wrote knowledgeably on various aspects of Indian problems, ranging from fertilisers to family planning. It was a useful source not only for his views but also for the latest production statistics. All these men had had to travel widely over India to inspect the many installations, farms and factories set up in India by them on behalf of their governments.

The Commonwealth group observed a sort of inner unity. There was also a beginning to the Association of Southeast Asian Nations (ASEAN) group but this was rather affected by the Sabah dispute as well as Singapore's execution of two Indonesian marines. Personal relations, however, were not affected. For instance, the tall and distinguished veteran Indonesian ambassador and I took care to be seen together in amicable conversation even as the Indonesian flag flew half-mast for a week to mourn the marines. He was firmly of the view that no white man should be given the opportunity to gloat over differences between ASEAN countries. The two Indonesian saboteurs had been arrested during Sukarno's Confrontation between Indonesia and Malaysia for exploding a bomb in MacDonald House in Orchard Road in March 1965, killing three innocent civilians and injuring 33 others. Over 40 other saboteurs had been caught exploding bombs on beaches and elsewhere in Singapore but as these caused no fatalities, they were released by the Singapore government when the Confrontation ended. But the two marines were tried as criminals and though found guilty, they were not executed till their appeals had been rejected by the Privy Council. Had they been shot soon after arrest, there would have been no problem. Just before their execution, President Suharto himself had appealed to the Singapore government and the rejection of this appeal, which I myself thought unwise, roused a great deal of Indonesian resentment.

Singapore's decision was legally unassailable but politically dubious though if the marines had been spared, Singapore's future action against sabotage by persons of any nationality might have been compromised. Would it not also be thought that Singapore had yielded under pressure? Was it not necessary for Singapore to demonstrate to the world her determination to see justice done? At any rate, such were the arguments advanced to justify the execution. Though I thought the sentence should have been commuted to life imprisonment, once President Suharto had made his appeal, I did my diplomatic duty of standing by and defending my government's decision.

The Indonesian ambassador and I agreed that the incident should be seen in its long-term perspective and we showed the usual friendliness to each other under observant eyes. We often conversed in Malay by ourselves in the presence of others. This was rude but it did discourage questions and much later, several diplomats said they were puzzled but impressed by the friendship between the Indonesian ambassador and me. There were rumours that Indonesian students would demonstrate at the Singapore High Commission in Ring Road but the ambassador saw to it that this did not happen. All members of the Indonesian embassy I happened to meet socially were friendly and the only hostility I encountered was from passing visitors. There was an interesting difference of views among the ambassadors — every white Commonwealth high commissioner held that we had done the right thing as it was legally justifiable. Every African and Asian diplomat either hinted or said that we had not acted with wisdom!

India in 1967

India depends on regular and abundant rainy seasons to ensure her food supply. Two poor monsoons had brought near famine to vast areas of the country but tons of wheat rushed especially from the United States had saved many lives. It is useful to remember that though all geography books speak of India as a subcontinent, as it is indeed a vast country taking days to cross by train and several hours by air, the country has to support 15 per cent of the world's population on about 2.4 per cent of the world's land area. It is less than a third the size of the United States or Canada but has more than three times the population of the United States and more than 30 times the population of Canada. In 1970, only China had a higher population of some 800 million (now 1.3 billion) as against India's 500 to 600 million (now 1.26 billion) but China is three times the size of India, so the population density of India is more than twice that of China. It has further to be remembered that India's economy, like most of Asia's, is basically agricultural on a soil that is less fertile than in most countries. A flight by day over most of India lays bare the wrinkled old land below, its shrivelled streams, denuded mountains and barren plains overgrazed by cattle and over-cultivated by man. Fifty-five thousand babies are born every day and the annual population increase, despite the high death rate, is 12 to 13 million. That is an addition of the whole population of Malaysia and Singapore combined or the whole Australian population every year. There is no doubt that this is India's most serious problem. The Indian plan was to stem the population increase by lowering the birth rate from 41 per 1,000 in the mid-1960s to about 25 per 1,000 by the mid-1970s, stabilising the population at about 670 million by the mid-1980s. The rate is now about 22 per 1,000. Indian efforts at encouraging birth control by sterilisation, the loop, and the pill are becoming steadily more effective in the cities where the sign of the red triangle (the symbol of family planning) is ubiquitous. But India is not her cities but her villages.

There are 600,000 villages in which four-fifths of her people live. These stretch from the clusters of boats on the lakes of Kashmir to the mud hovels of Bihar and the palm-thatched huts of Kerala in the far south. Villages and cities teem with people. Villagers are largely illiterate. Poor farmers believe in large families in almost all developing countries. In Cameron Highlands, where I spent the Japanese Occupation, and which is one of the main vegetable-producing areas in Malaysia, families of six to seven children were common and despite some family planning propaganda, I see no signs of any desire for smaller families. The whole family is up early in the fields, and except during the Chinese New Year festival, it is early to bed and early to rise to work in the fields where more hands mean more work done. The Indian farmer is no different.

Soon after independence in 1948, the Indian government with Nehru as prime minister had allocated 40 per cent of the first five-year plan provision for agriculture to increase acreage as well as the yield by irrigation, mechanisation and fertiliser production. In fact, over the years, food grain production has steadily increased and has nearly quintupled since 1950 when it was about 50 million tons. This green revolution is a notable achievement and would indeed have made India self-sufficient in food but for the phenomenal population increase. Though much has been done by irrigation, both by massive dams and simple wells, to increase agricultural acreage, modern machinery cannot be fully used as 41 per cent of the farms are under two acres (0.81 ha) and there are recurrent periods of drought and near famine once every five years or so. One-third of the farming population owns no land and land rent was as high as 50 per cent of the total produce when I was there. When there is drought, there is migration to the already congested cities in search of work. At the time of my arrival, India was recovering from the 1965 to 1966 drought, and much was said about the need to store grain to meet future monsoon failures. But it was not only the question of storage space which was being increased and which had to be vermin-proof. It was roughly estimated that 5–20 per cent of wheat and rice was lost to rats annually! The intricacies of statistics remain mysterious to me, but one may suspect that the wide variation in the estimate suggests mere guesswork. Another major problem is that of distributing grain on time to the famine areas. Incidentally, the Indian government dislikes the use of the word "famine" and prefers to speak of "shortages" and foreign correspondents are usually blamed for exaggeration.

Times of food shortage intensify parochial feelings. Those states that produce grain are reluctant to sell it to the needy ones at controlled prices as the wheat or rice could be more profitably black-marketed. Artificial food shortages are also sometimes created by speculators and hoarders. Central government control along with anti-hoarding campaigns and the establishment of ration shops become necessary, but by all accounts corruption makes much of all this ineffective. The lower-paid Indian staff in the different embassies were very vocal in their complaints about the poor quality of the rationed grain. But most Indians working with foreign embassies were well paid compared to the government or private sector.

Our High Commission paid its Indian staff the minimum they would accept and did its best to avoid paying overtime to its drivers. Although the servants received no more than from about S$40 to S$70 each (at that time, the Singapore dollar was worth 2.6 rupees), the Ministry of Finance was only concerned about saving money and not about the image Singapore should project abroad as a fair-minded employer. It was true, however, that because of the caste system, the number of servants was unnecessarily large. For instance, there had to be a sweeper who was of the lowest caste and whose work no one else would do. We learnt this when we engaged a Muslim "bearer", Iskandar, who moved into the residence we had rented a few weeks before I could move in, as it was unfurnished. When the first secretary visited the house a week after the servant had moved in, he was surprised to find the house had not been swept. Daily sweeping is essential in New Delhi as the city is near the Thar desert and fine dust is almost always in the air except during the monsoons. Layers of dust accumulate rapidly. There was Iskandar leaving his footprints everywhere on the dust-laden floors. He would not touch a broom, though as a Muslim he should not have been caste-conscious. However, it would have meant a loss of status and he could not have faced his fellow servants. Yet, the same Iskandar tried to take the shoes off my feet when I returned from work and would have done it without loss of dignity if I had allowed it!

A sweeper had to be engaged, a gardener, a cook, Iskandar the bearer and a chauffeur. It then became a task for my wife to keep peace between all these servants. A crisis flared up now and then, the most serious being an attack by the drunken cook on the bossy chauffeur. Early one morning, shouts of anger and screams for help got me scrambling out of bed only to see my irate cook, *parang* (chopper) in hand, chasing the chauffeur round and round the house. Fortunately, the chauffeur was the speedier of the two, so no harm was done. Gregory the cook had to be sacked. We then advertised in Singapore and found an excellent cook but he lost his way on arrival in New Delhi as he had found to his joyous surprise that whisky on a plane was free. He had consumed a bottle on the flight and naturally lost his way on landing. An unpromising start, but Pereira's dishes were delectable. Besides, drink made him most amiable and never aggressive like Gregory. Pereira, whose parents had originally migrated from Goa to Singapore, became a severe critic of India after his pocket was picked clean of his month's wages on his day off when he had joined his so-called friends' illicit liquor party. He was also convinced that Iskandar was a government spy, so relations were often strained. Iskandar never touched strong drink but was an inveterate smoker. He was exceptionally honest unlike the chauffeur, David Starr.

David was used to living by his wits of which he had more than a fair share. He was tall, well-built with the bearing of a soldier, and the commanding bark of a sergeant, where the other servants were concerned. I was told he extracted "coffee money" from them just as skilfully as he extracted petrol from my car. He informed me with justifiable pride that he was the dean of diplomatic chauffeurs, having driven for 11 other ambassadors and high commissioners. He disdained to drive for any diplomat of lower rank. The Nigerian high commissioner, his previous employer, informed me that David resigned when the high commissioner decided to keep the petrol tank key and to send an official along each time petrol was required. The high commissioner had good reason to do this but David felt it was all an unwarranted affront to his dignity. David was even suspected of having substituted worn-out shock absorbers for the good ones in our Mercedes. Eventually, after I left India, David was trapped by the first secretary in doing just this and was promptly sacked. I would like to record that David was efficient, knew every nook and corner of New Delhi and was always on time. He could not, however, resist overtaking the Nigerian high commissioner's car, if he ever caught sight of it anywhere, especially if the road ahead was a dusty one!

A Brief Conversation with Mrs Gandhi at Palam Airport

I was at the airport for the visit of General Ne Win, the head of the Burmese government. Only Prince Prem Purachatra, the Thai ambassador, was there along with Hla Maw, the Burmese head of mission. The president, vice-president and Mrs Gandhi were also present, of course. The other diplomats absented themselves as they disapproved of Ne Win's dictatorship.

Mr T.N. Kaul, the permanent secretary of the Indian Ministry of External Affairs, introduced me to Mrs Gandhi as the "shy professor from Singapore". She chuckled and said she had a professor in her cabinet "who is by no means shy — far from it!" (Professor Rao, minister of shipping and transport). Mrs Gandhi was very relaxed and charming — a warm personality with no airs about her for such an important public figure. She chatted about her son Rajiv's wedding to an Italian girl who had suffered from acute pain from appendicitis during the wedding reception! She had to be operated on urgently. Mrs Gandhi said that she enjoyed the wedding and was not in the least concerned that her daughter-in-law was not Indian. She said that she was till receiving letters of complaint from those she forgot to invite to the open-air reception. Many had been overlooked in the rush as she wanted it to be over while the weather was still cool enough to hold the party outdoors.

Mrs Gandhi said that there were striking resemblances between the social customs of Indians and Italians — for instance, the bride refused to walk ahead of the groom as this was not done in Italy. I commented on how Indian the bride had looked in her sari.

I remarked on the rowdy and aggressive scenes in Parliament. She said that "the level of debate" was "very low". It was true, she said, of both of the opposition as well as the government benches. I had attended several sessions of the Lok Sabha and watched from the visitors' gallery. It was often a riotous assembly with a desperate speaker yelling to keep control.

When General Ne Win's plane touched down, we went to the tarmac to receive him. The general disliked formality. He rushed down the gangway and shook hands down the line before the chief of protocol caught up with him and led him back to be photographed with the president, vice-president and Mrs Gandhi. Then he walked rapidly down the short line shaking hands, leaving his wife far behind! He looked cheerful but a little embarrassed. He was a well-built big man but rather unmilitary looking, I thought. He appeared anxious to get into his car and move off to his hotel. Dictators look quite ordinary and even benign — like Stalin, who could be mistaken for someone's gentle uncle. He murdered millions including his closest revolutionary comrades. Sometime in the 1980s, when I returned to Malaysia as high commissioner, I once found myself on the tarmac of the Kuala Lumpur airport chatting with Pakistan's General Zia-ul-Haq who had hanged Prime Minister Zulfikar Ali Bhutto. The general was most amiable, chatting about his family with a perpetual smile on his face! Looks are deceptive and as Hamlet observed, "one may smile, and smile, and be a villain"!

There were a number of visits to India by heads of governments like President Nixon and the Shah of Iran. Such visits were invariably celebrated by splendid banquets, the first given by the host country and the second by the visitor. The Shah of Iran flew out plane-loads of food and his cooks from Tehran for the dinner which all resident ambassadors, high commissioners and Indian ministers, and India's president attended. Amidst all the stately splendour and ceremony the ladies in their glittering saris and evening dresses outshone the men in their usual dinner jackets. Everything went well till the turbaned and smartly attired waiters brought in the dessert. Then it happened. An Indian waiter accidentally tipped the contents of his tray on the lap of the Pakistan diplomat's wife. All conversation came to a standstill. As the relations between India and Pakistan were tense as usual, some wondered whether what had happened was no accident! But the poor lady's green and gold sari was ruined as I'm sure her evening was too. The untoward event was the fodder for diplomatic gossip for a while. The Shah's banquet was the best ever dinner served in New Delhi during my two-year sojourn.

Beyond New Delhi: Kashmir, Tamil Nadu and Kerala

Once the calls on heads of missions and the leading ministers were over, I had to visit various Indian states, especially those in the south like Kerala, Tamil Nadu and Andhra Pradesh. These are the states from which most of the Singapore Indians or their ancestors had come from. Accompanied by my wife, I had to make courtesy calls on the chief ministers of these states as well as Maharashtra which is served by the great port of Bombay (now Mumbai). I also managed to spend a fortnight in cool and scenic Kashmir, staying at the state resthouse in Srinagar while Delhi was sweltering in the heat of summer. My wife and I visited the famous lake with its houseboats so popular among tourists, as well as the resort of Gulmarg among the mountains where we stayed in the Maharajah's cottage. We were even given a licence to fish the trout streams, milky white with melted snow. Kashmir, the most beautiful of the Indian states, often compared to Switzerland with its lakes and snow-capped mountains, is unfortunately a bone of contention between Pakistan and India. The population is mostly Muslim but the state is part of India, so the area is rife with discontent. There is the ever present Indian army to keep law and order. But for its political instability, Kashmir would be India's top tourist attraction.

The Indians are hospitable and everywhere my wife and I went we were warmly welcomed and looked after very well throughout our visits. Madras (now Chennai) was the first on our list. We found the city in the midst of a cultural festival during which the Tamil language and Tamil literature were celebrated with speeches, poems and plays. Throughout, a strong anti-Hindi feeling was displayed, especially in a play which showed how a wicked Aryan chief minister in the court of a Dravidian king exerted an evil influence on the virtuous ruler played by the famous actor M.G. Ramachandran ("MGR") who was destined one day to be Tamil Nadu's chief minister. I was amazed at the hatred against the northerners shown by the Madrassis. On the walls of buildings "Down with Hindi" was chalked up in large letters in English! The central government was attempting to promote Hindi as the national language in the 1960s to give India a greater sense of unity amidst the diversity of its peoples and their languages. India is not as fortunate as China which has a common script despite numerous spoken dialects. The Tamils are exceedingly proud of their language and culture with its famous epics like the *Ramayana* and the *Mahabharata*, epics which have influenced Southeast Asia including Indonesia. The emotional reaction against Hindi was a great surprise but perhaps, given time, the use of the national language would spread and become a bond of unity in the Indian subcontinent.

My wife and I were invited to visit several ancient temples and the impressive sandstone sculptures in Mahabalipuram after our courtesy call on the chief minister who was a popular and highly respected figure. He was unfortunately suffering from cancer and died in Madras later that year. A monument was erected in his memory by the citizens of the state.

One of the odd things about my trips to the Indian states was the fact that from time to time I was mistaken for the Indian high commissioner to Singapore because of my appearance. My hosts were invariably pleased to learn that my mother's parents had emigrated from Madras to the Malay States late in the 19th century.

One of my most enjoyable state visits was to Kerala with its capital Trivandrum on the southern coast of India. Kerala, one of the smallest states, is only 15,000 sq. miles in area or 38,850 sq. km. Uttar Pradesh, India's largest and most heavily populated state, is 113,500 sq. miles in area or 294,000 sq. km. Singapore is 227 sq. miles (704 sq. km.), a mere dot on the global map. The natural scenery of Kerala, with its tall and graceful coconut palms, its extensive rice fields and its hot and humid climate reminded me of Malaysia. The state of Kerala was established in 1956 when the three provinces of Malabar, Travancore and Cochin, all inhabited by Malayalam-speaking people, were integrated. Kerala, which has the highest literacy rate in all India, is highly cultured, practises religious tolerance and is free of the communal strife so common in other parts of India. We visited the excellent beaches of Kovalam and the southernmost point of India, Cochin, but we missed the well-known Periyar Game Sanctuary around Periyar Lake with its variety of wildlife including wild elephants.

At the time of my visit, Kerala was ruled by a freely elected communist government. The only other Indian state to elect communists into power was West Bengal. Kerala's chief minister was out of town, so I did not pay him the customary courtesy call, but all tours were arranged for me and every kindness shown as in the other Indian states I visited. I was impressed by the skill of the artisans in a wood and ivory carving factory. I bought some beautiful pieces of ivory and wood carving. Ivory carvings are no longer permitted in India as the worldwide agreement to protect elephants and wildlife generally has been signed by India.

Tun Razak's Visit to India

Sometime in mid-1968, Malaysia's deputy prime minister Tun Abdul Razak and his wife Toh Puan Raha stopped in New Delhi for a day. He had visited London, Copenhagen, Amsterdam and Paris to encourage the "Aid Malaysia Club". I was at Palam Airport to meet him along with the Indonesian ambassador Razif, Prince Prem Purachatra of Thailand and the Malaysian high commissioner Zaitun Ibrahim. Tun Razak was his usual friendly self. He invited me to visit him for a chat at tea-time in his suite although he was staying only one day in Delhi. The Indian protocol chief was surprised at having to fit me in between ministerial calls. Razak had called on Mrs Gandhi and had been visited by the home minister Chavan and the defence minister Swaran Singh whom I met as he was on his way out of Razak's suite. Razak was scheduled to see Deputy Prime Minister Morarji Desai and the president before attending a dinner hosted by Desai.

We discussed the failure of the merger and the separation of Singapore from Malaysia. Razak thought that perhaps the merger was too early and too hasty and recalled with amusement what difficulty he had in his efforts to get Lee Kuan Yew accepted by the Tunku who tended to be suspicious of the Singapore PM's motives. Razak told the Tunku that there was no need for fear as Lee Kuan Yew could never get power in Malaysia "except through us". Razak acknowledged Lee Kuan Yew's talents and "brilliance" but felt that he misunderstood the Malay people and their psychology. UMNO, Razak said, was a "loose organisation". There was always "plenty of talk" but in the end the members all listened to him and the Tunku. There was no great pressure even from extremists like Syed Albar. Razak said that he felt close to Goh Keng Swee, Lim Kim San and Eddie Barker. He considered that Toh Chin Chye had been unfairly treated by the Prime Minister who had "demoted him". Razak thought that in Toh Chin Chye's place he would not have accepted the change. Toh Chin Chye had been the deputy prime minister but that post was abolished and he was made minister for science and technology and vice-chancellor of the University.

Tun Razak believed that where defence was concerned, Malaysia and Singapore were indivisible. The two countries had to stand together — nothing else was practicable. Whatever the differences in policy, whatever the disagreements, we had to stand shoulder to shoulder in defence.

Razak mentioned the emergence of a new party, the Gerakan (Parti Gerakan Rakyat Malaysia or the Malaysian People's Movement Party) led by Syed Hussein Alatas, Wang Gung Wu, Lim Chong Eu and Dr Tan Chee Khoon. It was a moderate party and its leaders were well-meaning, he thought. He did not appear to fear it although it posed a challenge to the Alliance Party which Razak thought moved at times "too slowly".

Before I said goodbye, Razak suggested that I should be posted to Malaysia to help to improve the rather "touchy" relations with Singapore. I could speak directly and frankly to him. Curiously enough, this was to happen in 1969 after the May 13 racial riots.

Accreditation to Nepal and Recall Home

In March 1969 our Ministry of Foreign Affairs informed me that Singapore had decided to establish diplomatic relations with Nepal which lies between India and Tibet and that I would be accredited to that country. I was excited about visiting that mountain kingdom, the home of the Gurkhas, famous for their indomitable courage and loyalty as soldiers. In Delhi my residence was guarded by Gurkhas and in Singapore the prime minister's house was once guarded by them. When all arrangements had been made, I flew to the ancient city of Kathmandu accompanied by my wife and the second secretary Harry Crabbe in a small Fokker Friendship. In those days the Kathmandu airport was too small for larger aircraft. We were put up in the only hotel in Nepal's capital, although a second and better hotel was nearly ready. We were soon informed by the Nepalese protocol chief that His Majesty the King of Nepal was not ready to receive us till the following week when two other ambassadors would also present their credentials. The king quite sensibly wanted all three ceremonies staged one after the other on the same day. We didn't mind the delay as this gave us more time to explore the ancient city and its environs. The buildings and temples were hundreds of years old and impressive but we were struck by the total absence of drains. It was like being in the Middle Ages in Europe. We were told that no improvements had been made as the country was too poor but I understand that things have now finally changed for the better.[2]

We went for a long drive in a ramshackle taxi on the narrow precipitous road built by the Chinese communist government as a goodwill gesture to Nepal which is very much in the sphere of India's influence. We drove

---

[2] The reign of the House of Shah ended after 239 years with the abolition of the monarchy in Nepal in May 2008. (*Source*: Telegraph Media Group Ltd)

up to the Tibetan border across a river over which the Chinese had built a "Friendship Bridge". Armed Chinese guards prevented us from going over despite the bridge's name! About halfway to the Tibetan border we had come across the corpse of a pregnant woman beside the road. On the way back the flyblown corpse was still there. Our Nepalese driver refused to stop as he claimed that the woman was dead and anyway he would be in trouble with the police. Later we learned from the newspapers that the peasant woman had jumped off a moving truck and was killed. We never found out why she had leapt to her death.

The day finally dawned when I was presented to His Majesty the King who was a gentle and gracious personality. He was curious about Singapore so I had to do quite a bit of talking. He complained that most ambassadors to Nepal were accredited from New Delhi and they visited Kathmandu only twice — once to present their credentials and a second time to say farewell. I waxed eloquent on why I would not do the same as Singapore was a small new nation that valued its relations with friendly countries. This assertion of mine proved to be ironical because when I returned to New Delhi, a letter from our minister for foreign affairs was awaiting me, informing me that I was to be appointed to Malaysia. I was instructed to pay my farewell calls as soon as possible and return home quickly.

The reason for the sudden decision was the outbreak of the terrible May 13 racial riots in Malaysia, which affected us seriously as many Malaysian Chinese fled to Singapore. It was necessary for our government to have up-to-the-minute reports on developments in our nearest neighbouring country. Our leaders had assessed that Tunku Abdul Rahman, Malaysia's prime minister, would hand over power to his deputy, Abdul Razak. Singapore's leaders, who knew all about my close friendship with Razak, perhaps thought that I would be a useful link in difficult times as I would have direct access to the person who would soon be the prime minister. I did indeed, as Razak never forgot his friends even when he became the prime minister, and was always the same warm, approachable human being.

The news of my recall was unexpected as I had not had time to visit half the Indian states and had barely got to know a great country with its profound culture, its great art and architecture and its endless problems.

It would take one the greater part of a lifetime to really get to know India and I had spent barely two years there! I had not even had time to visit Orissa (now Odisha) where the famous sculptures celebrating sex adorn a temple in Khajuraho. The Hindus, like the Greeks, did not regard sex as sinful but as a god-given gift. The greatest of the Greek gods, Zeus, or Jupiter as the Romans called him, often descended from Mount Olympus and fell in love with beautiful girls. He transformed himself into a bull or a swan or even a shower of gold to consummate his desires with these maidens. John Dryden, the 17th century poet, satirist and dramatist, wrote a play called *Amphitryon*, a hilarious comedy in which Jupiter assumes the form of Amphitryon, a general who is away on the battlefield, to seduce his wife, Alcmene. Hercules was their son. The great Irish poet W.B. Yeats wrote a brilliant poem entitled "Leda and the Swan" about yet another of Jupiter's exploits. The Hindu classic and instructional manual on sexual positions, *The Kama Sutra*, is world famous.

But to return to my recall. I had little time to say goodbye to a few of the heads of missions of countries important to Singapore before partaking of the farewell dinner hosted by India's foreign minister Shri Dinesh Singh and attending the traditional farewell ceremony hosted by the dean and the diplomatic corps. In a sense, it was a relief to leave India as there were more than 100 foreign missions established in New Delhi because of India's importance as a non-aligned country at that time. The great number of diplomatic missions meant that at times one had to attend up to three cocktail parties a night! It became something of a joke running into the same diplomats twice or thrice on some evenings. Except for Sundays, no day was wholly free of diplomatic functions, especially as conferences were held in Delhi and ministers of different countries visited India often. As a university lecturer who had enjoyed peace and quiet in Singapore, I found the Indian diplomatic circuit too much of a strain. As Malaysia in the late 1960s and early 1970s had fewer than 30 missions in Kuala Lumpur, I expected to attend far fewer cocktail parties. However, Singapore's relationship with India was happy and relaxed and I had only one minor crisis to deal with. This happened when we were considering the question of citizenship and there was danger of serious unemployment when the British Labour government under Harold Wilson decided to close down its naval and military establishments in Singapore. As about

40,000 civilians were employed in the naval base, most of them Indians who had not accepted Singapore citizenship, one of our ministers said in a speech that there was a possibility of their repatriation to India. This upset the Indian government and I had to explain the situation to Mr Chagla, the then foreign minister. The minister, a well-known lawyer, spoke of how the skies, which had been so sunny on his visit to Singapore in 1967, had suddenly clouded over with the threat of a downpour and how this had saddened him greatly! I was able to assure him that although we were in economic difficulties, the problem would be resolved if the naval base workers made up their minds to accept Singapore citizenship. Eventually, the matter was amicably resolved and I was even able to arrange a successful visit to Singapore by the Indian Prime Minister Mrs Gandhi — the only such visit by India's leader to Singapore till 1994. So apart from the minor misunderstanding, it was roses, roses all the way as far as the relationship between tiny Singapore and the giant India was concerned.

As for Nepal, I informed our minister for foreign affairs about my conversation with the King of Nepal. He understood my reluctance to return to Kathmandu to bid farewell so soon after presenting my credentials. He decided my successor would be entrusted with the task

Picture 12: MB presenting credentials to the King of Nepal, June 1969.

Picture 13: MB and Mrs Barbara Baker with the Foreign Minister of India, Dinesh Singh, at Singapore's National Day reception in New Delhi, 1969.

of apologising to the king. I was certainly grateful for this decision which spared me some embarrassment. It was Mr Punch Coomaraswamy, the distinguished speaker of Parliament, who succeeded me in India and was also accredited to Nepal, and later to Sri Lanka too.

Prime Minister Mrs Indira Gandhi's Visit to Singapore

Early in 1968, Mr K.C. Nair, joint secretary of the Indian Ministry of External Affairs, told me that Mrs Gandhi would like to visit Singapore. Diplomatic courtesy demands that the host country should issue an invitation to make it appear that it is its own idea to invite the dignitary of another country. Accordingly, Singapore sent a formal invitation to the Indian prime minister welcoming a visit from her.

The official visit took place on 19 and 20 May 1968. Mrs Gandhi arrived accompanied by a dozen officials. She paid the usual courtesy call to President Yusof Ishak and Puan Noor Aishah at the Istana, followed by her call at 7 p.m. on Prime Minister Lee Kuan Yew for discussions, before the banquet hosted by him and Mrs Lee at the Singapore Conference Hall. Our prime minister made a superb speech at the dinner which the Indians appreciated greatly as he paid tribute to India and the impact of Indian culture on Singapore. This is a contrast to the present overwhelming emphasis on Confucian culture. The speech also reveals Singapore's educational and economic plans and hopes in 1968. I want to quote most of what he said as reported in our newspapers:

> "Prime Minister, Your Excellencies, Ladies and Gentlemen,
>
> It is more than courtesy that makes Singapore extend a warm welcome to you. You are the head of a government which represents a people who have given us a part of ourselves and more than part of our inspiration. May I recount some of the things for which we have borrowed and for which we are indebted to India.
>
> First, our name Singapura is Sanskrit. It was given to us by Indian traders centuries before the Europeans came.
>
> Next, our earliest public works and monuments were built by Indian labour and skills, albeit forcibly brought here by the British Raj. Among other projects, 146 years ago the British brought Indian convicts to build Government House, where you are now staying.
>
> And woven into the fabric of Singapore society are many strands that come from India, mainly from the south, Madras and Kerala, but more than a few silken threads from Bengal, Punjab, Sindh and Bombay.
>
> I hope you will get a flavour of Singapore during your brief stay. We have been the confluence of three great Asian civilisations brought together under the aegis of a great European civilisation. Here the British brought together the Chinese, the Indians and the Malays. The British had a few schools to produce English speaking clerks and junior staff but otherwise left the different ethnic groups to tend their own language and culture.
>
> By the time we achieved political power, we found our society permanently encrusted with several languages and

their literatures — literatures which carry with them memories of past glory, some history, part mythology. No community was willing to give up its rightful heritage, although all agreed that it was necessary to find common ground.

So about a decade ago, despite all the inevitable complications and tiresome duplications of multi-lingual and multi-cultural education, we allowed free choice and free competition to establish the common denominators. Every parent could and can choose whether to send his child to an English, Chinese, Malay or Tamil medium government school. For these are our four official languages. Whichever school a child goes to, he or she is tutored in two languages, one of which must be the mother tongue. Now by common experience everyone finds it convenient to continue English as the language of administration and as the channel to the scientific and technological era we hope to break into.

I am not familiar with the experience of other communities as a result of trans-marine migration. But I can speak of our experience in Singapore, that without the contribution we have had from India, her rich and enduring past, her sagacious and enterprising people, we would have been that much the poorer. For it was the continuous inflow of fresh blood that brought the stimulus of fresh ideas. These have contributed to the verve of a busy trading, and now manufacturing, transportation and communications centre.

We have not kept everything of the old. You may find Singapore Indians look like Indians, speak like Indians, but those who have been born and educated here, as you get to know them, you will find they are no longer Indians. Caste and customs, rituals and taboos which inhibit innovation and modernisation have been discarded under pressure of the competing influences from other cultural and value patterns and religions all seeking pre-eminence in the context of modernity.

So too with the Chinese. We look Chinese. We speak Chinese. But if a man from China speaks to a Singapore Chinese, he will discover that the Singaporean is already a distinct and different type.

Prime Minister, you have come to visit us on the eve of momentous changes, about to take place in the region. These changes India initiated when she obtained her independence in 1947.

Only recently all were subject peoples of European empires. We now find, however, that our hopes of universal brotherhood among fellow Asians dispelled as old feuds are resumed, and new ones are pursued. Still worse, the traditional buffers to conflict, the oceans, rivers, desert and jungle, are no longer impenetrable to armies equipped with modern means of transportation. Now over two decades later we have to adjust and adapt ourselves to the post colonial era as we search for security and economic progress in rapidly changing conditions.

The peoples of the region wanted to be rid of Western domination. India and her leaders played a consistent and significant role in settling the mood of world opinion which in turn affected the policies of the imperial powers of Europe and led to an earlier liberation of Asia and Africa.

There can be no going back to status quo ante. Whatever might have existed before the West came, Asia has got to live with the present, irrevocably altered, after four centuries of Western domination.

Like India, we are going through similar difficulties in modernising and educating our multi-racial, multi-lingual population into the secular values of a modern nation state. Like India in the past decade, we have had many difficulties and some successes.

As contemporary form is to magnify India's food and political problems, and to belittle her achievements, I found it refreshing that our High Commissioner in Delhi, to support his sanguine outlook for India's future, referred to analyses made by critical Western observers of India's economic performance. The present bumper harvest, it is said, may mark a turning point in the problem of overall economic growth which has not been adequately recognised.

We have had long trade ties with India. But the pattern of economic relationships is altering as we proceed with our industrialisation plans. We welcome India's participation in these industrial projects. For nothing reinforces sentiment better than bilateral economic advantages. We would like to multiply these ties to mutual advantage.

But it is the future that consumes all our attention and energy, as we seek continuing security and stability that will enable us to forge ahead with our economic and social plans.

Recently, we had the privilege of welcoming a flotilla from the Indian Navy. We hope it is the first of many visits. This harbour will always be a friendly haven for Indian naval units. It is not just for reasons of sentiment. Placed as we are, with one avenue looking westwards into the Indian Ocean and the other eastwards into the Pacific, not unnaturally we feel more relaxed and comfortable when there is no oppressive and over-powering hegemony by any single power.

Your visit re-affirms our affinity in many respects. May I express our hope that it will lead to more meaningful co-operation for the greater security and economic prosperity of both our peoples."

On Monday, 20 May, Mrs Gandhi visited the Housing and Development Board, the Jurong Industrial Estate and the Botanic Gardens, where an orchid was named after her. After a luncheon hosted by our Joint Chamber of Commerce and a reception by the Indian high commissioner in her honour, she left Singapore on an Air India flight at 9.40 p.m. The visit was brief but significant and certainly the highlight of my term as Singapore's first high commissioner to India.

Many favourable comments were made about our PM's speech. Mrs Alirajpur, the Indian high commissioner's wife, who sat next to me, was very impressed, calling it "a most excellent speech". Mrs Gandhi's lady-in-waiting expressed her joy at the PM's speech pointing out that it was the fashion in journalism to spotlight Indian failures and disasters while ignoring her achievements. I'm sure Mrs Gandhi must have felt the same because she has constantly both in private and in public made the same point. The Indian government, like most governments, appreciates foreign understanding of its difficulties and a word of praise for its achievements.

Mrs Gandhi was much loved by the crowds especially at the National Theatre. She asked me whether it would be all right for her to walk along the restraining police cordons to greet the crowds and she proceeded to do so to the consternation of the security officers, one of whom complained to me that she had "thrown security to the winds". Later, on the drive back to the Istana when the crowd surged round her car, Mrs Alirajpur, who was in the car with her, said that Mrs Gandhi was moved to tears by the enthusiasm of the people.

Parting Thoughts

My two short years in India were educational. I learnt something of the ancient culture, the religions, the myriad languages and dialects, the graceful dances, the intricate and exquisite handicraft, the immense sculptures and architecture of the temples and palaces in this vast land of contrasts. If only I had had another two years in India I would have travelled further and learnt so much more! I missed going to Karnataka with its famous cities of Mysore and Bangalore when my wife contracted hepatitis after the tickets had been booked and all the arrangements made. It was a great disappointment.

My diplomatic stint in India made me realise what a cultural treasure house the country is with its ancient and chequered history. What a tiny young country Singapore is by comparison! It is a very humbling thought. There is so much one can learn from civilisations such as India's or China's. It is a wonder that though the histories of India and China are full of examples of man's inhumanity to man, replete with murder and mayhem, bloody wars and slaughter by marching armies and tyrants, the art, literature and architecture, especially of places of worship, remain imperishable monuments to man's love of beauty. Perhaps India remains unrivalled in its superb temples such as the man-made cave temples of Ellora and the Buddhist sculptures and frescoes of Ajanta. The epics of the *Ramayana* and the *Mahabharata* are among the greatest literary achievements of mankind.

One of the sad things about India is the extreme poverty made worse by the rapidly increasing population. The struggle for survival imbues some Indians with a good deal of cunning and dishonesty. Corruption is as rife in India as it is in some other parts of Asia and Africa. Everyone who does a service in India expects a tip or a bottle of whisky for services rendered. Even the postman, the electrician or the telephone repairman has to be tipped or else your letters will be missing and your telephone will suffer frequent breakdowns.

Salaries of public servants in India are low compared to salaries of their counterparts in Singapore. That accounts for some of the corruption in the cities of India. The contrast between the rich and the poor is far greater than in Singapore and painfully visible to the visitor. The rich Indians seem so indifferent to the poverty around them. I suppose seeing so much of it all the time hardens their hearts. I found it impossible to ignore the beggars, especially the little children in the streets who stretch out their tiny hands at the traffic junctions. One should keep an ample supply of coins and notes to hand out. This eases one's conscience a little.

Chapter 5

High Commissioner to Malaysia and Return to Academia
August 1969–August 1971 and 1972–June 1977

P RIME MINISTER LEE Kuan Yew, Foreign Minister S. Rajaratnam and Finance Minister Dr Goh Keng Swee briefed me on what was required of me as high commissioner to Malaysia. They were all worried about the effects of the Malaysian race riots on Singapore. It is no surprise that disasters of this nature in Malaysia are likely to have repercussions in Singapore. It is essential to have first-hand information quickly to take countermeasures. What we feared most after 13 May 1969 was the possibility of a great flood of panic-stricken Chinese rushing to Singapore. We had also to be on guard against racial outbreaks on the island. In fact, one such attack by the Chinese on Malays in Singapore had been swiftly dealt with. There were strong rumours that the communists would exploit the racial riots to the utmost to create chaos.

Trouble was expected on 31 August, Malaysia's National Day, so it was decided that I should present my credentials before that date. The only difficulty was that Malaysian protocol insisted that the incoming ambassador or high commissioner should wear formal morning dress at the presentation ceremony although a top hat was not required. The only tailor in Singapore at that time who could do the job was Ah Chum in Orchard Road. He did this very quickly indeed, and I am glad to say that the outfit was paid for by the government. I had been allowed to wear a dark lounge suit for the ceremony in India although Indian protocol accepted this with some reluctance. The Malaysians, however, had a king and royalty, and insisted on formal British clothes including white tie and tails for dinners at which the king would be present. It is remarkable that, though countries like India and Malaysia became independent of Britain, they insisted on the trappings of Western civilisation for diplomats though these were far from comfortable in tropical climates. Formal attire was de rigueur on important ceremonial occasions. This custom was observed for several years before the practice was relaxed for diplomats from countries like Vietnam and Iran. Diplomats from the Philippines and Thailand were more sensibly clad in their national dress designed for the tropics.

My wife and I arrived at Kuala Lumpur airport to be surprised by a group of local reporters. I had not expected to face a barrage of questions on the strained relations between Malaysia and Singapore as my arrival in India had been a quiet one. I was questioned as to what I was going to do to solve the difficult problems. I indulged in the usual spiel about the need for good relations between such close neighbours with a common history. I emphasised the need to talk to resolve differences and stressed that a common defence was imperative in the long term. Next morning *The Straits Times* printed a large photograph of me on the front page with the caption "Talk, talk, talk …"!

The large photograph had the advantage of alerting old schoolmates and friends of my presence in Kuala Lumpur. The most surprising outcome was a letter from Kuantan in Pahang from the daughter of a lady who, as an orphan, had been adopted by my mother. She had stayed several years with us as a member of the family. Later I was able to visit her and her two daughters who were bright and cheerful girls with a great sense of humour. One had a notice on the back of her car with this warning, "Overtaker beware! I shall see you at the undertaker!!" The mother recalled how upset I had been as a boy when she had unwittingly killed my ducklings by putting a wooden box over them at night. They had all suffocated to death! I remembered the incident and the tears I had shed over my poor dead ducklings.

The friendship of former schoolmates and Raffles College graduates was of great help to me in my two difficult years in Malaysia.

The shock of the unexpected expulsion of Singapore from Malaysia in 1965 had bred great bitterness in the Singapore leaders. They had worked hard and long to convince the people of Singapore of the need for a merger with Malaysia and had repeatedly asserted that the island had not much of a future apart from Malaysia. The Malaysian leaders, and especially Tunku Abdul Rahman, the prime minister, were bitter too with the "Malaysian Malaysia" concept preached by Lee Kuan Yew which stated that the other races had as much right to be in Malaysia as the Malays. Malaysian leaders had to adjust to the idea of a sovereign state of Singapore not inferior to Malaysia. It is likely that the Malaysians believed in what the Singapore leaders had often said — that the city state could not survive economically without Malaysia. They were therefore tempted to impose tariffs on Singapore products. Singapore retaliated in kind. Among my first duties was to try and resolve the "chicken and pineapple" skirmish between the two countries.

Throughout 1967 and 1968, despite a "golfing summit" in Cameron Highlands in February 1967 at which Tunku Abdul Rahman, Tun Razak and Tun Dr Ismail met Prime Minister Lee, Dr Toh Chin Chye, Dr Goh Keng Swee and Mr S. Rajaratnam — the first friendly meeting of the top leaders since the separation in 1965 — difficult problems arose. By November 1966, some 700 officers and men who were Malaysian citizens in the Singapore Armed Forces were sent back on mutually agreed terms. In April 1967, the Singapore government sacked Malaysian citizens in the Singapore Police Force — 427 of them according to the Malaysians but 365 according to Singapore. Singapore claimed that it had tried to get Malaysia to re-employ them as early as December 1965 but to no avail. Malaysia denied any knowledge of this but nevertheless it could do no less than accept them into the Malaysian Police Force. It was natural that Singapore should ensure that nobody with a divided loyalty be employed in a security-sensitive area. But Malaysia was upset. Next, the Singapore government announced that it would issue special passports for travel to Malaysia only. Malaysia too decided on restricted passports for Malaysians to travel to Singapore effective from 1 July 1967 (later postponed to 1 September). Singapore refused to extend the implementation date. *The Straits Times* editorial of 30 June 1967 was critical of Singapore's refusal from the point of view of many people who had not been issued the special passports as yet. Next, citizens of both countries were only allowed a stay of two weeks although an extension could be obtained at immigration offices. What with increasing friction between the two countries, a reporter asked the Tunku if he thought the two countries were drifting further apart. "They can drift apart only as far as the Straits of Johor," replied the Tunku. When the immigration barriers went up at the Causeway, *The Straits Times* came out with the headline:

> A 44-year link has now become a frontier post

The article pointed out that before 1923, when there was no causeway, ferries were in use. Rail traffic between the mainland and Singapore had been conveyed by train ferries. In 1917, 54,000 rail trucks had to be ferried across the Straits. So the governments of the Federated Malay States and Singapore decided on a causeway, work on which commenced in 1919. The cost was $17 million. It was completed in 1923. The retreating British army blew up part of it on 31 January 1942 to check the Japanese advance but Japanese engineers repaired the damage very quickly.

From time to time, Tunku Abdul Rahman and Tun Razak suggested in press interviews that Malaysia–Singapore relations were on the mend and that the "teething troubles" of the 1965 separation were over. It was accepted that, in the interests of the people in both territories, there should be cooperation between the two countries. Nevertheless, there was friction from time to time. One problem I was asked to solve was the stoppage of pineapples from Johor to the Singapore factory.

I decided to host a dinner at my residence for Tun Razak, Tun Dr Ismail and Tun Tan Siew Sin — the deputy prime minister, the home minister and the finance minister respectively — on 20 October 1969. I invited my old Raffles College friends Tan Sri Kadir Yusof, the attorney-general and Tan Sri Raja Mohar, secretary-general of the Ministry of Commerce and Industry, the key person involved in the prickly pineapple issue.

The high commissioner's residence was a charming old-style double-storeyed house built on land leased from the Royal Selangor Golf Club just next to the club entrance. My predecessor, Mr Lien Ying Chow, the well-known banker, and his beautiful wife had furnished the house attractively. The dining room was large and had a long table which could seat 24 — ideal for diplomatic entertainment. All the guests were accompanied by their wives. It was a friendly and enjoyable gathering. I chose a moment in the presence of Tun Razak and Tan Sri Raja Mohar to bring up the pineapple question. The secretary-general of Commerce and Industry, who was usually the soul of courtesy, blurted out that Singapore's bureaucrats were often trying to outsmart Malaysia's but since I had made the request he would look into the matter.

The very next day I received a full explanation of the situation in great detail which I need not relate here. He proved that there was no discrimination in the supply of smallholders' fruits to the Singapore factory as an average of five lorry loads per day were despatched. There were three canneries in Johor which shared the smallholders' fruits. There was no reason for the Singapore authorities to suspect that the Malaysians were deliberately forcing the Singapore factory to close down. I give this as an example of suspicions on both sides on similar minor issues like vegetables, chickens and eggs.

My first impression on arrival in Malaysia was that Kuala Lumpur was a wounded city. Though three months had passed since the bloodletting, the streets were half-empty by day, and dead at nightfall. A close friend from Raffles College days invited me to a well-known Chinese restaurant one evening. His family and mine were the only diners that night in that spacious restaurant. Rumours ruled over the city. A chicken hawker on a bicycle whose basket of chickens fell off chased his fowls. This brought down the shutters of the shops. Anyone running to catch a bus could cause a panic! Fear gripped the people. A single fire cracker exploding in the night was believed to herald the return of the terrorists from the hills to avenge the Chinese victims of the riots. The silent city, after dark, reminded me of the night of 15 February 1942 when the British surrendered Singapore to the Japanese after two weeks of relentless shelling and bombing which tore the city apart. The silence on the 15th was stunning. There was a curfew on in Kuala Lumpur but only between 2 a.m. and 4 a.m. as the government was reasonably confident that there would not be a repetition of May 13. The deputy prime minister, Tun Razak, and the home minister, Tun Dr Ismail, who had been recalled from his private practice as a doctor to rejoin the cabinet during the emergency, dealt with the rioters firmly. Tun Dr Ismail later said that he had shown no mercy to the rioters no matter whether they were Chinese, Indians or Malays. He had them arrested and confined in Pulau Jerejak near Penang. It was perhaps mainly Ismail's decisiveness and his no-nonsense attitude which ended the riots swiftly and returned the country slowly to normality.

Why did the riots break out in the first place? Tunku Abdul Rahman put the blame squarely on the communist terrorists who had murdered an United Malays National Organisation (UMNO) worker in Penang. On the day before polling day, 10 May, the Labour Party (synonymous with the communists for the Tunku) had held a funeral procession in Kuala Lumpur for a Chinese worker shot by the police while resisting arrest. The demonstrators carried red flags and even portraits of Mao Tse Tung! While these acts roused Malay feelings, the real reasons for the outbreak lay deeper in the distrust between the Malays and the Chinese. On the one hand, the Malays feared that the Chinese, who already dominated the economy, aspired to political supremacy as well. This they would not tolerate in the country which they regarded as their own. They considered the Chinese and Indians as immigrants. The results of the May 1969 elections appeared to threaten Malay political control in the states of Selangor and Perak, while Penang was lost to the new multiracial Gerakan party which captured 16 of 24 seats. The UMNO–MCA–MIC Alliance (the coalition made up of the United Malays National Organisation, the Malaysian Chinese Association and the Malaysian Indian Congress), which had won all previous elections handsomely, was shocked by the collapse of the MCA which won only ten of the 33 federal seats it had contested, 14 less than it had won in the previous election in 1964. The Democratic Action Party (DAP) won 13 seats as the Chinese voters deserted the MCA for this party which put forward the concept of a "Malaysian Malaysia", and blamed the MCA for giving up non-Malay rights to UMNO. This idea, originally promulgated by the People's Action Party (PAP) of Singapore, was anathema to the Malays and had led to the separation of Singapore in August 1965. Although the UMNO–MCA–MIC Alliance won 66 federal seats of which UMNO held 51, the coalition had won 89 seats in the 1964 elections and 74 in 1959. In the 1969 elections the Alliance won only 49.1 per cent of the vote. It had a simple majority but lost its two-thirds majority. This erosion of the coalition's strength was seen as leading to the eventual loss of the political power of the Malays to the "immigrant" races. This belief was reinforced by the results of the state elections. In Selangor, the Alliance won exactly half the seats, 14 out of 28, although UMNO won 12 out of the 13 seats it contested. The MCA, which had won eight out of 12 seats in 1964, now lost all but one seat! The DAP won nine, Gerakan four and an independent one. In Perak, the Alliance won 19 of the 40 seats, the rest being divided between four other parties.

The election results led many UMNO activists to have doubts whether democracy was right for Malaysia. Democracy could lead to political power passing from the hands of the Malays to the Chinese and Indians. So, as the Chinese and Indian voters had let down the MCA and MIC, some UMNO supporters wanted to ally themselves with the extremist Muslim Pan-Malayan Islamic Party (later PAS), which controlled Kelantan and had won Terengganu, to ensure Malay political supremacy. The alternative was to abandon democratic elections and rule the country by other than democratic means as was done in Indonesia, to ensure the political supremacy of the Malay race.

The multiracial population consisting of Malays, Chinese and Indians represented very different cultures, languages, religions and personal attitudes and habits. The Malays were entirely Muslim, the Chinese were mainly Buddhists or Taoists and the Indians Hindus — four very different religious beliefs. The Malays equalled roughly in number the Chinese and the Indians combined. Their languages differed greatly and even their food preferences were distinct. The Chinese loved pork which was taboo to the Muslims. Chinese women wore cheongsams, the Malays the *baju kurung* and the Indians the sari, but the men usually adopted western apparel. The racial set-up in Malaysia with its complications has far greater potential for racial explosions than, say, Switzerland which is made up of German-, French- and Italian-speaking peoples who are, however, all Europeans. But until politicians began exploiting racial and language issues to gain votes, the country had remained at peace. The leadership of the country was in the hands of Tunku Abdul Rahman, Tun Razak and Tun Dr Ismail representing the Malays, Tun Tan Siew Sin representing the Chinese and Tun V.T. Sambanthan representing the Indians, who were all good friends working to keep the country united. There was also the good sense and tolerance of the populace until the extremist politicians brought to the forefront the deep differences in order to get themselves elected. The result was the May 13 cataclysm.

While the Malays were worried and anxious about the election results, the arrogance and boisterous behaviour of the Gerakan and DAP supporters on 11 and 12 May 1969 while celebrating their startling success in Kuala Lumpur proved provocative. They hurled insults at the Malays. They were reported to have yelled taunts such as, "This is not a Malay country", "Malays have lost power, now we are in control", "*Melayu boleh balik kampung*" (Malays can go back to the villages), "*Kuala Lumpur sekarang China punya*" (Kuala Lumpur is now Chinese). In fact, UMNO had not been defeated in the elections, so the Malays decided to hold an UMNO counter-demonstration on 13 May. A crowd of about 5,000 highly emotional UMNO supporters gathered on the grounds of the residence of Dato' Harun Idris, Menteri Besar of Selangor (which then included Kuala Lumpur). When news came that UMNO supporters had been attacked in Setapak on the outskirts of Kuala Lumpur, the enraged crowd dashed out despite Dato' Harun's appeal for calm. This was what he told me when I called on him.

The riots began with the killing of two Chinese passing by in a van outside Dato' Harun's residence. An orgy of killing, looting and arson by Malays and Chinese followed in the city. The police, despite all efforts, failed to bring the murderous riots under control so the army had to be called in. A curfew was imposed by 8 o' clock on the night of 13 May. Tunku Abdul Rahman in his book, *May 13 – Before and After*, recalled, "Kuala Lumpur was a city on fire. I could clearly see the conflagration from my residence on top of the hill and it was a sight that I never thought I would see in my lifetime. In fact, all my work to make Malaysia a happy and peaceful country through these years, and also my dream of being the happiest Prime Minister in the world, were going up in flames." Despite the courageous efforts of the police and the army, roving gangs of Chinese and Malays murdered and set fire to houses, shops, vehicles and whatever crossed their paths. Mob violence continued on the 14th in the city and its suburbs, so on 15 May a nationwide state of emergency was declared.

Parliament was suspended and party politics banned. An eight-man National Operations Council (NOC) under Tun Razak was set up to restore law and order swiftly. Two non-Malays, Tun Sambanthan and Tun Tan Siew Sin, were members of the NOC. The Tunku, who needed an eye operation urgently, had planned to fly out to Britain but the outbreak of the riots forced him to change his plan. He appointed Tun Razak as director of operations also because the latter was experienced in dealing with security problems during the communist troubles. Some non-Malays were unhappy with the appointment of Tun Razak as director of operations as they thought he was anti-Chinese. But this was certainly not true. Tun Razak, whom I had the privilege of knowing for many years, certainly wanted to uplift the Malays from their poverty, but he was not anti-anybody. He had close friends among all nationalities. Unlike the more extreme Malays or "ultras", he was realistic. He knew that no one race could have a monopoly of power in multiracial Malaysia. He was too intelligent and humane a man to harbour racial prejudices. The welfare of all Malaysians was what he strove for but he was aware that it was the Malays who needed help the most.

I knew when I arrived to take up my post that there was a group of "young Turks" in UMNO critical of the Tunku's leadership. He was thought to have favoured the non-Malays at the expense of the Malays. This group, dubbed the "ultras", which wanted to assert Malay political supremacy, saw the Tunku as an obstacle and decided that he had to be forced off the political scene. The "ultras" felt that the Tunku had given in too much to the MCA demands too often, especially on the language issue. They wanted Malay as the sole medium of instruction in schools and the sole medium in the administration.

Many poison pen letters attacking the Tunku were circulated blaming him for pampering the "immigrants" meaning the Chinese and Indians and "giving too much face to them" so that "they had the liberty to insult the Malays". The Tunku was also accused of neglecting the welfare of the Malays who were in danger of "becoming refugees in their own country like the Arabs in Palestine". He was even blamed for giving away Singapore ("our property" to immigrants!). One such letter was signed "Sharp Bamboo Command"!

The University of Malaya Malay Language Society organised demonstrations within the campus and called for a boycott of lectures. A Malaysian Students Action Front called upon the Tunku to resign, giving a number of reasons why he should. It claimed that the May 13 riots proved that the Tunku had failed to create national unity. It blamed him for not making Malay the sole official language by 1967 and for failing to improve the economic position of the Malays. The document rejected the Tunku's "policy of compromises and sweeping problems under the carpet" as well as his "feudalistic and intuitive approach to politics".

Another paper called for support for the NOC and expressed "faith in Ismail ... as a strong and disciplined leader" and "in Razak and believe that he is a sincere leader". It hailed "Ghazali Shafie as a wise man and a competent administrator" and gave support to "Kadir Yusof because he does not put self-interest before anything else". It condemned strong supporters of the Tunku by name as "avaricious renegades and traitors". It asserted that the masses supported Musa Hitam and Dr Mahathir who had been "victims of the cruel and power-crazy Abdul Rahman". It called for a "scientific government not an intuitive one" and insisted that "Abdul Rahman must go!"

Dr Mahathir bin Mohamad, an up and coming young leader, had written a letter to the Tunku dated 17 June 1969, calling on him to resign as UMNO president and prime minister. Dr Mahathir was against MCA participation in the cabinet at that time. The letter was widely circulated before it was banned by the police. But Dr Mahathir had widespread support among school teachers, university lecturers and students. The Tunku managed, with Razak's and Tun Dr Ismail's support, to have Mahathir expelled from UMNO.[1] In that same year, Dr Mahathir lost his parliamentary seat in Kota Setar Selatan, Kedah to Haji Yusof Rawa of PAS. Tun Dr Ismail told me once that what Dr Mahathir had done to the Tunku was "unforgivable" but he said that Musa Hitam, who had been sacked by the Tunku from his job as assistant minister to Tun Razak, had been sent to the United Kingdom for higher studies, "to keep him out of the way of the angry Tunku".

There was a strong feeling among the "ultras" that the country should be ruled by the Malays alone but the moderates, led by the Tunku, were supported by the military who were represented on the NOC by the chief of the armed forces. "The moderates under the leadership of the Tunku," said Tun Dr Ismail over Television Malaysia on 2 August 1969, "firmly hold the view that in the Malaysian multiracial society such a theory is not just a harmless pipe dream but an extremely dangerous fantasy of absolute rule by one race." He went on to warn extreme racialists that he would not hesitate to exercise his powers under the law — that is to arrest them if they caused trouble.

---

[1] Khoo Boo Teik (1995). *Paradoxes of Mahathirism: An Intellectual Biography of Mahathir Mohamad.* New York: Oxford University Press, p. 23.

Efforts were made to restore peace among the races by establishing National Goodwill Councils all over Malaysia in July 1969. Later in January 1970, a Department of National Unity and the National Consultative Council were set up to discuss racial problems that affected the country and to find solutions so that racial rioting would never occur again. The Department of National Unity headed by Tan Sri Ghazali Shafie drafted the national ideology called the *Rukunegara* to bring about national unity and maintain democracy.

The *Rukunegara* involved five principles — belief in God; loyalty to King and country; upholding the Constitution; rule of law; and good morality. These principles were not new, but they were codified for the first time. The *Rukunegara* aimed to work towards sharing the national wealth equitably, ensuring the preservation of the different cultural traditions and building "a progressive society which shall be orientated to modern science and technology". These principles were clarified further. While Islam was the official religion, all other religious beliefs could be practised peacefully. All citizens were expected to be loyal to the King. The letter and spirit of the Constitution was to be understood and respected — "the position of the Rulers, the position of Islam as the official religion, the position of Malays and other Natives, the legitimate interests of other communities, the conferment of citizenship". The right of free speech was guaranteed subject only to limitation imposed by the law. All citizens were equal before the law and their fundamental liberties were guaranteed. Finally, it was stated that individuals and groups shall conduct their affairs in such a manner as not to violate any of the accepted canons of behaviour or offend the sensitivities of any group. No citizen should question the loyalty of another citizen on the ground that he belongs to a particular community.

This carefully worded document was, I suspect, mainly the work of the intellectually brilliant Tan Sri Ghazali Shafie, Professor Syed Hussein Alatas and Ungku Aziz, the vice-chancellor of the University of Malaya. It attempted to resolve the difficulties of Malay–Chinese relationships; it ensured the continuance of parliamentary democracy and it assured the Chinese that their culture was safe. At the same time, the Chinese were bound by the Constitution to accept Malay as the national and official language, and respect the special position of the Malays and other native races. On the other hand, the loyalty of the Chinese or Indians could not be questioned because of their ethnic origins.

The *Rukunegara* was promulgated on 31 August 1970, Malaysia's National Day, and supported by all Malaysian political parties. Nevertheless, the return to democracy was delayed till after the elections in Sabah and Sarawak which had been postponed on the outbreak of the racial riots. The results of these elections restored the confidence of the Alliance as all 16 seats in Sabah were won by the United Sabah National Organisation (USNO) and the Sabah Chinese Association. In Sarawak, the Alliance parties did better than expected and Tun Razak returned happily from Kuching where he had succeeded, he said, in persuading the Sarawak United People's Party (SUPP) to align itself with the Sarawak coalition government. The Alliance now had a total of 91 seats in the 144-member Parliament and was confident enough to restore democratic government. This took place on 23 February 1971 when the new Parliament met after 20 months of NOC rule.

Deputy Prime Minister Tun Razak

Two days after our arrival in Kuala Lumpur, Tun Razak and his wife invited my wife and me to tea at his residence. It was an occasion to renew old friendships and recall our London days and how we had upset the British with The Malayan Forum and our Bulletin *Suara Merdeka* which was the Malayan students' mouthpiece for independence. We did not discuss the immediate problems Malaysia faced or its tense relations with Singapore. It was a friendly get-together and typically Tun Razak did not bring up serious issues. Names of mutual friends cropped up and Razak said that he had gathered together all the able Raffles Collegians in the country and given all of them useful work to do. He was happy with many but complained about one or two who had disappointed him and failed to live up to his expectations. He had to transfer them to less responsible positions. In Singapore, an inefficient civil servant would have been requested to retire prematurely in the interests of the state but in Malaysia he was found some sinecure to save him from public humiliation. Razak did say that he was tempted to sack one of the top civil servants who was "hopeless" but the Tunku intervened on his behalf as he was one of his "poker *kakis*" (poker buddies)! The Tunku valued his friends, even the corrupt ones, unfortunately. He disliked wielding the big stick to hurt his colleagues or the civil servants. He went so far as to protect two menteris besar who were targeted by the anti-corruption investigators — one was quickly sent abroad as an ambassador and the other was allowed to retire on grounds of ill health! The most well-known case was that of former Singaporean Chief Minister Lim Yew Hock who had emigrated to Malaysia and was sent abroad as high commissioner to Australia. There, the high commissioner allegedly became enamoured of a dance hostess and disappeared from his chancery for nine days. His wife reported him missing and the ensuing scandal hit the headlines. Lim Yew Hock was recalled but the Tunku made a humorous defence of him in Parliament, reduced everyone to laughter, and so closed the whole embarrassing episode. Lim Yew Hock had done a good job for Malaysia by explaining the country's policies in numerous speeches all over Australia during the confrontation by President Sukarno of Indonesia.

When the Tunku retired and became the secretary-general of the Organisation of the Islamic Conference (now the Organisation of Islamic Cooperation) in Jeddah, he took Yew Hock, who had become a Muslim, with him. Later, Yew Hock was made executive secretary of the Muslim Welfare Organisation of Malaysia (PERKIM[2]) whose president was the Tunku. The Tunku remained Yew Hock's steadfast friend till Lim Yew Hock's death in 1984.

Tun Razak was a much more demanding leader and insisted on his cabinet colleagues and civil servants doing their job well. He did not hesitate to show his displeasure. He used to travel by helicopter to many state capitals and towns to check on his civil servants. Sometimes, he said, he had to reprimand lazy state officials whose desks were cluttered with files which had not been cleared. He inspired fear in the civil service. I noticed that at some of the parties I organised for him in my residence, senior officials tended to keep their distance from Tun Razak. When I inquired why, they replied that he would often question them about their work!

Tun Razak demanded efficiency from the civil servants, many of whom, he complained, had what he called "outdated attitudes". Some of them both at state and federal levels appeared to regard the civil service as an organisation set up merely to hand monthly pay cheques to themselves

---

[2] Pertubahan Kebajikan Islam Malaysia.

and pensioners! He insisted that top civil servants should not only work hard themselves but ensure that those below them carried out orders and implemented decisions made by the cabinet. He wanted civil servants to stand up to politicians; to present all the facts of a case without bias and leave it to the politicians to make the decision. After all, politicians come and go but the civil servant is pensionable and has a duty to perform in a democracy. He should not be tied to his files and his desk. He was appalled to find, when he had granted $1.4 million in 1966 to improve the amenities of rural people in Johor, nothing had been done for a year and the money was lying idle! He demanded implementation of the plans without delay.

Once, on a visit to a Land Office, he said that he had noticed the flag flying at half-mast. He wondered who had died. When he inspected the Land Office, he realised that no one had died but it was an appropriate symbol that the flag should fly at half-mast as everyone in that Land Office was half-dead anyway![3]

Tun Razak often made his point in a witty manner. He evoked laughter but his humour had a sharp edge to it.

Tun Razak loved informal parties where he could relax among friends, especially his old Raffles College mates and those who had been in England with him from 1947 to 1950. He would himself hold such parties in his residence for a small group of about 15 to 20 of us. Once a year, he would host a large dinner party at the Lake Club for his friends, at which Tan Sri Taib bin Haji Andak was the master of ceremonies. Everyone relaxed and had a happy time. With his usual sense of humour, he held this get-together on 1 April ostensibly to celebrate his birthday which was on 11 March! At times, Tun Razak used to worry about his friends. For example, Fred Arulanandom, the lawyer who was a close friend of mine too at Raffles College and later in the United Kingdom, used to drink rather heavily and become loud and boisterous. The good Tun feared Fred would wreck his health so he discussed with me whether he should give him a responsible job to check his drinking habit. He wondered whether he should send Fred abroad as an ambassador or make him a judge. I advised against the first option as alcohol was tax-free for diplomats and I had seen one or two

---

[3] Morais, John Victor (Ed.). (1969). *Strategy for Action: The Selected Speeches of Tun Haji Abdul Razak bin Dato' Hussein al-Haj*. Kuala Lumpur: Malaysia Centre for Development Studies, Prime Minister's Department, p. 169.

diplomats in India who did not hold their liquor too well. Eventually, Tun elevated Fred to the bench in the teeth of opposition from the then chief justice who was an upright man. Fred turned out to be a sober and wise judge who earned the respect of the bar. He was sent first to Kelantan on the east coast of Peninsular Malaysia which was strictly Islamic and where alcohol was frowned upon. Tun Razak was amused by the "sufferings" of Fred who had to keep himself under control as he was expected to set a good example. Later he was tranferred to Ipoh, and finally to Penang where he died of throat cancer in 1982 at the age of 60. Tun Razak cared for his friends and went out of his way to lend them a helping hand when it was needed but he drew the line at the corrupt and the lazy.

Tun Razak's affection for Fred was made widely known when, on his birthday broadcast to the nation in September 1970, he actually named his three closest friends from his college and London days as Taib Haji Andak, Fred Arulanandom and Maurice Baker "who is here as Singapore's high commissioner to Malaysia". This broadcast by the prime minister made me the envy of my colleagues in the diplomatic corps and gave me great encouragement in the difficult task I faced attempting to improve relations between the two countries mutually suspicious of each other and ready to interpret every move as probably hostile. As I said earlier, Singapore's leaders had worked hard for a merger as they did not believe the island could survive on its own. The only person who thought otherwise was Singapore's first chief minister and renowned lawyer, David Marshall, but no one had agreed with him.

There was a programme broadcast by Singapore called *What Others Say* and run by Alex Josey, who was the prime minister's press secretary. This programme picked out items of world news critical of Malaysia — and there was much hostile journalism after the riots — and other items complimentary to Singapore to show how poorly Malaysia was governed compared to Singapore! Selected pieces were printed in *The Mirror*, a publication of the Ministry of Culture to be distributed to all missions abroad for general circulation. When I was high commissioner in India I did not allow any distribution of the newssheet as I was sure it would reflect more badly on Singapore than on Malaysia. It was obviously a mean attempt to denigrate Malaysia.

When I was asked to move from India to Malaysia as high commissioner in June 1969, I wrote to the minister for foreign affairs to say that unless this programme which was offensive to the Malaysians was stopped, I would rather not go to Kuala Lumpur. The minister promised that he would consider the matter and in due course modify the programme. But very little modification took place. So at a private luncheon hosted by Tun Razak, Ghazali Shafie tackled me on *What Others Say*, pointing out that there was a contradiction between professing to promote good relations between the two governments and peoples while simultaneously encouraging the opposition parties in Malaysia, especially the Democratic Action Party, by continually mocking the Malaysian government. He certainly had a point. Ghazali was then secretary-general of the Ministry of Foreign Affairs but was later invited by Tun Razak to join the cabinet — a thoroughly well-deserved promotion in view of his talents. Many considered him as a potential prime minister but Ghazali was too proud to play to the gallery or gain popular favour to win votes in UMNO. He had no time for fools and made no effort to mix with all and sundry. I think this attitude cost him the highest political position. He was considered arrogant and unapproachable but no one could deny his abilities.

Ghazali Shafie was the only secretary-general that I knew well who moved into the political arena. Others who had been with me in Raffles College between 1938 and 1941 such as Sheikh Abdullah bin Sheikh Abu Bakar, who was secretary-general of the Ministry of Foreign Affairs under Tun Dr Ismail, Syed Zahiruddin Syed Hassan and Sheikh Hussein remained in the civil service. Some like Syed Zahiruddin Syed Hassan and Hamdan bin Haji Tahir, became governors of Malacca and Penang respectively on retirement. All these friends from Raffles College days were very helpful and always accessible when I needed to see them. Tan Sri Kadir Yusof, who was the attorney-general, later joined the cabinet as a full-fledged minister, while the brilliant Kadir Shamsuddin, a contemporary of Tun Razak at Raffles College, led the civil service, and Tan Sri Raja Mohar remained a civil servant. Tan Sri Raja Mohar on retirement held several important positions of great economic importance and was eventually made a Tun — the highest honour the government could confer on its citizens.

Picture 14: MB with Tan Sri Sheikh Hussein, Secretary-General of Education, Malaysia (in white) and Minister of Health Chong Hon Nyan at a cocktail party in Kuala Lumpur.

Picture 15: MB having dinner with Tun Syed Zahiruddin Syed Hassan, Fourth Governor of Malacca.

Long-Haired Crisis

I thought that a meeting of the two prime ministers face-to-face might help to lead to better understanding and improve relations between Singapore and Malaysia. The plans were made and set in motion for Lee Kuan Yew to visit Kuala Lumpur. But an unfortunate incident ruined our plans and set back the visit till after I had left Kuala Lumpur and returned to teach at the University of Singapore in 1972.

The Singapore police had received information that a gang of youths, probably secret society members, would meet in the Orchard Road car park (now no more) which at night flourished as a hawker centre. By an unfortunate coincidence, three long-haired Malaysians, two of whom were university undergraduates from Kuala Lumpur and who were on a visit to Singapore, had decided to have a meal at the hawker centre. The local detectives promptly arrested them and, despite their protests that they were Malaysians who had left behind their passports in their hotel, the detectives hauled them to the Central Police Station, forced them to have a haircut and locked them up for the night! They were searched but no drugs were found on them. The next day the police realised their mistake but it was too late. The high-handed action of the detectives was to have severe repercussions as the undergraduates from the University of Malaya at Pantai Valley in Kuala Lumpur decided on a huge demonstration against the Singapore High Commission which was then located at the fifth floor of the Straits Trading Building on Market Street (now Jalan Leboh Pasar). They came by the busload. The secretary-general of the Ministry of Home Affairs, Sheikh Abdullah, who had been a year my senior at Raffles College, telephoned me before the demonstrators arrived assuring me that the police, both in plain clothes and in uniform, would be present to keep control and that nothing untoward would happen apart from some clamour. On this occasion and on several others when I was faced with demonstrations during my two terms as high commissioner in Malaysia, the police kept the demonstrators under firm control and did not permit any disorder or violence. Their armed presence alone was enough to deter even the most indignant and vociferous in the crowd from becoming violent. The Malaysian police were thoroughly efficient and deserved high praise.

The students sent five representatives to see me in my office — the delegation included a Chinese and an Indian undergraduate. My first secretary, Mushahid Ali, sat with me. At first the students appeared belligerent, the Chinese and Indian being more aggressive than the Malay representatives. It is usual in Malaysia for the Chinese and Indians to impress the Malays with their enthusiasm. The Malays usually remain more polite. I listened to them and then explained that the policemen involved in the arrests were detectives who were low ranking, not too well-educated and possibly even reformed ex-criminals — "set a thief to catch a thief" — and their rash action in no way represented government policy. Malaysians should not place too much importance on the unfortunate incident for which the Singapore authorities had apologised. The students relaxed and appeared to be satisfied. They asked me whether I would go down to be photographed with them but I regretted that I had to decline the invitation. They left quite appeased but later we could hear the mass of students booing their representatives. I don't know what they had expected of their delegation.

The proposed talks between the two prime ministers in Kuala Lumpur had to be postponed and *The Straits Times* of 20 August 1970 commenting on this, called for a curb on "over-zealous CID officers". "Policemen must not let themselves be carried away by distaste for hippie hair or anything else." Meanwhile, the secretary-general of the Malaysian Ministry of Foreign Affairs exclaimed, "My God, has it come to this? We must consider whether or not to advise our Sarawak brothers through Tan Sri Temenggong Jugah that anyone there with long hair should stay on their plane on transit in Singapore." Temenggong Jugah was an Iban minister and Ibans in Sarawak often grew their hair long!

Meanwhile in Kuala Lumpur, the Singapore High Commission was subject to abusive, and at times threatening, phone calls. The police had to monitor all calls to my residence. Among several letters I received were cartoons of our prime minister depicting him as bald-headed. There were donations of locks of hair including pubic hair! An example of a hardly literate threatening letter:

> "Awak punya consul boleh close. Go home Israel Asia. Lee datang sini akan di-tembak. Kepala kasi botak. One day Malaysia Black Commandos akan rampas Singapura. Go to hell Israel Asia.
>
> from Malay Black Commandos"

While on my way to official functions in my car with the Singapore flag flying, I was booed and shouted at for a while.

I was also handed a strong protest note by a Foreign Ministry official expressing its "most serious concern" at the "ill-treatment" of the three Malaysians by Singapore police officials. This was "contrary to the spirit of goodwill which underlies the relations between the two countries". "It is the view of the Malaysian Government," the note continued, "that since the bulk of interstate relations is conducted at the level of day-to-day contact involving citizens, the attitude and behaviour shown by public officials should be such as to be conducive to the promotion of good relations between Malaysia and Singapore." The protest note sought "full clarification" from the Singapore government.

The Singapore authorities, who believed that the Malaysian press had blown up the incident out of proportion, apologised "if the three Malaysians had been wrongly and poorly treated", and reiterated that Malaysians were welcome to visit Singapore. But Lee Kuan Yew decided to postpone his visit for "a more propitious moment" to avoid embarrassing both governments although Tun Dr Ismail had assured me that the students would be under strict control. In answer to questions regarding Singapore's decision to keep "hippies" out of Singapore, the prime minister insisted that he was convinced the policy was for the good of Singapore.

The Malaysian Ministry of Foreign Affairs soon announced that it was fully satisfied with the explanation given by Singapore that over-zealousness on the part of a few police officials, who should have acted more tactfully, was responsible for the incident. "The Singapore note reiterated their apologies in regard to the hair-cutting incident and further said that no malice was intended to the three youths concerned." The whole affair was declared closed. I breathed sighs of relief!

The Tunku's Retirement

Malay "ultra" politicians who were critical of Tunku Abdul Rahman claimed that the May 13 riots proved that the Tunku's policies had failed to meet the aspirations of the Malays whose economic position had not shown any significant improvement during his term as Prime Minister. So the time had come for him to step down and hand over the reins of power to Tun Razak, his deputy. Although the Tunku had announced his intention to retire, he was obviously not happy to do it so soon. Tun Razak was in no hurry to become the prime minister. He used to say that he regarded the Tunku as his political father but there was no way of ensuring that the Tunku could continue in power. So all he could do was to ease the departure of Malaysia's Father of Independence as much as possible. An honourable exit was found for the great man when he was invited to be the first secretary-general of the Organisation of the Islamic Conference with his office in Jeddah, Saudi Arabia. Razak told me that he did not think the Tunku would last as secretary-general, but he had accepted the post "as an honourable way out".

The Tunku always wanted to mould a nation out of the diverse races of Malaysia but he was aware that the indigenous people had to have preferential treatment to haul them up to the economic level of the others. But while he wanted more to be done for the bumiputeras (the name used to describe the Malays and other indigenous people), he disliked the constant emphasis on the rights of the bumiputeras as this upset the other races. He wanted more action and less talk as he wished the whole population to think of themselves as Malaysians first whatever their ethnic origins. The ultras among the bumiputeras were, however, impatient with the Tunku's policies. They wanted tangible results quickly. So he had to make way for the younger Tun Razak. The Tunku believed that the cooperation of the other races was essential if the bumiputera economic position was to be improved. If the Chinese and Indians were made to feel that they were foreigners and unwanted, why should they cooperate with the government?

The Tunku, despite nationalist pressure on promoting the Malay language, stood firm on the need for English in higher education, especially in the teaching of mathematics and science, while the official language should be Bahasa Malaysia. He refused to give way on the language issue at the risk of unpopularity, and for this principle he was prepared to make sacrifices. After his retirement, Malay politicians exploited the language issue to gain popularity. Many years later, in 1993, Prime Minister Mahathir Mohamad reiterated the need for English if the country were to remain internationally competitive. The wisdom and courage of the Tunku was thus vindicated after his death. He was a man of principle who put the interests of the country before his personal popularity and he paid the price for it.

The Tunku's retirement worried the non-Malay population as he had gained the confidence and affection of the Chinese and the Indians with his friendliness and geniality. He was a moderate statesman who made intuitive decisions. He had little time for theories and ideologies, except that he was whole-heartedly anti-communist, unlike Tun Razak who preferred to call Malaysia "non-communist". Razak was more analytical than the Tunku in developing his external policies and was keener on Afro-Asian ties than the Tunku who was decidedly pro-Western. The Tunku rated personal friendships very highly. I recall Tun Razak complaining privately that whenever he suggested dismissing a civil servant for inefficiency, the Tunku would intervene. "How can you do such a thing to hurt the poor fellow?" and stop him from proceeding further.

As I have indicated earlier, the Tunku was the most loyal of friends, even when it was politically unwise and the person unworthy of his friendship. In my experience, Malays are firm and loyal friends who never forget you even when they reach the heights of power.

Tun Tan Siew Sin, who was the president of the MCA and Finance Minister for 15 years — a remarkable record — ascribed the success of the Alliance government in its early years to the Tunku's personality and his leadership — "a warm, human personality who is generous and loyal to a point which sometimes become an embarrassment even to himself".[4] Then again, "It was his superb leadership and his unique ability to generate not only trust and confidence but also affection and respect, that enabled this country to weather those first crucial years without serious incidents apart from the events of 13th May 1969."[5]

Malaysia owes a great debt of gratitude to the Tunku for his leadership at a crucial period in its history. He was selfless in his devotion to the people of his country.

During his retirement, the Tunku lived in Penang but visited Kuala Lumpur from time to time. He stayed at his residence provided by the government in Bukit Tunku (formerly Kenny Hill). He had his own office

---

[4] Morais, John Victor (1981). *Tun Tan: Portrait of a Statesman*. Singapore: Quins, p. 37.
[5] Morais, John Victor (1981). *Tun Tan: Portrait of a Statesman*. Singapore: Quins, p. 39.

adjoining his residence where he worked on his weekly articles for *The Star* newspaper of which he was chairman. He received his visitors including foreign diplomats at about 4 p.m. after his usual afternoon nap. He was always accessible and I called on him many times during my second tour of duty as high commissioner to Malaysia from 1980 to 1988. He had interesting views and made candid comments on political events and personalities of the day. One of the visits I remember best occurred after Prime Minister Tun Hussein Onn, who succeeded Tun Razak in 1976, had decided to retire on medical advice because of a weak heart. Tun Hussein Onn had to choose his successor from one of the three UMNO vice-presidents who were elected by the whole UMNO Assembly. At that time, the three men in order of the votes they had garnered were Ghafar Baba, Tengku Razaleigh and Dr Mahathir, in that order. The choice was the prime minister's to make and he had chosen the third man, Dr Mahathir. Tun Hussein decided, as a matter of courtesy, that he should inform the Tunku of his decision before making a public announcement. So he called on the Tunku, knowing well that Malaysia's elder statesman had no love for Dr Mahathir whom he held responsible for his downfall. The Tunku, chuckling at the memory, gave me an amusing account of Tun Hussein's visit. He said, "The poor man was clearly nervous. I knew what he wanted to tell me but he looked here and there, avoiding my eyes, drank his tea, picked up a biscuit, fiddled with it and couldn't bring himself to tell me. He was sitting right where you are sitting now on the couch, shifting about uneasily, talking of nothing in particular. You know he is naturally a shy fellow but of course he knew me well enough not to be shy. But he must have felt very guilty and didn't want to upset me. I was sorry for him but also I thought it was all rather funny you know. Believe it or not, Hussein finally said goodbye and left me without telling me whom he had chosen to succeed him! Poor man, poor man!" So commented Malaysia's first premier on the country's third prime minister. Tun Hussein Onn told me that he was too embarrassed to inform his great predecessor. He was sensitive to the Tunku's feelings and just found it impossible to reveal his choice of a successor.

A couple of years after Tun Hussein Onn stepped down in favour of Dr Mahathir, I called on him. He was then chairman of Petronas,

Picture 16: MB with Tunku Abdul Rahman at a cocktail party in Kuala Lumpur, 1970.

Malaysia's huge oil organisation. I visited him regularly twice a year in his office to seek his views on developments in Malaysia.

Both former prime ministers in their retirement were approachable, so I was able to listen to their views from time to time to report back their comments on the political and economic developments in Malaysia. But, as I mentioned earlier, all this happened during my second term as high commissioner to Malaysia from 1980 to 1988.

The Accreditation Ceremony, 24 August 1969

The chief of protocol, (later Dato') Abdullah Ali, who had been at Raffles College a year or two my junior, had briefed me on the formalities of the presentation of credentials to the Yang di-Pertuan Agong at his palace in Kuala Lumpur. The Agong was then the Sultan of Terengganu who was almost at the end of his five-year term of office.

I was accompanied by the first secretary, Mr Kajapathy, who was rather nervous. After the formal entry walking in step, there was a lot of bowing involved. The Letter of Credence I had read was drafted by our Ministry of Foreign Affairs though I was permitted to contribute to it. I quote it below as an example of an accreditation speech.

"Your Majesty,

It is a great honour and privilege for me to be received in audience today by Your Majesty to present my Letter of Credence, accrediting me as the High Commissioner of the Republic of Singapore.

I am honoured to be able to convey to Your Majesty the sincere wishes of the President of the Republic of Singapore and of the Government and people of Singapore for your good health and the continued prosperity of the Government and people of Malaysia.

The destinies of our two countries will always be interrelated. What happens in one country has impact on the other. The ties of history, geography and family between the peoples of Singapore and Malaysia make it so. Though we may take different political approaches, our relationship will remain close and intimate in all fields and I am particularly happy the leaders of Singapore and Malaysia have repeatedly stressed this fact and the need for close co-operation between our two countries in as many fields as possible. For rapid changes around us in Southeast Asia can be expected in the near future and this will make it even more vital that we work closely together to create conditions of stability through economic progress. Singapore for its part recognises that co-operation must be preceded by the conviction that success in certain spheres of activity, for example, in the economic field, can be more smoothly and rapidly achieved through co-operative effort rather than individually. If the will is there, it should not be difficult to identify a wide variety of areas where it may be mutually beneficial for our two countries to work together.

In the discharge of my responsibilities as Singapore's High Commissioner in Malaysia, I will be assisted by my personal knowledge of Your Majesty's territories. I shall always be at the disposal of Your Majesty's Government and shall endeavour to promote the closest co-operation between Your Majesty's Government and the Government of Singapore. I am equally hopeful that Your Majesty's Government and the people of Malaysia will extend their understanding and co-operation to me in the discharge of my responsibilities.

I should like to conclude by expressing my sincerest wishes for Your Majesty's very good health and happiness and the everlasting prosperity of the Government and people of Malaysia."

Once the Agong had read his speech, we had to bow and step backwards out of the hall. The first secretary was excited and continued bowing to the amusement of His Majesty. I had to signal him to stop! Dato' Abdullah Ali, who had a great sense of humour, never tired of recounting this incident later, accompanied by gales of uproarious laughter!

Soon after the accreditation ceremony in August 1969, I called on other heads of missions. On 3 September 1969 the British High Commissioner Sir Michael Walker thought that the worst of the consequences of the racial riots were over. "Razak has got on top of the situation now. He is more confident and not as depressed as he was." He remarked that Malaysian ministers were very sensitive to foreign press criticism as the visiting journalists who poured into Malaysia after the riots had given highly exaggerated and pro-Chinese reports of that catastrophe. He added

Picture 17: MB, accompanied by Ghazali Shafie, Minister of Foreign Affairs (on his right) and Abdullah Ali, Chief of Protocol (on his left), to present credentials to the Yang di-Pertuan Agong of Malaysia, August 1969.

tactfully that Singapore's *What Others Say* programme was "damaging relations". Both the Australian and New Zealand high commissioners were of the same view, and as Britain and these two countries were committed to the defence of Malaysia and Singapore, it was essential to pay heed to these views. The Japanese ambassador was pessimistic. He thought the growth of the "ultras" and the resurgence of the communists would end in a disastrous civil war in the country!

Later in September two of our ministers, E.W. Barker and Lim Kim San, came to Kuala Lumpur. Tun Razak hosted a private lunch at his residence Seri Taman at which Tan Sri Ghazali Shafie and I were present. At this time Singaporeans were sensitive to any sign of the "big brother" pose of Malaysians so when Tun Razak lit Kim San's cigarette, the latter thought it was a good indication that he was being treated as an equal! (This was in the days long before anti-smoking campaigns were launched — first by Singapore after I had personally attacked glamorous TV advertisements of cigarettes in Singapore in a speech made to a Higher School Certificate audience. Lee Kuan Yew called me up, accepted my criticism and suggested that I should persuade Malaysian ministers to ban cigarette adverts on TV simultaneously with Singapore. I found support only from Tun Tan Siew Sin and Khaw Kai Boh who were both non-smokers. Tunku Abdul Rahman, who loved his cigarettes, simply laughed at the very idea, arguing that people would smoke, advert or no advert! Singapore went ahead with its ban.)

The discussion between the ministers was mainly on defence. Ghazali thought that talks on defence between our two countries should precede joint talks with other partners. Razak felt that Australia and New Zealand would remain only if Britain retained some forces here and thought that if the Conservatives won the elections there, there was a greater likelihood of a token force remaining in Malaysia. Ghazali suddenly launched a vigorous attack on our *What Others Say* programme. He accused Singapore of indulging in "double-talk" and insisted that no one, including Australia and New Zealand, would be convinced of Singapore's sincerity on defence or anything else if government media made propaganda statements against Malaysia. He claimed that foreign diplomats often drew his attention to items as examples of the strain in relations to test his reactions. "What business is it of Singapore to taunt and mock Malaysia?" he asked. He felt that the hostile broadcasts gave good enough reason for diplomatic protest and severance of relations! Razak nodded in agreement but made no comment on this distasteful subject. Both Barker and Lim Kim San promised a change of content and tone in the programme very soon. Such problems should be solved amicably, they said. They were clearly embarrassed.

There was also some discussion of the communist threat on the border with Thailand and the inability of the Thai government to enforce cooperation between their officials and the Malaysians at lower levels. The terrorists had increased in number from a low level of 400 to nearly 7,000. It was therefore a serious matter. It was suspected that some Thai officials in Songkhla were in the pay of the terrorists. In an emergency they could not be contacted, and when Malaysian troops crossed over into Thai territory in hot pursuit, strong protests followed!

I hosted a dinner at Temasek, our residence at 400 Jalan Pekeliling (later Jalan Tun Razak), for Tun Razak and the Singapore ministers at which the communist terrorist threat was again discussed, and a possible joint Singapore–Malaysian military manoeuvre on a small scale was even mentioned. Razak felt that ultimately a Malaysia–Singapore fight against the terrorists would take place. Razak was grateful for the visit of our two ministers as a gesture of friendship. He said he was likely to visit Singapore soon in return.

Tun Tan Siew Sin

Although I had met Tun Tan Siew Sin at cocktails and dinner parties, I had not made my courtesy call on him as required by diplomatic practice. My call came at a dramatic moment as the day before *The Malay Mail* had headlined that 2,000 Singaporeans had been turned back at the causeway on their way to work in Johor. In the late 1960s many Singaporeans continued working in Malaysia as they had done before and during the merger with Malaysia. Tun Tan immediately pointed out how the press tended to exaggerate matters. The actual number was not 2,000 but 237 Singaporeans who had been refused permission to work in Johor. Tun Tan said he was puzzled by the action of the Immigration Department. Later, the minister in charge, Tan Sri Manickavasagam, told me that it was Singapore that had started "the whole business of work permits causing a lot of unnecessary suffering". The minister said that employers had been given a year's notice but had not taken the trouble to renew work permits for essential staff from Singapore. They had assumed that the government would change its mind at the last moment but in fact the decision was irreversible. However, special arrangements would be made for our Public Utility Board workers to look after Singapore's waterworks in Johor. Over the years, with Singapore's growing industrialisation and increasing prosperity, large numbers of not only Malaysians but others from neighbouring countries have found employment in Singapore.

Tun Tan Siew Sin was generally more suspicious of Singapore than the rest of the Malaysian cabinet because he believed that during merger the PAP had attempted to persuade Tunku Abdul Rahman to let the PAP displace MCA in the Alliance cabinet. Another reason for his attitude was the fact that the Singapore High Commission's first secretary, Mr Kajapathy, had many useful contacts in the MCA so he was able to report what was going on within the party very effectively. Tun Tan claimed that he had "incontrovertible evidence" that Kajapathy had obtained secret MCA information. Tun Tan thought he was a spy when he was actually doing his diplomatic duty. I managed to get Tun Dr Ismail to explain this to Tun Tan, who in fact became quite friendly later, especially during my second tour of duty. He was then the Malaysian chairman of the multinational Malaysia company Sime Darby.

During my courtesy call in early October 1969, we got down to discussing the racial riots in May. Tun Tan put the blame squarely on "Chinese cultural arrogance". He said that it was all right for people to be proud of their culture but unfortunately the Chinese despised all other cultures. This was evident even in their language where all other races were referred to as "devils". He said Thailand had "tamed" the Chinese in the 1930s by closing Chinese schools and forcing ethnic Chinese to adopt Thai names. His father, the famous Tun Tan Cheng Lock, had tried to persuade the British to take control of Chinese schools but the colonial government refused. So the Chinese schools developed independently with the children being taught to regard China and not Malaya as their mother country. Even Chinese parents who wanted permission to send their children to Malay schools when no other schools were available were not allowed to do so. It was part of the British "divide and rule" policy.

And now Malaysia had suffered the consequences. "The chickens have come home to roost," he said.

Tun Tan pointed out that during the riots it was in the towns, especially in Kuala Lumpur, that the worst took place. The rural areas where the Chinese were isolated, as in Terengganu and Kelantan, remained peaceful during the worst of times. The Malays were a proud and sensitive people who could not tolerate the cultural arrogance of the Chinese.

Tun Tan praised the Singapore government's courage in making Malay the national language despite a 75 per cent Chinese majority. He was also impressed by the firm way in which communists in schools and Nanyang University were dealt with. He was critical of the recent rapid implementation of Bahasa in Malaysia under the new minister of education, a Sarawakian who, he felt, would have to be brought under control soon by the government. He favoured a more gradual implementation of the language so as not to lower educational standards.

The late Tun Tan was a noble son of Malaysia, a man of integrity who never played up race and language issues in order to win popularity. He was incorruptible. He fought for the rights of all Malaysian-born Chinese to be recognised as citizens and to be given the right to vote at the time of independence when the British and some Malays were opposed to this. He had his way because the Tunku, Tun Razak and Tun Dr Ismail were farsighted leaders who realised that it was the only way to have unity in multiracial Malaysia. The Tunku, who liked Tun Tan, once said of him, "He is absolutely honest but sometimes tactless. He is not an astute politician. He has done a lot for the economy but he is sometimes too rigid."

The Tunku used to joke about Tun Tan's parsimony. He loved to tell a story of how he visited Tun Tan's home in Malacca. His host at the end of dinner offered Tunku a cigar. Tunku bubbled with laughter as he recounted how because the cigar was too old, the smoke spouted out in several spots when the cigar was lit! There was another favourite story of his about Tun Tan. He said that he had advised the finance minister to take a holiday as he had been working long and hard. Tun Tan Siew Sin agreed but suddenly asked, "Who is going to act as finance minister when I'm away?" The Tunku replied, "I will." Tun Tan immediately shook his head and said, "No, no. I'm not going then!" The Tunku would chuckle delightedly while recounting this anecdote.

Call on Tun Razak

In September 1969, I called on Tun Razak. He wondered whether democracy was the most effective form of government for developing countries. He felt there was a need for discipline which the communists had been able to impose in China but he felt that discipline was lacking in democratic India. He said that it was necessary in Malaysia "to draw up some ground rules" and get them accepted. For instance, no party should be permitted to make religious or racial appeals. He remarked that the Pan-Malayan Islamic Party(PMIP) in Kelantan had turned from religious appeals to extreme Malay nationalism for its support. He thought that democracy would only work with a reasonably well-educated population which had been brought up in the democratic tradition. How could there be democracy when as in Sabah and Sarawak votes could be bought and the native population did not have an inkling of what democracy meant?

Razak went on to discuss a major problem he was faced with. The younger Malays from the rural *kampungs* were coming in droves into the towns looking for work. There was a lack of jobs for them so they envied the Chinese and Indians who seemed to prosper in the urban areas. These young Malays were disenchanted with the government and the anti-Tunku feeling was an expression of their desire to find a scapegoat for their disillusionment. These young men did not seem to know of the Tunku's great contribution to the nation as the father of its independence. Nor were they aware of the Tunku's heroism during the Japanese Occupation. The feeling against the Tunku, Razak said, was "gathering momentum" and was strongest in Kedah, the Tunku's home state. The cabinet had decided to keep the Tunku in power for a year or so, as yielding quickly to pressure would affect successive leaders in the future. The older Malays understood what was happening and appreciated Razak's loyalty to the old man.

Razak brought up the opposition DAP and said that its connection with Singapore was an "irritation". Some cabinet colleagues of his suspected that the DAP was financed by Singapore through contacts with businessmen during the elections. But he conceded that some of the younger DAP intellectuals were genuine nationalists. This was typical of Razak's fair-mindedness. He was critical of the MCA which had concentrated on businessmen, "money-makers" instead of attracting younger intellectuals into its ranks. The Alliance Party, Razak believed, should open its membership to the intellectuals of all races. He complained that during the elections the DAP line had been racially vicious, even to the extent of claiming that the Chinese would be compelled to wear the Malay sarong and *baju* and that they would be forbidden to eat pork! Incidentally, this was confirmed by the British High Commissioner Sir Michael Walker who said that all political parties played the racial line but the DAP was "by far the worst". Razak said that PMIP was also guilty of racial propaganda. He did not mention Gerakan. It was well known that Razak respected Dr Lim Chong Eu, the Gerakan leader, for his abilities but considered Syed Hussein Alatas something of an idealist. The able Sarawakian minister Ong Kee Hui in the federal cabinet once affectionately described Professor Alatas to me as "Sir Galahad in search of the Holy Grail"! It was not long before Professor Alatas gave up politics which he found too unprincipled for his taste.

As the Singapore government was concerned about the attitude of the Malaysian army after the May riots and feared the possibility of a military takeover, I brought up the subject. Razak assured me that the top military brass from colonel upwards were wholly reliable but he was not so sure of the lower echelons. However, he sensed no danger from the military provided there was a firm government in control. Chaos could, of course, lead to a military coup.

Razak commented on Malaysia's neighbours. He said that he had high regard for Adam Malik, the Indonesian foreign minister and for General Suharto. He thought Singapore's decision to execute the Indonesian marines who had bombed MacDonald House during the confrontation and caused some deaths, after President Suharto's personal appeal on their behalf, was a serious mistake. At least some delay and reconsideration would have saved Suharto's face. Razak felt that the Malay mentality would ensure that the insult would be remembered for a long time. He was right.

Razak was all praise for the Indonesian cooperation with Malaysia in its fight against the communists at the Sarawak borders with Kalimantan, but he was unhappy about the lack of cooperation on the northern borders with Thailand. The threat there was more serious.

Razak felt certain of a US withdrawal from Vietnam as South Vietnam could not resist the northern communists for long. In the event of a communist takeover of the south, Razak believed that Thailand would be neutralised. Then Malaysia and Singapore would be in danger. The presence of the British, Australian and New Zealand armed forces would be all-important but only a Conservative electoral victory would ensure that the British would stay. If Britain moved out, Razak thought that Australia and New Zealand would move out too. Razak was quite concerned about such an eventuality becoming a menacing reality especially as President Nixon appeared to be playing down the Chinese threat to justify US withdrawal from Vietnam.

It was essential for Malaysia and Singapore to work together on defence matters in the light of the potential dangers. He was aware that Singapore had a vital interest in the survival of "the present moderate government" in Malaysia. Lee Kuan Yew had assured him about it. But Singapore had to be careful in its comments on Malaysia and show its goodwill in "practical ways". "I think there is ground for hope of better understanding between the two countries," Razak concluded.

I kept notes of the above meeting with Tun Razak and some of the key ministers in the Malaysian cabinet to help me in my efforts to bring about a better understanding between the two countries. As I had been born in British Malaya, brought up and educated there, it was natural that I should love the country although I owed allegiance to my adopted country Singapore and served her as high commissioner. I felt it my mission to do what I could to iron out difficulties and resolve misunderstandings between the governments of the two countries. Both prime ministers appreciated my honest efforts though one or two of the Singapore ministers were critical of my attitude. They thought I was too sympathetic to the Malaysians.

Call on Tun Dr Ismail, Minister of Home Affairs, October 1969

Tun Dr Ismail was the strongman in the Malaysian cabinet in the time of crisis. He had rejoined the government to deal with the May 13 riots and he rapidly gained control of the situation by his decisiveness.

Tun Dr Ismail said that the situation in the country appeared to be normal but there was as yet no restoration of confidence or goodwill between the communities. One reason for this was the fact that the "ultras" on the Malay side and the Chinese secret societies were intent on keeping up the tension for their own purposes. He was also worried by the Malay students in the university and higher institutes of learning who were creating "*kampungs*" in these institutions and ganging up against the Chinese and Indians, whereas Malaysian students abroad were more united. He found that the students in London thought that the main cause of the May 13 riots was economic and not racial. The blame for the student problem in Malaysia, said Tun Dr Ismail, had to be placed on the lecturers at the tertiary levels in Selangor who had stirred up the students. The Tunku wanted drastic action to be taken against both the students and the staff but Tun Dr Ismail decided that he had to move with some caution "despite the Tunku's impatience". (In fact, it was not till the mid-1970s that legislation was passed which brought the university student body under control after Tun Dr Ismail's untimely death.) Tun Dr Ismail in 1969 said that he was more worried by the students than by the peasants.

It was during this call of mine that Tun Dr Ismail mentioned that he thought Dr Mahathir, the ringleader of the anti-Tunku "ultras" was "something of a fascist"! He argued that Dr Mahathir was "logical but argued from a false premise". However, he had decided that it would be a mistake to arrest him as that would "make him a martyr". I found it significant that Tun Razak did not criticise Dr Mahathir even privately and it was Razak who brought him back in 1972 into the UMNO fold and in 1974 into the cabinet. This was eventually to lead to the highly successful premiership of Dr Mahathir during which the country developed economically by leaps and bounds in the 1980s and 1990s and the urban Malays emerged as highly successful bankers and businessmen.

Tun Dr Ismail, like Tun Razak, believed that it was absolutely necessary to grant "special privileges" to the Malays, to uplift them economically. He claimed that the Malays "lacked that extra something" which the Chinese possessed. He did not know whether it was biological or environmental, or whether it was the "home background and philosophy" that was responsible for this. He said that when he had mentioned this bluntly in a speech to the students in London, they were angry. A Chinese undergraduate had pointed out that the Alliance government's special privileges policy had benefited only a few Malays at the top. A Malay student had insisted that no one should question the special privileges. Tun Dr Ismail had seized the opportunity to point out the basic difference of views of the two students from different communities.

Tun Dr Ismail referred to the Tunku's shock at the Malay criticism of his policies which had led to the riots. This caused the Tunku to write a book blaming the communists for the riots. Neither Tun Dr Ismail nor Tun Razak could stop him from doing it. At times the Tunku refused to listen to advice and even thought of inviting the Federal Bureau of Investigation from the United States to probe into the poison pen letters which appeared at every UMNO election! The Tunku's book was burnt by the university students, which upset him even more.

I found Tun Dr Ismail to be a frank and forthright man. He was highly regarded by Singapore's prime minister and other top men such as Dr Goh Keng Swee. Unfortunately, Tun Dr Ismail suffered from throat cancer which required treatment in London and he had a coronary problem as well. "I am a doctor," he used to say. "I have no illusions about the state of my health!" He died of a heart attack in 1973, much to the sorrow of Tun Razak whose right hand man Tun Dr Ismail had been. His death was an irreparable loss to Malaysia. He was a man of action invaluable

Picture 18: MB with Tun Dr Ismail, Deputy Prime Minister of Malaysia, at Singapore's National Day reception in Kuala Lumpur, 1970.

in a crisis. The minister for public works, Tan Sri Manickavasagam, gave me an example of how strict Tun Dr Ismail was on punctuality. Once Manickavasagam came a few minutes late to a committee meeting chaired by Tun Dr Ismail. The Tun paused, looked at his watch and asked, "Manicka, do you have a watch?" "Yes, Tun," was the reply. "Well, you better get it adjusted or repaired!" Tun remarked and continued with the business in hand.

Tun Dr Ismail's view that the Malays "lacked that extra something" which made it difficult for them to compete with the immigrant Chinese is dwelt upon more fully in Dr Mahathir's provocative and challenging book *The Malay Dilemma*. Dr Mahathir argued that while the Malays who settled in the river valleys and plains did not have to struggle for a living, the Chinese immigrants who had survived feast and famine and the depredations of warlords and corrupt officials had found life a continuous struggle in China. The weak in mind and body had perished and only the fittest had survived as in Darwin's theory of evolution. While the Malays, especially in the rural areas, preferred to marry relatives like first cousins, Chinese custom forbade marriage within the same clan. The Chinese as a result of cross-breeding produced hardy and more resourceful people than the easy-going and tolerant Malays whose hereditary and environmental influence was debilitating. Malaria and other tropical diseases affected the ability to work among the rural Malays who lived on the paddy they planted and harvested, contented with little whereas the Chinese in the urban areas worked hard to accumulate wealth. The *kampung* dwellers were cut off from developments in the outside world though the few urban Malays who enjoyed better health did benefit by mixing with other communities. Like Tun Dr Ismail and other Malay leaders, Dr Mahathir was convinced that the Malays had to have preferential treatment to be brought up to the economic level of the immigrant races. There was no other way, as the Malays were too heavily handicapped to compete on equal terms with the Chinese and the Indians who had great business acumen and controlled trade and commerce in the country.

Although Dr Mahathir's view that part of the Malay problem could be hereditary is controversial and even depressing, it is interesting that Tun Dr Ismail, another medical man, held the same theory as Dr Mahathir.

Chinese businessmen during the British colonial period continued to increase their economic dominance in the country, except for the big British import–export houses, the larger rubber estates and tin mines. Totally committed to making money, the Chinese left the administration to the British and the Malays to keep law and order. Dr Mahathir pointed out that the Chinese even displaced Malay skilled craftsmen, such as carpenters and builders. Even the petty traders in their small retail shops were ousted by the Chinese. More and more Malays moved out of the towns to their *kampungs* where food was plentiful and an attap hut was all the shelter they needed. As the Chinese would not employ Malays or in fact any non-Chinese in their enterprises, large or small, the only satisfying employment an urban Malay could find, apart from menial jobs, was in government service. The Chinese employed relatives in their shops or members of their clan in larger enterprises. They were loyal to family, clan and race and shut out all others. Dr Mahathir admitted that the Malays, who were by nature tolerant and easy-going, did not fight back. The Chinese with their work ethic and business acumen became the most successful entrepreneurs of Southeast Asia. So when the two races came into contact, the Malays were inevitably on the losing end. Thus any government which wanted the races to achieve equality would have to set about improving the economic status of the Malays one way or another if democracy was to prevail and racial riots like the one on May 13 were to be avoided. It had to discriminate in favour of the Malays, such as in the four-to-one quota in the civil service and in the awarding of scholarships. As the best schools were invariably in the towns, the rural population was educationally handicapped in addition to all the other handicaps the Malays suffered from. Education had to be greatly expanded to help to improve the position of the Malays and this happened with the coming of independence from the British. Education for the poor Malays had to be subsidised to give them a chance to catch up.

The above situation in the 1950s, 1960s and early 1970s changed for the better in the 1980s and early 1990s. By then, Malays were well represented academically on the staff of universities in Malaysia. They were on the boards of directors of many companies and had companies of their own. Many in the cities became millionaires in their own right. Expanded educational facilities at all levels including the establishment of more universities increased the number of Malay graduates although too few studied science and technology and too many chose Malay Studies and the arts generally. In fact, when Tun Hussein Onn was minister of education in the Razak government in the early 1970s, he told me once that it was difficult to place Malay and Islamic Studies graduates in good jobs. It was undeniable that preferential treatment for the Malays had only gone some way to counter the superior position of the non-Malays in the field of education and made the situation less unequal or more equitable. The very best Malay students were sent abroad to Britain, the United States and Australia on state scholarships. The rest were given tertiary education at local universities. The majority of the graduates were absorbed into the government service. Others like lawyers, accountants, architects and engineers went into private firms and banks.

Both Tun Dr Ismail and Dr Mahathir believed that for a start, and in order to bring about eventual racial harmony, Malays had to be given jobs even if efficiency in government and industry should be slightly affected. The government involved itself in economic activity, in order to ensure a just distribution of jobs among the population. Tun Dr Ismail once said that although total efficiency was ideal, "because of special factors in Malaysia, efficiency should not be the sole objective of those in the private sector at the expense of other more important objectives". The labour force should reflect racial proportions even at the cost of efficiency. Otherwise in the long run racial strife would ruin the country. The long-term objectives of peace and harmony should not be sacrificed for short-term bigger profits.

There was obstruction in the private sector in the early days. The Tunku told me how the Chinese businessmen had quietly organised a boycott of cigarette firms which employed Malays at higher levels. Such economic pressure had to be faced and dealt with.

There was certainly some loss of efficiency when most of the "rest houses" in small towns along the highway, which were run very well by the Chinese, were handed over to inexperienced Malays who had little idea of how to run them. In 1992, I arrived at the Tapah Road railway station from Cameron Highlands. As I had a first class ticket, I wanted to use the waiting room which was padlocked. I approached the station master who was in conversation with two of his colleagues in his office.

One of the officials reluctantly opened up the room. I found that it hadn't been swept for a long time. There was a pile of wood-rot in one corner. The washbasin was filthy and the toilet broken down! Obviously the station master had not ensured the cleanliness of the waiting room or the rest of the railway station for that matter. During the British regime the railway stations were well looked after with attractive plants like crotons which decorated even the smallest railway station. There was a curious reluctance among higher Malay officials to enforce their authority on their subordinates to ensure that a job was well done.

Singapore–Malaysia Problems

Newspaper and Magazine Circulation

When I took up my post as high commissioner, the newspapers and magazines published in Malaysia and Singapore circulated freely in both territories. But soon the Singapore government became uneasy about the impact made by the most influential of the Bahasa Malaysia papers, *Utusan Melayu*, on Singapore's Malay population, especially when the new Malaysian minister of education launched a powerful nationalistic campaign to promote the use of Malay at the university and in the administration. The special treatment of the Malays in Malaysia for good economic reasons could not be pushed in Singapore with its 75 per cent ethnic Chinese population, though there was free education for the Malays all the way up to and including the tertiary level. The Singapore authorities felt it was necessary to ban circulation of *Utusan Melayu* on the island.

I was instructed to inform both Tun Dr Ismail and Tun Razak before the ban was imposed. I told Tun Dr Ismail that if *Utusan Melayu* wanted to circulate in Singapore it would have to be published in Singapore and be subject to the country's laws. Tun Dr Ismail accepted Singapore's decision with little comment but Tun Razak, while saying that what we did was our affair, looked uneasy as he would come under pressure to react to our ban. Eventually Malaysia banned a long list of Singapore's magazines and newspapers. Malaysia's newspapers simply ignored developments in Singapore and reported only happenings such as fires, rapes and violent crimes! Singapore, however, continued to publish political and economic developments in Malaysia while not allowing Malaysian papers to enter Singapore.

The Malaysia–Singapore Airlines Dispute

The multimillionaire Robert Kuok, as fine and considerate a gentleman as one could hope to meet, was chairman of the joint venture, the Malaysia-Singapore Airlines (MSA). He was as keen as I was that every effort should be made to preserve this link between Malaysia and Singapore, but we failed. The Malaysians were unhappy that nearly all of the staff at the MSA headquarters in Singapore were Singaporeans and that Malaysian citizens were prevented from working in Singapore. Secondly, the Malaysian government was under pressure to develop domestic routes, especially to Sabah and Sarawak, whereas Singapore was only interested on increasing the international routes which were more profitable. In short, the Singapore government was determined on commercial success and had no interest in service to the Malaysian public which was unlikely to be profitable.

In the end, it was decided to break up MSA into two national carriers. Singapore tried to expropriate the initials MSA but Malaysia claimed $72,675,000 as goodwill and was prepared to resort to legal action. Singapore then decided on SIA — Singapore Airlines — and gave up MSA. Malaysia at first decided on MAL (Malaysian Airlines) but woke up to the fact that *malus* in Latin is the opposite of *bonus* (good). So words such as "malnourished", "malodorous", "malpractice" and "malefactor" all suggest evil. I think it was Tan Sri Ghazali Shafie who spotted this and concluded that some Europeans might dislike the name. It was decided to call the airline MAS — Malaysian Airlines System. The word *emas* means "gold" in Malay.

There was much discussion and disagreement as to how many flights each airline should have to the other's capital. Singapore's attempt to fly to Penang, Sabah and Sarawak was denied. It was only in the early 1980s during Tun Hussein Onn's administration that SIA was allowed to fly to Penang. This improved tourism in Penang and was highly profitable to SIA as well as MAS which continued to enjoy full flights. The actual break-up of MSA occurred in early 1972 when I had left Malaysia to return to my teaching job at the University of Singapore.

Common Currency

Divergent national policies, bitter disappointment at the way Singapore was cut off from the merger with Malaysia and perhaps personal animosities influenced the leaders of both countries to make the separation complete. All bonds were to be severed in the early 1970s. In ending the common currency, Malaysia took the initiative and surprised Singapore, giving it only half-an-hour's notice of the termination. The interchangeability arrangement which allowed the use of Singapore dollars in Malaysia and vice versa ended on 8 May 1973 at 4 p.m. However, both governments announced that until 7 August Singapore and Malaysia dollars would remain interchangeable at par.

The Malaysian Finance Minister, Tun Tan Siew Sin, in announcing the change explained that interchangeability was only a transitional phase right from the beginning and because the economies of the two countries were different — Malaysia being a producer of primary products and Singapore being a city state that depended on trade and services — "monetary union can be likened to a pair of Siamese twins trying to grow together normally". He concluded that the arrangement was unnatural and could not continue indefinitely. He also announced that Malaysia would have its own stock exchange.

Singapore's finance minister, Hon Sui Sen, while regretting Malaysia's unilateral action which severed an economic link between the two countries, put an end to speculation that Singapore would devalue its dollar. The strength of a nation's currency is based on its economic performance and Singapore was doing very well industrially and had built up good reserves. Those who believed that Malaysia, with its enormous natural resources, would outstrip Singapore economically were proved wrong. In the course of time the Singapore dollar proved to be the stronger currency.

But there was some confusion when the Malaysian government changed its mind about the 7 August date for the interchangeability at par and suddenly set the date as 19 May! Singapore, however, stuck to its initial decision. *The Straits Times* revealed on 22 May that Malaysians who had been hoarding Singapore currency rushed to exchange 93 million Singapore dollars for ringgit! This compared with the S$19 million collected by the Singapore Currency Board during that period.

The dollar split had been timed when both countries were experiencing boom conditions so that any detrimental impact would be minimal.

The Stock Exchange

On 4 May 1973, Malaysian MPs called for a separate stock exchange but the Finance Minister Tun Tan Siew Sin told the Dewan Rakyat that a separate exchange was not feasible "because there are not enough shares to have more than one exchange" but he agreed to consider it "when the time comes". The time came within a few days — on 9 May when Tun Tan announced that a separate exchange would be established! The end of the currency interchangeability arrangement was announced at the same time, within five days of his previous statement that a separate exchange was not feasible. The decisions on the currency and the stock market must have been reached sometime before 4 May! Tun Tan on the 9th said that the new stock exchange "makes sense because the majority of the shares listed on the present exchange are those of companies incorporated in Malaysia". Of the 223 companies listed, 152 were Malaysian incorporated.

Meanwhile, the Singapore-based *The Straits Times* in an editorial written on 5 May agreeing with what Tun Tan had said on the 4th thought that "the enormous confusion which would surely arise from any decision to split the equity market is too frightening even to contemplate!" By the 9th, the newspaper had overcome its fright, for it stated that "the effects on Singapore are likely to be neither long-term nor major". Such is the way of the media!

The Return to Parliamentary Democracy

When I presented my credentials on 24 August 1969, Parliament had been suspended so the newly elected MPs did not take their seats. The country was ruled by the NOC headed by Tun Razak. It was an authoritarian body which had to restore order after the riots. It was the right set-up to deal firmly with racialists and gangsters who were intent on exploiting the chaos caused by the riots. But there was international pressure especially by the Western media to restore democratic rule in the country. Malaysia's leaders were acutely aware of this, and the Tunku was so upset by the media that he once angrily said that the foreign media and the communists were the worst enemies of the country!

Tun Razak in private conversation showed that he did not believe that British parliamentary democracy could be practised in its entirety in a country without the educational levels and the requisite traditions. Then again, racial and religious issues could be exploited by candidates to win votes. The solution lay in a restricted or limited form of democracy. Malaysian leaders and intellectuals met in the National Consultative Council to draw up some rules on "sensitive" subjects which could not be discussed. First of all the *Rukunegara*, the national ideology, was promulgated after a three-day session. Tun Razak identified the *Rukunegara* as "a signpost and guide" to establish a united and progressive nation.

Tun Razak promised to provide an effective opportunity for the underprivileged to find their rightful place in commerce and industry. The uplifting of the economic position of the Malay population had always been one of Razak's ambitions as he believed that their economic backwardness was the main reason for the May 13 outbreak. On this subject of the special privileges of Malays, Tun Dr Ismail used an effective image. He said that it was akin to a golf handicap which enabled a weaker player to compete more fairly with a better player. But typically, Tun Dr Ismail insisted that the Malays should not perpetuate the handicap but should strive to improve their game and thereby reduce and finally remove their handicap completely. This special position of the Malays was considered a sensitive issue not to be criticised by anybody or even brought up for discussion. Equally, the position of the Sultans was beyond question. The implementation of the Malay language at all levels of education and administration was to be accepted fully. The citizenship of non-Malays was not to be challenged by anyone.

Once these principles were emphasised and re-emphasised, Tun Razak and Tun Dr Ismail began to talk about the possibility of restoring Parliament. Both were cautious. Tun Dr Ismail said that the ban on politics would be relaxed a few months before Parliament was reconvened and people would be able to discuss soberly the government's proposals to entrench sensitive issues like Malay rights and the national language in the Constitution. But he warned that no one would be allowed "to inflame the public". He thought that while no date was set, it was time to prepare for the reconvening of Parliament though he predicted that it would take from six months to a year before it could happen. Meanwhile, the NOC would introduce a sedition ordinance making it an offence for anyone to stir up communal trouble.

The successful Sabah and Sarawak elections had given the Alliance a two-thirds majority in Parliament so that any constitutional amendment could be carried through against any opposition. The Tunku stepped down as prime minister on 21 September 1970 when his nephew the Sultan of Kedah became Malaysia's fifth Yang di-Pertuan Agong, and Tun Razak became the second prime minister of Malaysia. Privately he remarked, "What's the difference? I have been doing all the work anyway as DPM. Only now I have a new title!" Tun Razak was 47 and had been minister of education, minister of foreign affairs and deputy prime minister. Tun Razak had also engineered a successful rural development programme as minister for rural and national development. He had proved his brilliance and dynamism in administration during a decade and half as the Tunku's deputy. His task was to bring unity to the nation and resist the pressures of Malay extremists and Chinese chauvinists. He lacked the Tunku's charisma and he was essentially not an outgoing warm personality like the Tunku. He was also considered, unfairly, of being too pro-Malay by some Chinese and Indians and had to win their confidence by his tolerance and impartiality.

Picture 19: MB paying a courtesy call on the fifth Yang di-Pertuan Agong, the Sultan of Kedah, October 1969.

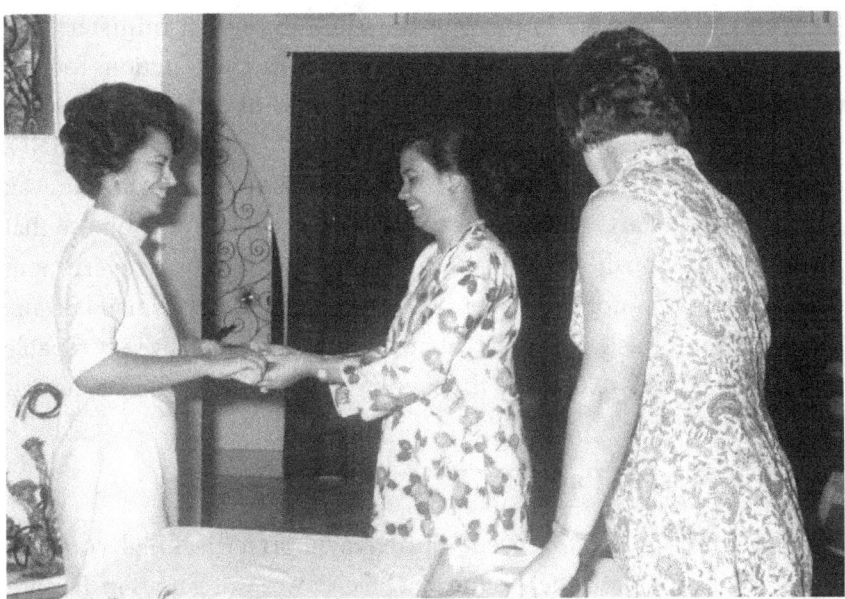

Picture 20: Toh Puan Raha (Tun Razak's wife) receiving her graduation certificate from Mrs Barbara Baker at the Kuala Lumpur Ladies Speakers' Club, 1970. (On the right: Mrs Fruin from the Dutch Embassy)

Picture 21: Tun Razak telling MB about his visit to Sarawak where he succeeded in persuading the Sarawak United People's Party (SUPP) to align itself with the Sarawak Coalition government, 1971.

Tun Razak kept all but one of the Tunku's cabinet ministers and brought in Tan Sri Ghazali Shafie as minister of special functions to head the Department of National Unity in the Prime Minister's Office. Hussein Onn, a lawyer and the son of Dato' Onn Jaafar, the founder of UMNO, became the minister of education. Dato' Ong Kee Hui of the Sarawak United People's Party (SUPP) became minister without portfolio so that his party, previously in opposition, became an Alliance government supporter though not a member of the Alliance. Tun Dr Ismail became deputy prime minister. Thus the cabinet was strengthened by very capable men to help Tun Razak govern the country at a difficult time in its history.

Exercise Bersatu Padu, 1970[6]

One of the most interesting events during my short term as high commissioner to Malaysia was the staging of a Five-Power war games in Terengganu in June 1970. The Singapore Armed Forces (SAF), established after Singapore's independence, started with two infantry battalions, 1 SIR and 2 SIR. When national service was introduced in 1967, its fighting force increased rapidly with the majority consisting of national servicemen. In 1970, the SAF participated in its first large-scale military exercise involving the armed forces of Singapore's defence allies.

As the British military forces planned to withdraw from Singapore in 1971, it was agreed during the Five-Power Ministerial Meeting held in Kuala Lumpur in June 1968 that a joint exercise would be held in Peninsular Malaysia to demonstrate military support for Malaysia and Singapore in the event of an attack by enemy forces on their territories. Called Bersatu Padu (Malay for "Solidarity"), it involved 25,000 soldiers, 200 aircraft and 50 ships from Britain, Australia, New Zealand, Malaysia and Singapore. Singapore supplied 900 men from 5 SIR, most of whom were national servicemen, with regulars being senior commanders and non-commissioned officers. To prepare for the Five-Power Exercise, the Singapore troops underwent six weeks of jungle warfare training in Johor.

The scenario for Exercise Bersatu Padu involved a supposed enemy, an imaginary country called Ganasia situated between Thailand and

---

[6] Liew, Derek (1970). Exercise Bersatu Padu. *MINDEF History*, 10(4).

Malaysia, which had infiltrated into Terengganu and had occupied part of the state. The aim of the exercise, which began in April 1970, was to stop the growing aggression of Ganasia and to recapture the lost territory.

The main exercise called for the capture of Penarek Airfield and enemy bases. Singapore's forces together with some British units as well as Malaysian, Australian and New Zealand troops successfully recaptured Penarek Airfield and four enemy bases. At the end of June 1970, Singapore's forces participated in the final attack on the enemy stronghold manned by the British Royal Marine Commandos who played the role of the Ganasians. The attack was carried out successfully, with equal losses on both sides. Singapore's 5 SIR had 105 troops "killed or wounded in action" while the British Royal Marine Commandos had 102 "killed in action".

For the 5 SIR, it was a remarkable achievement because the majority of its troops were young, inexperienced national servicemen who "fought" against more experienced combat forces. As a matter of interest, the British Royal Marine Commandos were later sent to the Falkland Islands where they served with distinction in the Falklands War. The successful participation of the 5 SIR in Exercise Bersatu Padu proved that with proper training and excellent leadership the citizen soldiers of the SAF could hold their own against more experienced foreign military forces.

The overall success of Exercise Bersatu Padu demonstrated how effective the military support provided by the Five-Power Defence Agreement had been. In case of an enemy attack, the forces of the Five Powers would react and defend Malaysia and Singapore.

On a personal note, as I was Singapore's high commissioner to Malaysia at the time, I accompanied Mr Lim Kim San, the defence minister, and Mr George Bogaars, the permanent secretary for the Ministry of Defence, to visit our troops in Terengganu during the exercise. A helicopter with a British pilot flew us to Terengganu. We were supposed to be dropped somewhere near where our troops were based, but when we landed we discovered we were next to a river and were nowhere near where we should have been. We were lost! We decided, the three of us, to stay put in the hope that in due course our troops would discover us and not the Ganasian forces who would have "captured" us. That would have surely been a great embarrassment for the whole exercise. Fortunately, one of the commanders of our troops realised that we were unduly delayed and set out to search for us. He eventually found us and took us back to where the troops were camped. We had lunch and met the men of the 5 SIR.

An interesting thing I observed was that the British officers were provided with air-conditioned quarters to keep them comfortable in the very hot and humid weather. I thought it most peculiar, but then it was merely during a military exercise and not the real thing.

Return to Academia

I had no contact with the University after June 1967 until my return in 1971 to head the University of Singapore's Department of English as an associate professor after Professor D.J. Enright's resignation in 1970. Enright was a popular head of department who got on well with the staff and students. Two expatriates resigned along with him. Later when I returned, I asked Vice-Chancellor Dr Toh Chin Chye why Enright had left. He said that Enright had offered to resign "once too often so I called his bluff". I must say that I liked Enright and got on well with him. In fact, all the English professors from the time of Raffles College had no racial prejudices. They mixed well with the local staff and undergraduates. This was true of professors Casson, Morrell, Brian Miller and Dennis Enright. Perhaps it was the love of literature which influenced them. They were all warm and friendly personalities. Three of the younger Englishmen who were lecturers in the English Department fell in love with and married local girls who were all university graduates, two of whom held honours degrees in English.

A potential scandal was avoided when the University authorities refused to extend the contract of a Sri Lankan lecturer who fell in love with a pretty Indian undergraduate. He was married to an European lady and had two children. The girl left the University for India. When, in 1968 as high commissioner, I paid a courtesy call on one of the governors of an Indian state, I discovered that the young lady was happily married to the governor's son!

There were other scandals and divorces especially when married expatriates fell victim to oriental charms. Anyone acquainted with David Lodge's comic novels of goings-on in university circles would not be surprised at such happenings in Singapore's University. There was at least one bachelor who was a great comfort to neglected wives with his sympathetic and understanding ways.

I remained at the University until June 1977 when I was persuaded to resume my diplomatic career as Ambassador to the Republic of the Philippines.

Chapter 6

Ambassador to the Republic of the Philippines
June 1977–August 1980

SOMETIME IN 1976 the permanent secretary for foreign affairs, Mr Chia Cheong Fook, impressed upon me that Singapore needed an experienced diplomat to head our embassy in Manila. Our ambassador to the Philippines, an ex-deputy commissioner of police, had already completed a six-year term. Mr Chia believed that as ASEAN was moving ahead, Singapore needed to be effectively represented in all ASEAN capitals. Mr Chia, a friendly and warm personality, was very persuasive but when I discovered that I would be paid less than the joint income of my wife and myself, I declined the offer. I had already served Singapore in India and Malaysia on low pay for four years, supplementing my income by renting out my house. The officials in the Ministry of Foreign Affairs inevitably put the blame for their stinginess on the Ministry of Finance. I called on George Bogaars, the permanent secretary for finance, and discovered that the question of my pay had never been referred to him! When I revealed this to Mr Chia he mumbled his apologies. Soon I was offered more reasonable terms. He suggested that I follow our prime minister who, accompanied by ministers Hon Sui Sen, S. Rajaratnam and Lim Kim San, was scheduled to visit the Republic of the Philippines from 16 to 20 January 1977. If I liked Manila, he suggested, I should accept the appointment.

The most memorable part of the visit was the entertainment on President Marcos' yacht, the *Pangulo* (note the resemblance to the Malay word *penghulu*, meaning headman), presided over by the President himself and his attractive wife, Imelda. Several Filipino cabinet ministers including the famous Carlos P. Romulo, the foreign secretary, and Juan Ponce Enrile, the defense secretary who was a close friend of Marcos, were present.

There was an extravagant display of food and drink. Music was provided by a live band which made the atmosphere festive and friendly while the ministers held serious private talks in the cabins below deck. Though most of those present were VIPs, they were relaxed and obviously enjoying themselves. I was to discover that the Filipinos, like the Malays and Indonesians, love to have fun and enjoy themselves. They make friends easily. I became acquainted with Francisco Tatad, the president's young press secretary (information minister) and his good-humoured wife who had heard that I was likely to be the next Singapore ambassador to her country. When in answer to her question I told her that if I accepted the job I intended to arrive well ahead of my wife who was a teacher, she gestured in comic alarm and exclaimed, "No, no, no! You better bring your wife along with you. We Filipino women are fast workers and you won't stand a chance!" and burst into gales of laughter. This comic warning gave me a fair idea of the Filipino sense of humour. They love to laugh at their own foibles but, I was told, they resent any foreigner commenting on their weaknesses such as their siestas and their unpunctuality.

Later on I was more than once told by eminent Filipinos that they had acquired their bad habits of not being punctual and of sleeping in the afternoons from the Spanish colonial masters who ruled the country for 300 years. Their numerous fiestas they blamed on the Spaniards too. "If only we had been colonised by the Germans or even the British we would have learned better habits! We would work harder and celebrate festivals less often," said an eminent Filipino. It is true that Filipinos have a far more relaxed attitude to life than Singaporeans. They seem to be in less of a hurry to get anywhere; as a result, punctuality is not a common virtue. Foreign Secretary Carlos P. Romulo was the exception. In fact, he jokingly claimed that the "P" in his name stood for "punctuality". Actually it stood for "Pena".

The highlight of the entertainment on the presidential yacht was the singing of Imelda Marcos, who had a good voice.

Imelda Marcos

A natural singer, Imelda Marcos received some voice training from a professional teacher while she was working in Manila as a sales assistant in a music shop. She could play the piano and sing, so she was a success but her father objected to the job. She then joined a bank as a clerk. After she married Marcos she sang her way into the hearts of the electorate during his presidential election campaign in 1964 which Marcos won. He said later that Imelda won him a million votes — which was actually more than the margin of his victory over the incumbent President Macapagal.

A trip was arranged to the well-known mountain resort of Baguio for Prime Minister Lee Kuan Yew to visit Singapore's three cadets at the famous Philippine Military Academy. A golf game for the prime minister and Marcos was also arranged. The most fascinating part of the trip in two small aircraft to Baguio was Imelda's description of the Marcos whirlwind courtship in 11 days. She gave a lively account of this to Mrs Lee Kuan Yew, in the presence of Lim Kim San, Hon Sui Sen and myself. The president and our prime minister had gone ahead in another plane. She recounted how, dressed in an old gown and in slippers, she had accompanied her aunt to the Congress building to pick up her cousin, Danding Romualdez, who was a Congressman. There she heard Marcos, then 37 years of age, holding forth eloquently on the floor of the House attacking President Magsaysay's budget. She had no interest in politics then and was bored. Besides, mosquitoes bothered her. So she and her aunt retired to the House cafeteria to have a drink. It was then that Marcos, accompanied by a friend, saw Imelda for the first time and was struck by her beauty. He was to admit later that it was love at first sight. He was introduced to her. She said that he practically besieged her, sending her roses and boxes of chocolates and telephoning her frequently. He then invited her to join him and his journalist friend on holiday to Baguio. After an initial refusal, she accepted the offer to drive up in Marcos' new car. He kept up the pursuit in Baguio and proposed to her. Under such pressure she accepted and married Marcos who was 13 years older.

A book entitled *The Untold Story of Imelda Marcos*, by Carmen Navarro Pedrosa, makes the blitzkrieg wooing of Marcos even more impressive as apparently she was in love with a handsome, well-educated suitor from a wealthy family when Marcos first met her. But the man was already married although he claimed that the marriage had never been consummated. He was waiting for an annulment while courting Imelda. Her family and especially her father, who was a fervent Catholic, were dead against her being involved with a married man. She did not tell us about this but concentrated on the 11-day Marcos courtship story. We were charmed by her dramatic version of the wooing.

Imelda belonged to the well-known Filipino Romualdez family, but to a poor branch of it. Her great-grandmother was the daughter of a Spanish friar. Her grandfather had been a teacher who had three sons, of whom the eldest, Noberto, was an outstandingly successful lawyer, an author, a justice of the Supreme Court and an assemblyman representing the district of Leyte. The second son became the mayor of Manila. Imelda was the daughter of the youngest son, Vincente Orestes, by his second wife, Remedios Trinidad, a girl from a Catholic orphanage. Remedios was not herself an orphan but she was left there as she had a mother who travelled a good deal selling jewellery. Vincente Orestes had already fathered five children, the eldest of whom was 17 and the youngest nine, when his first wife died. Vincente was a lawyer too like his brother but a less ambitious and a much less successful one, who preferred to stay by the sea in Leyte rather than in Manila. Remedios did not get on well with her stepchildren who rejected her. Eventually, she moved into the garage with her eldest daughter Imelda and her other children. She died when Imelda was only nine years old.

Imelda grew up in Tacloban in Leyte, poor but richly endowed in beauty. She was affectionately called "The Rose of Tacloban". She attended St Paul's College and graduated with a degree in education. She was a popular figure in Tacloban, often singing in concerts, taking part in school plays and so on. But the future lay in Manila for a beautiful girl with a good singing voice, so when her cousin Danding, who was a politician, suggested to Imelda's father that she should take singing lessons in Manila and could stay with him and his family, her father agreed. So at the age of 23 she landed in the capital city where she was destined to meet and marry a future president of the country. She arrived with a small bag of her clothes and five pesos! By the 1970s she was reported to be one of the 10 richest women in the world!

President Marcos

Ferdinand Marcos was born in Ilocos Norte, the northern province of Luzon, of school teacher parents. His father, Mariano, went into politics with initial success but serious defeats later. The Ilocanos are noted for their thrift and hard work; they are the Scotsmen of the Philippines. They are generally small, light brown in colour, short at about 5' 6" (1.68 m) but hardy and strong. Marcos himself was only 5' 7½" (1.71 m). He was an exceptionally bright child, usually at the top of his class. Later he graduated in law as the "topnotcher", that is, in first place in the whole of the Philippines under the most trying circumstances.

He had been charged along with his father and his uncle for murder of his father's successful political rival Nalundason. The case is a famous one in Philippine legal history. Ferdinand Marcos was arrested four years after the murder, just months before his final examinations and was in jail, missing his lectures for a whole term of four months. Because he was such an exceptionally brilliant student, he was released on bail after eminent citizens had appealed on his behalf to sit for his examinations in which he not only emerged first, but scored such high marks that the professors subjected him to an oral examination just to make sure he had not had access to the question papers before the examinations! Marcos was blessed with a photographic memory and he could quote whole pages from the textbooks! The high marks he scored have remained a record through the years.

Soon after the newly elected Congressman Nalundason had been shot through the heart while he was washing his mouth after dinner, the bullet having been fired from outside his window, the police arrested one Nicasio Layaoen, the campaign manager of the defeated candidate Mariano Marcos, but he was acquitted by the judge. Four years passed before the police found a certain Calixto Aguinaldo who was a key prosecution witness. Aguinaldo claimed that he was a friend of Quirino Lizardo, who had married Mariano Marcos' sister. Aguinaldo had borrowed a car to help in the election campaign and after the heavy defeat of Mariano Marcos, he claimed to have heard Mariano, his brother Pio, brother-in-law Lizardo and Ferdinand who was only 18 at the time, plan to avenge the defeat, especially as Nalundason's supporters had mocked the defeated candidate by parading a coffin in front of his house. Aguinaldo said under cross-examination in court that Ferdinand Marcos had offered to fire the shot instead of Lizardo, as he was a better marksman. Ferdinand was indeed an excellent shot and had won prizes for his skill with the gun. An eminent lawyer Vincente Francisco was retained to defend Mariano, Lizardo, Pio and Ferdinand. The last-named actively helped his counsel during the trial.

It was not only a criminal trial but a political one as well, as the government was upset that the assassination of an elected candidate for public office reflected badly on the Philippines in the eyes of the democratic world. Public sympathy, however, was with the defendants, especially as the trial took place in Ilocos Norte and there were demonstrations on behalf of the accused. The chief state witness, Calixto Aguinaldo, was cross-examined over 18 days but he stuck to his version of events about the murder. After a trial lasting two months, Ferdinand Marcos and Quirino Lizardo were convicted of the murder of Julio Nalundason. Mariano and Pio were acquitted. Lizardo was given a life sentence but Ferdinand was given a sentence of 17 years and 4 months. The judge said that he was impressed by Ferdinand's intelligence and legal knowledge. The judge recommended executive clemency which was eventually granted by President Manuel Quezon. Marcos refused the pardon as it implied his guilt, so he appealed to the Supreme Court where the lower court's decision was reversed and both Ferdinand and Lizardo were set free. The judge who heard the appeal was Jose Laurel who was later made President by the Japanese conquerors and became a controversial figure. Marcos was eternally grateful to the Laurel family throughout his rule from 1965 to 1986, even when one of the Laurels was opposed to Marcos. Gratitude is a strong Filipino characteristic — *utang na loob* — is a phrase treasured by all Filipinos. Marcos was only 23 years old then.

During the Japanese Occupation both Lizardo and Mariano, the father of Marcos, were said to have been killed by the conquerors. Ferdinand distinguished himself during the defence of the Philippines. He was captured and tortured by the Japanese but managed to escape to conduct guerrilla warfare. He ended up by winning more than 20 medals for his courage in battle. He was recognised as a war hero. His exploits are related fully in a book written by the American Hartzell Spence published by

McGraw-Hill in 1964 entitled *For Every Tear a Victory* in time for the Philippine presidential election that year when Marcos stood against the incumbent Macapagal. It is obvious that the book was dictated by Marcos. The book was revised and re-issued in 1969 under the title *Marcos of the Philippines* by The World Publishing Company. This was timely for the re-election campaign for his second term. The author of a book entitled *Waltzing with a Dictator* published in 1987 after the fall of Marcos alleged that many of the medal claims of Marcos were fraudulent.

Serving as Ambassador during the Marcos Administration

I prepared for the job of being ambassador to the Republic of the Philippines by reading books and articles about the country, its people and its ruler. By the time I arrived in June 1977 in Manila, Marcos had imposed martial law on the country from 1972 before the expiry of his second term as president. Martial law in the Philippines did not mean rule by the military as in Argentina or Chile. Marcos was in absolute control and ruled by decree as the Congress was dissolved and the armed forces took their orders from him. It was martial law with a civilian government, the cabinet ministers being appointed by Marcos. Critics of Marcos believed that the proclamation of martial law was designed to keep power in the president's hands as all Filipino presidents are limited to two four-year terms by the Constitution as in the United States — the only exception in the United States was Franklin Roosevelt's third term during World War II. Marcos played up the communist threat, blaming the New People's Army for a number of bombing incidents which were carefully staged so that only one person was actually killed and a few injured.

There was one serious incident at Plaza Miranda when the opposition Liberal Party leaders were injured by hand grenades hurled at them at the party rally. Nine people were killed. The communists were blamed for this outrage though the perpetrators were never discovered. Benigno Aquino, a Liberal Party leader and the likely presidential candidate of the party in the next elections, came late to the assembly and thus escaped the bombing.

Most of the leading opponents of Marcos were arrested when martial law was proclaimed. Aquino was still in prison in 1977 when I presented my credentials to President Marcos at the Malacañang Palace which had been built originally by the Spaniards. Marcos had retired a number of generals and colonels before proclaiming martial law in 1972, appointing more Ilocanos whom he could trust and who were obligated to him for their promotion. Whether the situation in 1972 warranted the declaration of martial law is debatable. In the southern island of Mindanao, conflict had continued between the Muslims and the Roman Catholic settlers who were granted huge tracts of land which traditionally belonged to the Muslims who had no legal papers to prove their ownership. They had resisted the Spaniards successfully for 300 years and kept their independence which they tried to preserve against the Philippine armed forces which supported the settlers. The conflict in Mindanao certainly posed a serious threat to the authority of the central government.

There were also student-inspired demonstrations against the Marcos administration in February 1970 and 1971 as a result of rising prices and a general economic crisis after the expensive December 1969 re-election of Marcos. The peso had to be devalued and the prices of all goods escalated. Six students died in clashes with the police and the military. Universities and schools had to be closed for a while. Marcos cracked down on militant student organisations while making some concessions. The students wanted reform in the administration, not revolution, but there was also an element of anti-Americanism in their protests.

Although Marcos made much of the communist threat which would inevitably ensure American backing, in August 1971 Brigadier-General Fidel V. Ramos, deputy chief of staff for home defence, said that there were between 600 and 1,000 insurgents. However, Marcos claimed that the New People's Army numbered 1,000 with 2,000 active supporters and a "mass base" of 50,000.[1] The US administration under all the presidents was fanatically anti-communist and supported right-wing dictators no matter what their human rights violations. Even President Carter, a Democrat, despite good intentions ended up supporting dictators who were anti-communist. When a left-wing politician like Allende was democratically elected in Chile the CIA engineered his overthrow and

---

[1] Adkins, John H. (January 1972). Philippines 1971: Events of a year, trends of the future. *Asian Survey*, 12(1), p. 81.

placed the military dictator Pinochet in power. It was the same story in San Salvador and Nicaragua. Marcos was a clever politician who knew how to manipulate the United States in getting huge sums of money as aid. He had the additional advantage of the American need for the Subic Bay Naval Base as well as the Clark airbase although Philippines nationalists wanted to be free of the American military presence. Ironically enough, even the Soviets preferred the Americans to retain the bases to restrain China. China also wanted the Americans in the Philippines after the Soviets moved into Cam Raan Bay when the North Vietnamese defeated the Americans. Japan favoured the US presence and so did ASEAN. Singapore was open about the need for the American presence to keep the peace in Southeast Asia. So Marcos had a winning hand in the naval and air bases in securing US support for his policies and ensuring a blind eye to human rights abuses and blatant corruption — corruption was endemic at all levels in the Philippines.

I was familiar with the background information when I arrived in Manila in June 1977 as Singapore's ambassador designate.

The embassy in Saludo Street occupied the sixth floor of the ODC Building in Makati which Singapore had wisely purchased before prices escalated as they usually do in major cities. The residence in Forbes Park was a double-storey five-bedroom mansion complete with two dining rooms and a swimming pool. Forbes Park was where many Filipino millionaires lived and several embassies were located there. Former President Macapagal was a close neighbour. The whole area was walled off and well guarded. I found that we had five maids and two gardeners to look after Singapore's property — in fact, the house swarmed with servants. As in India, the household staff were paid low wages in the Philippines. On the whole, the maids and gardeners were hardworking and obliging.

The presentation of credentials in Malacañang Palace was a curious mix of formality and informality. At the entrance to the palace I had to take the salute before the presidential guard commanded by General Ver, who I later learned was the man most trusted by Marcos. General Ver was also the chief of intelligence. Unlike the practice in India and Malaysia, I was not accompanied by my staff. Only the Chief of Protocol Mr Gonzales was with me in the hall of the palace. There were curtains all round and behind them the president and several ministers were chatting and laughing while the two of us sat down waiting. I sensed that Mr Gonzales was uncomfortable at the apparent discourtesy of keeping a foreign diplomat waiting, although I'm sure it was unintentional. Finally the curtains parted and there was President Marcos in the middle and his cabinet ministers on either side of him. I read out the letter of accreditation; then I was introduced to all the ministers, drank a toast with the president, delivered a special message from my prime minister and took my leave. Later at home in Forbes Park I hosted the customary champagne reception for the officials involved in the presentation.

The next day I had to face a more formal inspection of the guards at Fort Bonifacio accompanied by our Military Attache Colonel James Aeria, a very helpful and efficient officer. Rifles were fired off ceremonially. After this, I had to go to the Rizal Memorial to lay a wreath. I must admit that the two-day ceremonies took a good bit out of me! How much more pleasant and relaxing was my teaching job at the University!

Then began the usual courtesy calls, first on the Dean, who in the Roman Catholic Philippines was always the Papal Nuncio. Calls were made on the ASEAN ambassadors, of whom the Indonesian envoy Air Marshal Soedamorno was the one who had been the longest in the Philippines. He was a man of great charm and ability who had in his wife an equally attractive personality. Soedamorno was a great lover of horses so there were numerous sculptures and images of this noble animal in different postures in his house in Forbes Park. He was the Dean of the ASEAN diplomats in Manila and a very popular one. Incidentally, all the Indonesian ambassadors I met during my diplomatic days were very friendly, cheerful personalities whom it was a pleasure to work with. They were all retired military men who were rewarded with diplomatic appointments for their service to Indonesia.

Some countries tend to send defeated or retired politicians, businessmen or personal friends of ministers as their ambassadors. Some of these political appointees, especially those lacking tertiary education, have let their countries down. One I knew was an alcoholic who often abused his staff when drunk. He was also a womaniser. A fellow high commissioner said of another, "Never have I met a more helpless or a more hopeless head of mission in my life!" Yet the man who had high connections was regarded as a success by his country! There was an ambassador from the

Picture 22: MB presenting credentials to Ferdinand Marcos, President of the Republic of the Philippines, at Malacañang Palace, June 1977.

Picture 23: MB drinking a toast with President Ferdinand Marcos of the Republic of the Philippines after the presentation of credentials, June 1977.

Middle East who was treated as a joke by the Filipino ladies whom he relentlessly pursued. It is true that when too many political appointees are chosen, the professional officers are greatly discouraged as no matter how well they serve, they may never become heads of diplomatic missions. A careful balance should be maintained between the professional staff and the amateur political appointees.

Picture 24: MB welcoming the former President of the Philippines, Diosdado Macapagal, to a party at the Singapore Ambassador's residence, 1978. Foreground: Mrs Baker (left), Mrs Macapagal (right).

General Carlos Romulo

The ASEAN ambassadors as well as their staff and their wives formed a united group. The ambassadors held meetings chaired by Foreign Secretary Carlos Romulo on matters of common interest to us. Whenever Romulo left Manila, the ASEAN heads of missions invariably turned up at the airport to see him off and were there again to receive him when he returned. He was rather keen about our presence and sometimes had photographs taken of us standing beside him. In fact, he made no secret that we were a favoured lot. Occasionally, he ignored protocol at diplomatic dinners he hosted by placing the ASEAN envoys next to him instead of the more senior diplomats of other nations. This gave rise to some discontent as seniority according to the dates of accreditation to the host country is strictly observed at all formal diplomatic functions like the reception at airports for incoming VIPs such as heads of states or prime ministers and at dinners hosted by ambassadors.

General Carlos Romulo (he loved to be addressed by his military rank which had been assigned to him by MacArthur whose aide he was in the heroic defence of Bataan and Corregidor) was a colonel and later a Brigadier-General who was an exceptionally gifted individual. He had been a professor of English at the University of the Philippines and later its president, and a winner of the Pulitzer Prize for his journalism. He had predicted the Japanese invasion of Southeast Asia. Short in stature and somewhat plump of figure in his late 70s (he had been born in 1899), he was the soul of wit and good humour. He had a fund of jokes at his fingertips for all occasions, some fit for male ears only. He used to begin every conference or dinner he hosted with two or three funny stories to relax his audience. On one occasion while on the rostrum he peered at the lectern and asked, "Where are my jokes?" The paper with his jokes was missing! Everyone joined Romulo in laughter as he had made it appear that he needed no reminders to tell his comic stories on previous occasions. He enjoyed joking about his lack of height. There is a famous picture of General MacArthur who was well over six feet tall (over 1.83 m) wading through the waves to land in Leyte accompanied by several military officers. Romulo, in uniform and helmet, appears in the photograph. He said that the reporters had claimed that MacArthur had breasted through chest-high waves to the beach. Romulo chuckled that if the report was true he would have been drowned! The sea was only knee deep when MacArthur returned, as he had promised, to the Philippines.

General Carlos Romulo was the greatest Filipino I was privileged to meet. He had a distinguished career representing his country at the United Nations. He was involved right from the beginning, leading the Filipino delegation in setting up the United Nations and writing its charter. He realised that the colonial powers like France, Britain and Holland would want to cling on to their colonies even though the people there wanted independence and were prepared to fight for freedom. Romulo urged the colonial powers to see Asia through Asian eyes. He saw to it that the United Nations Charter would read that the non-self governing nations could aspire to self-government or independence. The great colonial powers wanted to limit the wording to self-government only. Romulo fought hard and long and in the end succeeded in having the words "or independence" in the Charter. Romulo considered this his greatest victory in the United Nations. The United States had, after the defeat of Japan, set 4 July 1946 as the date for Philippine independence but the other powers were not willing to follow suit. In fact, both France and Holland had to suffer defeat in Vietnam and Indonesia before they accepted the inevitable in Asia. The change of government in the United Kingdom, when the Labour Party under Clement Attlee defeated the Conservatives under the great war leader Winston Churchill, led to the freedom of India without strife. Later Burma and Malaya were granted their independence.

Romulo also tried in vain to prevent the right to veto which the United States, USSR, Great Britain, France and China insisted on maintaining. He foresaw that the use of the veto could neutralise the United Nations and at times bring it to a standstill, what with the Soviet Communist bloc confronting the democratic countries led by the United States. In fact, the veto affected Romulo's own career by preventing him from being elected the secretary-general of the United Nations, a post he coveted and which he well deserved. He had been the first Asian president of the UN General Assembly in 1949 and had acquitted himself with distinction. When he was nominated for the post of secretary-general with the support of the United States, the Soviet Foreign Minister Vishinsky, who liked Romulo personally, vetoed the nomination. Vishinsky apologised later in private. Dag Hammarskjöld of Sweden was elected as secretary-general. He was acceptable to both the US and Soviet camps. Romulo in conversation with ASEAN ambassadors once recalled his verbal clashes with Vishinsky in the UN debates but maintained that the Russian was a gentleman. He told us that when Vishinsky left for home he sent Romulo caviar and vodka and roses for his wife. In a book written by Romulo and his second wife Beth Day, published in 1986 after the great man's death in 1985 and entitled *Forty Years – A Third World Soldier at the UN*, it was stated that when Romulo visited the USSR with President Marcos in 1976, he laid a wreath on Vishinsky's tomb as a tribute to his "friendly enemy".

Romulo also recalled that Hammarskjöld was an unassuming and dedicated secretary-general who served the United Nations with integrity, refusing to be cowed by the great powers. Romulo said that, in his opinion, the Swede was the most dynamic secretary-general the United Nations had ever had. Hammarskjöld had tried to be neutral and fair but to the Soviets this was not good enough. One had to be with them, otherwise one was considered to belong to the American camp. Equally, the United States considered that to be neutral was to be immoral! The secretary-general was attacked by De Gaulle for the collapse of the Congo after the Belgian withdrawal because the French leader regarded him as pro-Soviet. He was regarded as pro-Western by the Soviets because the Russians supplied arms to the left-wing Prime Minister Patrice Lumunba of the Congo in his struggle for power against the moderate Congo President Kasavubu. Hammarskjöld wanted the supply of arms to stop. The Russian leader Khrushchev denounced him and asked for his resignation. But the General Assembly supported the secretary-general. Dag Hammarskjöld died in a plane accident in Rhodesia. Romulo considered his death a great loss to the United Nations. Indeed it was.

General Romulo also spoke to us about his experiences at the famous Bandung Conference — the first conference of the Third World underdeveloped nations, mostly former colonies, from which the Westerners as well as the Soviets were excluded. China attended, represented by Zhou Enlai, and Pandit Nehru came from India and Nasser from Egypt. Romulo got to know both Zhou and Nehru. He remarked that Zhou was a handsome and impressive figure who shrewdly kept in the background while he made use of Nehru to convey the message that China believed in non-aggression and in promoting good relations among Asian countries. Romulo had his doubts about this but nevertheless thought that Zhou was a great stateman. He had a private dinner with the Chinese premier the night before the Bandung Communique was to be issued. They agreed between them that the final statement should be dignified with no mudslinging against the colonial powers. They succeeded.

Romulo said that once he had clashed with Nehru in debate and in the heat of the argument he had predicted that India would one day be attacked from the north. Nehru dismissed this as absurd, but in 1962 China attacked and defeated the Indian army over territorial claims on their common border in the Himalayas. The Chinese army could have marched into Calcutta but desisted and withdrew unilaterally, having conquered the disputed area. Romulo recalled years later that, when he was invited to deliver a lecture series in the Indian capital, he called on Nehru who remembered how right Romulo had been at Bandung. Nehru had never thought China, which he considered a brotherly Asian nation, would ever attack India! Zhou had declared that China was not aggressive and would never declare war on a neighbour. But it certainly did and was to do so again in Vietnam. The peaceful professions of powerful nations should be taken with a pinch of salt. China claims the whole of the Spratly Islands including those claimed by Vietnam, the Philippines, Malaysia and Taiwan. This claim is likely to prove explosive in the future when China has strengthened her navy and become a world power.

Our ASEAN Standing Committee meetings chaired by General Romulo were always enjoyable as, after dealing with the meeting's agenda, we were regaled by his anecdotes. Once when he was convalescing in hospital after a gall bladder operation, he called a meeting. So there we ambassadors were, sitting around his bed, while he was propped up with the agenda in his hand. This was the only occasion when the ASEAN Standing Committee of ambassadors had its meeting seated around the foreign secretary who was lying in bed!

One of my favourite memories of General Romulo is of his face which lit up with joy when I informed him that Mr S. Dhanabalan would succeed Mr Rajaratnam as Singapore's Minister for Foreign Affairs. "At last," he exclaimed, "I can talk eye to eye with an ASEAN FM!" The talented Mr S. Dhanabalan was about the same height as the General. On another occasion, when our prime minister was on an official visit to Manila, General Romulo was ill at home. Lee Kuan Yew overruled protocol and visited the Philippine foreign secretary. Romulo was so moved by this gracious gesture that he had tears in his eyes when he greeted our PM. General Romulo always took the trouble on national day celebrations of the ASEAN countries to attend and make a speech before proposing a toast to the country. Foreign ministers in most countries usually delegate another minister to do this as they have no time to attend all the national day functions.

General Romulo was thought by many to be pro-American and indeed he did admire the American people, but he was also critical of the American belief that their concept of democracy should be accepted by all countries, some of which had wholly different cultures and histories. The desperate economic situation of some developing countries required strong rulers who could get things done without a carping opposition. He thought that some form of benevolent authoritarian rule could be acceptable to ensure economic success. He often cited Taiwan, Singapore, Indonesia and South Korea as striking examples. He pointed out that despite the profession of freedom and justice for all, there was widespread racial discrimination in the United States.

It was General Carlos Romulo who gave an important role to the Philippines in international affairs because of his vibrant personality, his eloquence, his good humour and his humanity. He chaired many UN conferences and committees and was elected president of the UN Fourth General Assembly from 1949 to 1950. It should be remembered that the Philippines had been the first of the colonial countries to fight for its freedom. It had achieved this in 1898 against the Spaniards led by General Aguinaldo, only to be robbed of its liberty by the Americans in 1901. During the Pacific War it was the Filipinos who fought the longest against the Japanese in Bataan and Corregidor and held up their rapid advance. So in a sense the Philippines had earned the right to lead the march to freedom of the colonies. In Romulo it found the right man to be its eloquent leader in the United Nations. It is also true that the United States was the first among the colonial powers to grant freedom to a colony whereas Britain, France and Holland tried to retain control of their colonial territories against the wishes of the people. The Philippines was

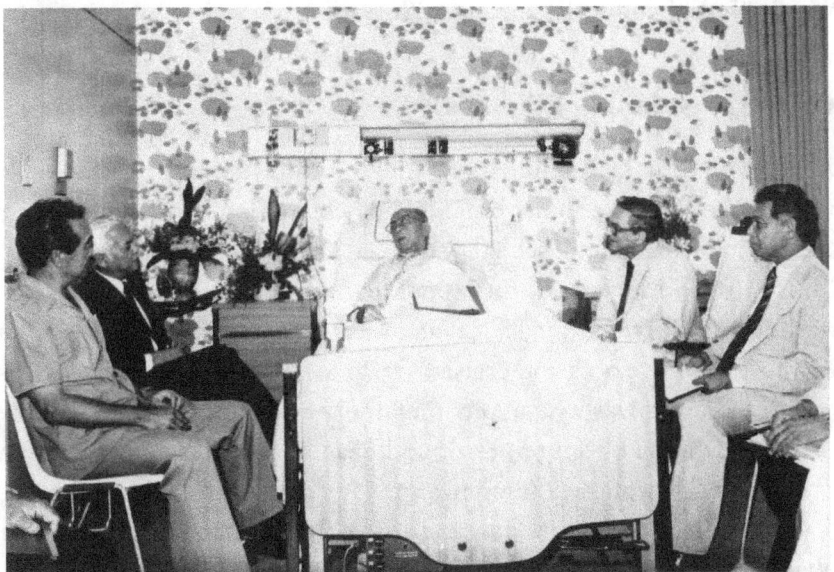

Picture 25: ASEAN Standing Committee. From left: The Thai Ambassador; Air Marshal Soedamorno, Indonesian Ambassador; General Carlos Romulo, Philippines Foreign Secretary (in bed); MB; Yusof Zainal Abidin, Malaysian Ambassador.

Picture 26: ASEAN envoys with General Carlos Romulo (with garland) between Philippines Deputy Ministers. From left: Thai and Indonesian Ambassadors; MB (on the right).

given its independence on 4 July 1946. So General Romulo could speak with authority and be listened to with respect.

Other Outstanding Filipinos

Apart from General Romulo there were some outstanding Filipinos who were in the Marcos cabinet untainted by corruption. Among these was Cesar Virata, the finance secretary who led a simple life and distinguished himself in the service of the Republic. He was highly successful in negotiating with the United States and was noted for his integrity. Marcos on more than one occasion praised Virata for his efforts on behalf of his country. Marcos was wise in retaining the services of men of the calibre of Virata who had been professor and dean of business administration at the University of the Philippines and later chairman of the Philippine National Bank. He was a friendly and approachable finance secretary. After I had left the Philippines in 1980 to return to Malaysia as Singapore's high commissioner for the second time, I heard that Marcos had appointed

Virata as prime minister under a changed constitution. Virata retained the post till the fall of Marcos in 1986 before going into private practice.

It is true that many associates of Marcos amassed great wealth during his dictatorship but some who did not allow themselves to be corrupted by power led blameless lives and did their best for the country. Cesar Virata was one of these, as was Arturo Tanco, the agriculture secretary for 15 years who died poor in 1985. It is said that he did not leave enough money for his funeral! Another who had an unblemished reputation despite being deputy armed forces commander under Marcos was General Fidel V. Ramos who was actually a cousin of Marcos. Some foreign observers were astonished that Ramos aspired to be president and actually succeeded despite his association with Marcos, but it was he and Defense Secretary Juan Ponce Enrile who risked their necks leading the revolt against Marcos. While the corruption of some of the military was public knowledge, Ramos was known to be clean. The surprising thing was not that Ramos won the election but that Imelda Marcos despite all that was publicised about her, garnered 2.3 million votes, about 10 per cent of the total in her presidential bid. Her glamour still had its appeal for the Filipinos for she was elected to Congress from Leyte despite being convicted for corruption but freed under appeal. She continued to live in luxury, being driven around in a limousine. The Filipinos did not believe that she would actually be sent to prison.

As I had got acquainted with General Ramos even before I made my official courtesy call on him, I asked whether he would let me off the usual inspection of the guard of honour before seeing him. He paused, smiled and said, "I'll do something special for you!" When I turned up accompanied by Singapore's defence attaché, I was astounded to find a wholly feminine guard of honour, smart and curvaceous in their uniforms waiting to be inspected. I was slightly embarrassed but it was certainly the best looking, the most unusual guard of honour I had ever inspected! The general asked me with a twinkle in his eye how I had appreciated his gesture and chuckled good-humouredly.

A most rewarding courtesy call was one on Jaime Cardinal Sin, the respected leader of the Roman Catholics in the Philippines who form about 85 per cent of the population which in 1983 was 50.4 million. The Cardinal was often critical of the authoritarian Marcos government and pursued a policy of "critical collaboration". Once, when Imelda Marcos began building a towering monument of the Infant Jesus to celebrate an expected visit of the Pope, Cardinal Sin in a pastoral letter to be read in all churches opposed it and suggested that the money should be spent on building hospitals instead. The monument was quietly abandoned. No other individual would have dared to oppose the First Lady.

Cardinal Sin was a portly figure with a brilliant mind and a witty tongue. He was blessed with a great sense of humour. He was the 13th child of a pagan Chinese father and a very religious Filipino mother. He rose rapidly in the church hierarchy. It was suggested to him that he should change the spelling of his name to Syn but he refused. He preferred, he said, to be the church's eighth cardinal sin and especially as his immediate predecessor was Cardinal Santos. When he was a child, he recalled, he asked the maid who looked after him, "Why am I my mother's favourite child?" Came the prompt response, "Because you are the ugliest!"

We discussed the Marcos regime. He was fearless in his criticism of the restrictions on people under martial law, of arbitrary detentions, of the use of torture and the arrests of priests suspected of cooperating with communists. He particularly condemned the excesses of martial law. In 1979, he called for martial law to be lifted but this didn't take place till early 1981 to celebrate Pope John Paul II's visit.

My wife and I were invited to lunch once by the Cardinal who told us that President Marcos visited him once a year to congratulate him on his birthday. On one such occasion he recalled that he told Marcos, "Mr President, I can understand what you are trying to do but I can't understand the First Lady." Marcos replied promptly, "Neither can I!" and laughed. The Cardinal delighted us with his witticisms. It was a most delightful lunch though the food was simple and plain.

The power of Cardinal Sin over the people was demonstrated in 1986 when Ramos and Enrile led the revolt against Marcos. When the army tanks moved into Manila, Cardinal Sin called on the people to turn out in the streets. They did in their tens of thousands. The tank commanders could not bring themselves to fire on their own people so Marcos and his closest associates had to flee in American helicopters. So ended the Marcos dictatorship after two decades.

Luis Taruc

One of the most fascinating personalities I met during my three years in the Philippines was the famous guerrilla leader Luis Taruc, commander-in-chief of the Hukbalahap — the People's Anti-Japanese Army — who had served 15 years in prison after his surrender which had been negotiated by a young journalist, Benigno Aquino, during the administration of President Magsaysay. Benigno Aquino was to become a great rival of President Marcos who imprisoned him under martial law. Aquino's eventual assassination at Manila airport led to the revolt and the overthrow of Marcos in 1986. Taruc had been promised amnesty but he was let down. He was actually sentenced to life imprisonment.

Luis Taruc was born into a peasant family in June 1913 in the province of Pampanga. It was a time of domineering feudal landlords who exploited the peasants ruthlessly. As a boy Luis witnessed the misery and despair of his parents and came to hate the landlords who even forced the children of the peasants to clean the homes of the landlords and chop firewood for them. There was deep resentment among the peasants at the way they were treated.

Even as a child Luis Taruc realised that he would have to educate himself to fight the *hacienderos* or land owners. He had to walk five kilometres to school carrying a little rice wrapped in a banana leaf for lunch as his poor parents could not afford to give him any pocket money. He was bright and did well in school. After school hours he used to go to a railway station to work as a porter to earn a few centavos. He completed elementary school and went on to a provincial high school in Tarlac where he boarded with a family. He did all the chores in the house, even cooking and washing dishes to pay for his keep. He graduated from high school in 1932 which was a year of strikes and hunger marches in Manila.

Taruc applied for entrance to the National University to study law. He looked everywhere for a job and finally found one as a ditch digger! Six months in the wet ditches affected his legs so badly that a doctor told him that he would be paralysed if he didn't give up ditch-digging. He then found work as a tool-keeper through a relative but he kept this job for only a year as, because of a change in the government, all in the department were replaced by relatives and friends of the new man. Taruc was then in the second year at the university attending night classes while working all day. There was no hope of finding work in Manila so he decided to give up his law studies and return to the province where his parents lived, to open a tailor's shop for a living.

Central Luzon, the main island in the Philippines, was seething with the discontent of land-hungry peasants and exploited sugar plantation workers. The Americans who had robbed the Filipinos of their newly won independence from the Spaniards who had oppressed them for more than 300 years, did nothing to change the feudal system. Under such conditions the socialists and the communists found ready support. Taruc was attracted by their philosophy so he joined strikes and started making speeches supporting socialism which he interpreted as working for the welfare of the peasants. He met an American socialist who argued convincingly that capitalism had had its day and socialism was historically inevitable. He also proved that American money controlled the Philippine economy, kept wages low to gain high profits, prevented the growth of local industries and impoverished Filipino workers.

Taruc believed that only through the efforts of the people themselves could socialism be attained, and he determined to devote his life to the cause of the poor. He joined the socialist movement which was led by a lawyer, Pedro Abad Santos, who had founded the Socialist Party in 1933. Santos was not a theorist but a pragmatic old man who wanted the peasants to be militant. Taruc became an active organiser under Abad Santos and stirred the peasants to demand a 50–50 share of the crops instead of 30–70 in favour of the land owner. He wanted to stop the exorbitant rates of interest demanded by the landlords on loans made to the peasants. He organised strikes. The landlords used the Philippine Constabulary and even hired thugs to break up the strikes. Gradually the unions grew more united and stronger. When the police arrested the leaders of strikes, all demanded that they be arrested too so that there was no place in the jails. This was what Gandhi and Nehru did in India against British rule. Taruc was imprisoned in 1938 for organising the strikes.

By 1940 the peasants and workers had made many gains and several socialist mayors had been elected in Pampanga alone and some communist mayors elsewhere. The socialists were persuaded to affiliate themselves with the Communist Party in 1938. The serious consequences of this are described by Taruc in his book *He Who Rides the Tiger* written while he was in prison and published in England in 1967 with the help of Douglas Hyde who was disillusioned with communism which he had exposed in his famous book entitled *I Believed*.

The Japanese invasion witnessed the birth of a movement which became known as the Hukbalahap — the People's Anti-Japanese Army, called "Huks", for short — to fight a guerrilla war against the invaders. The Filipino people had a long history of rebellion against the Spaniards as well as their own tyrannical rulers. According to Taruc, there were 200 such uprisings recorded in Philippine history. The great Filipino heroes like Rizal and Bonifacio had inspired Filipino rebellions against the colonial power of Spain. So the Huks found enormous support from the people especially the peasant unions, and the guerrilla movement with mass backing harassed the Japanese throughout the Occupation and often ambushed their foreign oppressors. But through inexperience some costly mistakes were made and some of the leaders who were arrested by the Japanese Kempeitai were tortured to death. The same sort of guerrilla warfare was carried on in Malaya by the anti-Japanese forces in the jungles. The Huks sometimes liquidated landlords who collaborated with the Japanese. But they treated the villagers well while eliminating the spies and traitors who informed on their movements, betraying the Huks to the Japanese army.

The Huks were led not only by peasant leaders but by men from the middle class like the scientist Vincente Lava, a chemistry graduate of American universities whose research work on the coconut gained him world renown. Mateo del Castillo, whose Spanish father was a liberal landowner, sympathised with the peasantry and cast his lot with the Huks when the Japanese came. There were other men and women leaders who were Filipino patriots risking their lives against the invaders. Being a guerrilla is naturally a hazardous life, facing constant danger of death and at times surviving under miserable conditions in the mountains, jungles and swamps.

Taruc said that he had several narrow escapes from the Japanese troops. But he was inspired by strong bonds of comradeship and the feeling of patriotism so that the guerrillas could endure hunger and starvation living on what the jungle could provide. As Spencer Chapman's famous book *The Jungle Is Neutral* makes clear, one can survive under the harshest conditions if one understands the jungle and adapts to it. It was the joy of comradeship, Taruc said, the feeling that the guerrillas were one family that enabled them to endure hardships, sharing a common crowded shelter, eating from the same pot on wild banana leaves. Taruc himself, though the commander-in-chief, often did the cooking, and with his tailoring experience mended the clothes of his comrades. He said with a grin that he really enjoyed cooking!

The Huks organised the villages or barrios so that there were at least two reserves in every village carrying out their normal peaceful pursuits, but who were trained and ready to take the place of a guerrilla who needed to rest or who was ill. In a sense two-thirds of the Huk army was undercover in the barrios, like an iceberg which is far bigger under water than above. The barrios also organised food supplies for the fighting Huks while denying rice to the Japanese. The rice was often hidden in drums and buried or taken into remote forest areas for concealment. The Huks formed a Cultural and Information Department which performed short plays in the barrios to improve the morale of the people and propagandise them at the same time. Typically, they composed Filipino songs, taking over tunes from the Americans and even the Japanese and adding their own verses. The "Hukbalahap Song" became quite well-known.

Apart from the Huks, there were other guerrilla units, some led by Americans who disliked the communist Huks, and sometimes fought against them. There was no united front against the Japanese. Both the Huks and the American-led units suffered losses because of this enmity. There were also bandits who exploited the situation for their own benefit, robbing and looting wherever they went and murdering civilians. The Huks, with 10,000 men in the field and another 20,000 in reserve, were the most powerful guerrilla force. This fighting force was backed by at least half-a-million people in the barrios under their control.

According to Taruc, despite the heroic achievements of the Huks against the Japanese, once victory was assured, the Americans turned against them and wherever possible disarmed the Huks and imprisoned them. In one instance the Americans disarmed Squadron 77 of 109 Huks who were then tortured and shot after being forced to dig their own graves! The murder was carried out by a Filipino, Carlos Maelang, and his men with the approval of the Americans. Taruc said this was similar to the

Nazi massacre of the Jews. Those who collaborated with the Japanese were preferred by the US forces and the Huks thought to be communists were suppressed by the post-war Filipino governments. Inevitably the Huks became reluctant rebels against their elected governments in which the Congress was dominated by the landlords who blocked every attempt at land reform even by such a well-meaning president as Magsaysay.

The Americans kept to their word in granting independence to the Philippines on 4 July 1946, but ensured that economic and military control of the country remained in their hands by the Military Bases Agreement and the Bell Trade Agreement. In the Philippine elections in April prior to independence, Taruc was elected to Congress by an overwhelming majority from his district but he was unseated in a few months by false charges of having used terrorism in the elections! Actually he was opposed to the special economic privileges given to the United States. This was followed by the murder of several Huks and their leaders. So the Huks reorganised themselves in the face of grave injustice and took to the hills again. Taruc claimed that he was forced into this act along with the peasantry who were members of the Communist Party. Taruc wanted genuine freedom for the people, free of rampant corruption and the injustice of the feudal landlords and profiteers. He worked for socialism and industrialisation to raise living standards of the workers but he was aware that the communists were using nationalism as a tactic to establish a dictatorship of the proletariat eventually.

For two years, from 1946 to 1948, much fighting took place with government forces until the then President Quirino realised that the rebels were getting more support and growing stronger. He decided that efforts at suppression of the rebellion had failed and granted an amnesty. During the fighting atrocities were committed by both sides and some innocents lost their lives. There were moderates as well as extremists on both sides. Some reactionaries on the government side continued their attacks on the peasant villagers who supported the Huks especially in Central Luzon while the dedicated communists among the Huks also resorted to violent methods. All along the government had offered a reward of US$50,000 for information for the capture of Taruc but he was never betrayed. The long-suffering peasants wholly supported the Huks and kept their morale high.

From 1948 to 1950, the Huks were well organised and well supported by the people whereas the military were a demoralised force. But within the Huk organisation there were differences between the concerned nationalists and the Marxist–Leninists who considered the moderate Taruc too idealistic. Taruc said that he was against the increasing ruthlessness of his communist comrades-in-arms who regarded the class struggle to be above morality as asserted by Lenin. So Luis Taruc said that he knew in his heart that sooner or later there would be a parting of the ways. However, he said the government forces were utterly ruthless in burning villages, raping and looting and torturing captives. The Huks retaliated in kind matching the cruelty of their enemies. The administration was corrupt, elections were dishonest with tampering of the ballots, terrorising the populace and assassinating candidates. This state of affairs continued through the years. Even when I was there between 1977 and 1980, I recall that the same corrupt tactics prevailed in an election. It was proudly announced that only 28 assassinations had taken place — the lowest count in the history of Philippine "democratic" elections.

The communists led by Jose Lava, who succeeded his more moderate brother Vincente, decided that the situation in the Philippines would be ripe for a revolutionary takeover by 1951, so everything should be done to improve military discipline. For a start, the Hukbalahap name was to be changed to HMB, the Tagalog initials for Hukbong Mapagpalaya ng Bayan or People's Army of Liberation. Jose Lava hoped to seize power by armed struggle of the Communist Party on its own. Lava's late brother Vincente had formed a United Front, a Democratic Alliance, and had allies in the Nacionalista Party. But Jose wanted to achieve revolutionary victory alone. Taruc argued that the Communist Party allies should not be discarded and that it should be a united effort to gain the support of all sincere Filipinos who wanted freedom but were not necessarily communists. But he was overruled and even his position as commander-in-chief was diminished as the general secretary, Lava, assumed absolute command over the HMB forces.

Taruc did not believe that the people as a whole were ready for a revolution, and that the great majority were indifferent. However, he went along with the decisions of the party leadership to preserve unity. Taruc said that the HMB did not have sufficient forces, for instance, to capture Manila. At most it could have about 4,000 men for this operation although it had about 15,000 well-equipped men spread out in various parts of the country. In 1950, several attacks were carried out successfully in different areas on army camps and small towns but these successes led to the Americans supplying the regular army with modern weapons and re-organising it. The appointment of the energetic Ramon Magsaysay as secretary of national defense led to the capture of the Politburo in Manila along with Jose Lava, the general secretary himself! The whole secret organisation in the capital was rounded up. It was a fatal blow to the Communist Party and its plans. There was a need for total re-organisation. Taruc himself was away in the field where his group suffered a surprise attack and lost weapons and supplies.

The third of the Lava brothers, Jesus, became the new general secretary. Taruc resigned his position as commander-in-chief officially, knowing that he had secretly been displaced anyway. Despite the disaster the communists had suffered, the new leadership stuck dogmatically to its original revolutionary plans.

The government forces, boosted by their success, became more aggressive. Magsaysay also carried out effective psychological warfare by treating surrendered Huks well which undermined the morale of the fighters. Previously, captured prisoners were tortured and imprisoned. Magsaysay disciplined the army to behave well with the peasantry instead of pillaging the villages. In attempting to expand its activities, the Huks suffered reverses and lost several leaders. Taruc preferred a more defensive policy and a dispersal of the leaders to various safer regions rather than concentrating in the capital. But the top men remained in Manila with the most dedicated of their followers whereas those who showed a certain independence of mind or a critical attitude were sent to the riskiest areas where there was a greater chance of their being captured or killed. Such was the way of dogmatic communism which was intolerant of criticism.

But eventually Taruc's suggestion to prepare for a "long and bitter struggle" rather than push for a quick victory was accepted by the leaders. Taruc led a group of 90 on a difficult march to the Sierra Madre mountains in very bad weather, suffering hunger, living on edible ferns and what the jungle could provide. Part of this group, including his third wife Liza (the first two had died young of disease), was ambushed and she was killed.

A moving account of this sad incident is recounted by Taruc in the sixth chapter of his book *He Who Rides the Tiger*. Taruc loved Liza very deeply so her death shattered him. He said that he lost the joy of living. He asked himself how many more lives would have to be sacrificed on both sides before the struggle would end. This irreplaceable loss and the fact that he had also lost the trust of the communist leaders who actually had him spied on (a typical communist tactic) led him eventually to give himself up. The man who was appointed to report on him confessed to Taruc what he had been told to do!

The government made unofficial efforts through well-intentioned emissaries to contact the rebels and induce them to surrender. Some of the Huk-HMB commanders did conduct peace negotiations in early 1953 with government representatives especially the president's brother Judge Antonio Quirino. These contacts were reported on the radio, much to the disapproval of both the army and the communist leadership. Most of these contacts came to nothing as the extremists on both sides were not prepared to make concessions.

Meanwhile, the army mounted a fierce campaign against the rebels. Taruc had a narrow escape when his group was completely surrounded in the mountains but eventually broke through the cordon. In the fighting the person running close to Taruc was killed but he escaped death. It made him wonder, he said, why he was spared! Had God a purpose for him? Taruc could never embrace the atheism of the communists and in fact, after his surrender, he became very religious. The faith of his parents and his boyhood as a Catholic were too strong for him to forsake.

Eventually one May day in 1954, given an assurance that he would be pardoned, Taruc surrendered. He was supposed to be taken to see President Magsaysay at the Malacañang Palace but instead he was locked up in jail as "a maximum security risk". A month later a meeting with the President was arranged. Taruc gives a fascinating account of this in the eighth chapter of his book *He Who Rides the Tiger*. Magsaysay was himself an unassuming man who sat near Taruc and listened to what he had to say. Taruc tried to convince the President that a general amnesty for the Huks would be the best policy as the rebels were really patriots fighting to give the long exploited peasants a better life. He argued that the problem could never be solved by military means but by providing land for the landless peasants and jobs for the unemployed workers.

Magsaysay saw the point but said that powerful forces that he could not ignore were against an amnesty. The only way out would be for the Huk leaders to surrender and face trial. After that the President could grant executive clemency. Magsaysay who knew that Taruc had been expelled from the Communist Party asked him to renounce communism for good. Taruc agreed but said that he kept the right to renounce the worst features of capitalism and feudal landlordism. If freed, Taruc said, he would devote himself to helping in development projects for peasants. He stressed the need for land reform and an industrialisation programme. The peasants' need for land was the basic cause of rebellions and unless this need was met and agricultural methods modernised, the communists would find support from the peasantry.

Taruc himself was disillusioned about communism. Whereas he had expected justice for the oppressed he found that the Communist Party itself exploited and oppressed the individual and sought to control his thoughts and feelings. In Taruc's day, Soviet and Chinese communism flourished but now communism has collapsed in the USSR, its greatest stronghold. In China, free enterprise is fast replacing state control in economic development. Vietnam too is opening up to capitalist enterprises and foreign investment after the poverty and misery brought about by communist principles. There can be little economic progress if there is no room for human initiatives.

Despite promises, Taruc was first sentenced to prison for 12 years. Then there was a second trial at which he was given not one but four life terms! So much for the promise of executive clemency! This, of course, ensured that the rebellion would go on, and it did. Taruc was released after serving 15 years. He became an earnest worker for social reform programmes in rural areas. I was privileged to meet and get to know this great son of the Philippines — a sincere and humble but charismatic man who lived, worked and suffered for his underprivileged brothers and sisters.

The above account of the Huk rebellion is wholly that of Luis Taruc. I have not given other views. Criticisms of communist rebellions are always presented from the state or capitalist point of view, so Taruc's account is interesting presented as it is from the opposite angle. It should be noted that Magsaysay's efforts at land reform met with little success as the landlords in Congress sabotaged the moves as usual. But he did open up Mindanao in the south for the Luzon farm families who were willing to settle there. This eventually was to lead to the Muslim reaction and insurrection. The Roman Catholic settlers were granted land which the original inhabitants, who were Muslims, claimed as their own. The Muslims had long resisted the Spaniards and the Americans. They organised themselves to resist the northerners and the Moro National Liberation Front (MNLF) came into being. It has cost the Philippines thousands of lives and much money and despite many attempts, no solution was found. Throughout my three years in Manila there were frequent reports of ambushes and clashes between the Moro rebels and the military. I sensed the tension in the air when I visited Mindanao and saw the huge banana and pineapple plantations owned by a rich Filipino as well as the American firm of Del Monte.

When I visited Davao and stayed for a couple of days at a seaside hotel, there were police in mufti in the garden for my protection. There were occasions when the Muslim guerrillas kidnapped individuals and held them to ransom.

The civil disturbances continued unabated throughout Corazon Aquino's presidency. It was only when General Ramos was elected president in 1992 for a six-year term that an agreement was reached in 1996 with Nur Misuari, the leader of the MNLF, and the fighting subsided.

Chapter 7

Return to Malaysia
September 1980–April 1988

I HAD BEEN succeeded by Dr Chiang Hai Ding when I left Malaysia in 1971. He stayed only two years before moving on elsewhere. His successor, Mr Wee Kim Wee, a well-known journalist, took Dr Chiang's place and stayed on for seven years. I was asked to succeed him as he was appointed ambassador to Japan. Our foreign minister, Mr S. Rajaratnam, asked me to return to Kuala Lumpur as high commissioner for three years from 1980. I accepted as I would have to retire from the University the same year, having attained the age of 60. I had many friends in Malaysia and some of the students whom I had taught at the University of Malaya in Singapore before the establishment of a separate university in Kuala Lumpur had reached high positions in the civil service. As Malays have a high respect for their gurus, I was sure they would be helpful in my work. This was important as relations between Singapore and Malaysia were often prickly.

The major change since my previous stint as high commissioner (from 1969 to 1971) was the new embassy building which was also located in Jalan Tun Razak. It was a well-designed two-storey structure surrounded by a wall with a large garden and staff quarters for lower ranking members of the mission. Once I had settled in, I planted four mango trees and two rambutan trees in the large empty spaces. In 1969 our embassy had been on the fifth floor of the Straits Trading Building which housed legal firms and dental clinics and other offices — not at all suitable from the security point of view. Another big difference was the fact that our diplomatic mission had twice the number of officers that it had in 1969 and in the 1970s. Our set-up in Kuala Lumpur was probably the largest of all our diplomatic missions. On the whole I was to discover that our diplomats were capable and hardworking, though one member told me that he had handed in his resignation and was emigrating to Australia as he was unhappy with the mission.

When I left Malaysia in 1971, Tun Abdul Razak, my good friend from Raffles College and London days, had taken over as prime minister from Tunku Abdul Rahman. Tun Razak died of leukaemia on 14 January 1976 at the age of 53 and Tun Hussein Onn, the son of the famous founder of UMNO, Dato' Onn Jaafar, had become Malaysia's third prime minister. He was deputy prime minister when Tun Razak passed away.

I got to know Tun Hussein Onn when he was education minister in Tun Razak's cabinet. He invited me to his office in 1971. He was worried about the exodus of science and mathematics teachers to Singapore partly as a reaction to the May 13 1969 riots but also because, he thought, of more attractive salaries offered by Singapore. He was unhappy about having to recruit too many teachers from Indonesia. I was impressed by his frank and sincere attitude, and reported back to the Singapore cabinet on the matter.

As prime minister, he was noted for his abhorrence of corruption and his caution in making decisions. One of his colleagues in the law firm he worked for told me that he used to underline important points in his legal briefs, in fact, in anything he read. He was by nature a cautious man, slow to make decisions. Unlike Tun Razak, he was not easily accessible. Even the deputy prime minister, it was said, had to make an appointment to see him. His closest adviser was Tan Sri Ghazali Shafie who was minister of home affairs up to 1978 and later minister of foreign affairs.

Tun Hussein Onn had been trained as a soldier at the Indian Military Academy at Dehradun in India and he brought the discipline of a military man into the administration. He was not ambitious, but always ready to serve the country in any capacity. He once said, "If I'm trusted, asked to serve, if the country wants me, I will not refuse at whatever cost to me. But to scramble for office at whatever cost, no." Although he gave the impression of being aloof, he was humble and never courted popularity. He was quoted as having said, "What after all is high office? It merely means greater responsibility. So why lose your head? I'm a somebody today. I may be nobody tomorrow. When you go up you must come down. That's life."

Above all, he was a man of high principles, of integrity and honour. He had been the first secretary-general of the United Malays National Organisation (UMNO), but when his father Dato' Onn resigned from the party he founded because he failed to get UMNO to open itself to non-Malay members, Hussein Onn also left the party and went off to London to study law. It was Tun Abdul Razak who persuaded him to rejoin UMNO and return to politics. Razak realised Hussein Onn's potential.

When I settled down in my job I soon heard rumours about Tun Hussein's health. He had a weak heart and had suffered two heart attacks. Early in February 1981 he went to London for a coronary bypass. I spoke to Tan Sri Kadir Yusof who was a cabinet minister and a friend of mine from Raffles College days. Kadir said that whether Hussein Onn would continue as prime minister depended on the result of the operation. If the prime minister did not feel that he was 100 per cent fit for the job he would not cling on to the premiership. It would be in character for him to step down and hand over the reins of power to his deputy, Dr Mahathir Mohamad. Sure enough, within three months of the operation, Tun Hussein Onn resigned on 16 May 1981. He had been prime minister for a little more than five years. He died in 1990, nine years after resigning the premiership.

Once, when I called on Tun Hussein Onn after he had retired, I asked him what led him to choose Dr Mahathir as his deputy. He sat back, sighed and said that he had had great difficulty in making a decision. He said that Dr Mahathir was "the steadiest of the three" vice-presidents. Ghafar Baba was an outstanding senior grassroots politician, a stalwart UMNO member, but he did not possess the necessary educational qualifications to represent Malaysia at international meetings. Tengku Razaleigh, though able and well-qualified, was a young man and a bachelor. So he had chosen Dr Mahathir who was a doctor, a sound family man and an experienced politician though as a young man he had been "something of a rebel" and "had unnecessarily upset the Tunku". Tun Hussein Onn was a rare prime minister who willingly handed over the supreme position to another because he believed that he could not do a full-time job in the service of his country. Having stepped down, he left the limelight to remain in the shadows. He never interfered in any way with the administration of his successor nor, to my knowledge, did he comment publicly on the policies of Dr Mahathir. He placed the good of Malaysia first and foremost when he stepped down. His farewell speech was an emotional and even tearful one. Such statesmen are a rare breed.

There were the usual exchanges of visits between the prime ministers of the two countries. The last visit by Tun Hussein Onn to Singapore was on 14 May 1980. At the meeting between the two prime ministers, the following issues were discussed:

- Tun Hussein Onn requested additional land in Woodlands for additional facilities for the Royal Malaysian Navy which was then based there. Lee Kuan Yew agreed to look into this favourably.
- The possibility of a second causeway was considered.
- Singapore Airlines (SIA) wanted more flights to Penang. Tun Hussein Onn agreed to consider this but made clear that flights to Sabah and Sarawak were non-negotiable.
- Singapore needed some land near the Tanjong Pagar railway station belonging to Malayan Railways for road expansion.
- Both prime ministers agreed that the question of who Pedra Branca (Horsburgh Lighthouse) belonged to should be settled amicably.
- An Inter-Governmental Committee (IGC) directly responsible to the two prime ministers was to be set up to solve problems as they arose.

The IGC was soon set up. Some of these issues were resolved after Dr Mahathir became prime minister but others like the question of Pedra Branca remained in limbo even in the new millennium![1] One issue that

---

[1] The International Court of Justice delivered its judgement over the three maritime features in the Straits of Singapore on 23 May 2008. It found that sovereignty over Pedra Branca belonged to the Republic of Singapore and that sovereignty over Middle Rocks belonged to Malaysia. The Court refrained from awarding South Ledge to either country, ruling that sovereignty over the low-tide elevation belongs to the State in whose territorial waters it is located. (*Source*: The Hague Justice Portal)

was resolved during Hussein Onn's premiership was the SIA flights to Penang. SIA got more flights to its benefit and to the benefit of Penang's tourism.

There was a major change in the Singapore cabinet when Mr S. Dhanabalan became foreign minister in place of Mr S. Rajaratnam who became the second deputy prime minister. Dr Goh Keng Swee remained the first deputy prime minister. Dhanabalan was in Victoria School when I was teaching there in 1953 and 1954 and part of 1955. Later, when I moved to teach in the Department of English at the University of Malaya in Singapore, Dhanabalan read English as one of his subjects along with economics. He was brilliant, and qualified easily to read for honours in both subjects. He came to me for advice as to which subject he should specialise in. He was certainly a potential first-class graduate in English but I advised him to do economics as Singapore was desperately short of good economists at that time. He applied to the Ministry of Education from which he held a scholarship to read for honours in English to be allowed to change to economics instead, but the request was turned down. When he told me about it I spoke to Dr Goh who called up the ministry to permit Dhanabalan to read for honours in economics instead of English. This was done. After he graduated I recommended him to Dr Goh Keng Swee who appointed him to the Economic Development Board. Later he was moved to the Development Bank of Singapore (DBS). He did so well that he was persuaded to enter politics.

Dhanabalan always said that if I had not intervened on his behalf he would have become a school principal. I think Singapore would have been the poorer for it.

As a banker he used to pick me up once a month in his chauffeur-driven Mercedes for lunch. When he became a minister he still invited me to lunch but he had to drive himself in a smaller car! This was a time when politicians made sacrifices in the service of Singapore. I enjoyed telling this story in Malaysia as it was a good example of the honesty of political leaders who did not go into politics to enrich themselves. Years later there was a major change as the Singapore cabinet decided to reward itself generously, so much so that the prime minister of tiny Singapore earned three times the salary of the President of the United States! Singapore has a cabinet of millionaires. It is no longer service before self but self before service. The reason given for the astronomical pay is that it is the only way to attract capable people into politics and to prevent corruption. The example of corrupt Asian governments is pointed at, but the example of good governments as in Sweden, Norway, Holland or New Zealand is conveniently ignored. Money values are what really count in Singapore.

But to return to my account of my sojourn in Malaysia. It was my old friend and golfing partner James Puthucheary who introduced me to Daim Zainuddin, a businessman and land developer, who was known to be close to Prime Minister Dr Mahathir. Both James and Daim were lawyers and long-term good friends. I often joined them for lunch at the Royal Selangor Golf Club. Daim is slight of build, sharp of intellect, and wholly unpretentious and good-humoured. He is naturally friendly. It was the most important friendship for me as he was always helpful and informative. He was accessible even when he eventually became Malaysia's finance minister and an eminently successful one. He was the best source on the intricacies of Malaysian politics that a diplomat could have. Rumour-mongering is a favourite sport in Malaysia and inevitably the rumours reached Singapore. I could and did often check with Daim about such rumours and could debunk them in my reports to our Ministry of Foreign Affairs.

There was one persistent rumour going around Kuala Lumpur that the Malays wanted to teach the Chinese yet another lesson as they had done on 13 May 1969. The rumours were so strong that I decided to check with Daim whether armaments had been brought in from the outlying areas, from Pahang to Kuala Lumpur. When I visited him in his house I brought up the subject. He confirmed that intelligence reports indicated that it was true that the Malays were preparing to confront the Chinese again. I reported this back to Singapore.

Later on, I discovered that two of the younger ministers had encouraged the Malays, which was very shocking. I was told that when Dr Mahathir, who was away in Canada attending a conference, was informed about the situation, he hurried back. He called up the two ministers responsible and reprimanded them very severely for what they had done. He took control of the situation before any trouble could begin. This is an example of the way Daim Zainuddin was able to help me sort out the truth from fiction. I was grateful to him for helping me many times in similar situations.

Dr Mahathir's Visit to Singapore, December 1981

Shortly after taking over from Tun Hussein Onn in July 1981, the new Malaysian prime minister, Dr Mahathir Mohamad, decided to pay the customary visits to the ASEAN capitals. First he went to Jakarta and then Bangkok. I was approached by the Malaysian chief of protocol to arrange for a date suitable for Dr Mahathir to visit Singapore.

A two-day official visit on 17 and 18 December 1981 was agreed upon. The purpose was to discuss bilateral and regional issues. Among the most important of the bilateral issues was a request by the Royal Malaysian Navy for an extension of another three to five years for the use of the Woodlands Naval Base as well as providing additional land at Woodlands for the Navy. This request had already been discussed by the IGC which had been appointed during Tun Hussein Onn's time. However, Singapore's civil servants could not come to a decision because they believed that Malaysia should pay more for the extension. But at the meeting which I attended, Prime Minister Lee Kuan Yew told Dr Mahathir that it was good for both the security and defence of Singapore that the Royal Malaysian Navy should stay for as long as possible. Therefore there would be no problem at all to grant the extension for as long as he was prime minister. This was a very gracious gesture on the part of Prime Minister Lee. In return, Dr Mahathir said that there was a piece of land called Khatib near Sembawang which the British had given to the Malaysian military. He said, "This piece of land is of no use to us. All we do is to maintain a watchman there to keep an eye on it. Therefore you can have it." This was the friendly spirit in which the meeting was conducted. Various other issues were brought up and discussed amicably. Prime Minister Lee Kuan Yew called it "a true meeting of minds".

In addition, Singapore said that it needed some land belonging to Malayan Railways (KTM) in Keppel Road for the development of the East Coast–Jurong Expressway. Dr Mahathir agreed that this would be looked into so long as the running of the railway was not affected. Mr Lee agreed that appropriate compensation would be paid. Another issue that was discussed was the fixing of the boundary between the two countries along the Straits of Johor. A joint hydrographic survey would be conducted.

I was informed by the chief of protocol that Dr Mahathir was keen to synchronise the time between East and West Malaysia. There was a half-hour difference. If Singapore wished to synchronise its time with West Malaysia, then it must move its clock half an hour forward. At first, Prime Minister Lee was concerned about schoolchildren having to get up earlier when it was still dark, but eventually he decided to accept Malaysia's time adjustment.

On 1 January 1982, Singapore, in line with Peninsular Malaysia, moved its clock forward by half an hour so that it would be in the same time zone as East Malaysia. The decision was generally welcomed by Singaporeans. Although minor difficulties were expected, adjustments to the time change would be minimal and mainly psychological. Both the Singapore International Chamber of Commerce and the Singapore Chinese Chamber of Commerce strongly supported the move as the time change would get rid of the inconvenience to be expected in the trading, commodity and finance sectors if Singapore were not to adjust its time to that of Malaysia's trading hours. Local stockbrokers and foreign exchange dealers were generally happy to avoid the half-hour difference. With Singapore clocks showing the same time as their Hong Kong counterparts, dealers expected some spill-over business which should boost foreign exchange turnover.

A major issue that was not resolved during Dr Mahathir's visit was Malaysia's wish to take control of the airspace over Johor. The issue of the air corridors remained to be worked out in detail. The existing arrangement then was that Singapore controlled, for flight information purposes, two air corridors stretching up to 90 nautical miles (166 km), used by aircraft approaching and departing from the island. As Malaysia was seeking to reduce the control to 35 nautical miles (64 km), it meant that an aircraft leaving Singapore would switch to Malaysian flight information control after 35 nautical miles but revert to Singapore Flight Information Region (FIR) beyond a certain point along the East Coast and over the South China Sea. Prime Minister Lee Kuan Yew conceded that Malaysia had every right over its own territory provided that flights coming into and leaving Singapore would not be endangered. PM Lee and Dr Mahathir agreed on the principle which officials could work on. Dr Mahathir was quoted in *The Straits Times* on 19 December 1981 saying, "We will make sure no problems arise from a switchover from Singapore Flight Information Region to Malaysia FIR. We don't think there will be any difficulty ... the officials must ensure the higher degree of safety for aircraft using this space."

In his speech at the Istana dinner given in his honour and that of his 18-member delegation by Mr Lee Kuan Yew, Dr Mahathir noted that though many of the Malaysian and Singapore ministers had developed close ties, since the days when they were in school or university together, and could easily contact and talk to each other over the telephone to resolve issues, this was no longer possible among the new generation of Malaysians and Singaporeans. It was even more necessary that there should be frequent contacts and meetings between ministers of both countries so that issues could be settled before they blow up.

Dr Mahathir spoke of his long association with Singapore. He himself had studied in Singapore and graduated as a doctor and made many friends over the last 30 years, some of whom had become prominent. He said that Singapore's economic and social successes could not but be a model for Malaysians and Malaysia would continue to have a happy and stable neighbour. He ended his speech on this note: "The development of Singapore and of Malaysia is a task not only of the leaders but the peoples of the two countries. Similarly, the development of a good relationship between the two countries is also a task for the leaders as well as of the people. I will try for my part, to ensure good people-to-people relations and I am sure this will be reciprocated." Mr Lee agreed with Dr Mahathir that there should be more contacts such as exchanges of visits between political leaders, members of Parliament, officials and students.

Following the meeting between Mr Lee and Dr Mahathir, in an interview with Dr Noordin Sopiee, group editor of the *New Straits Times*, Mr Lee remarked, "The state of relations between KL and Singapore is very good. They will improve further as the understanding which Dr Mahathir and I have achieved percolates down to senior and middle-level officials on both sides. It is usually at middle-level officials that differences emerge and problems first take shape."

He added, "The mass media can help to bring Singaporeans and Malaysians up to date on changes in each other's attitudes and circumstances. Perceptions each has of the other can change for the better." Mr Lee commented that what was important was that at their first meeting, "We resolved nearly all the bilateral issues besides reaching broad agreement on our perception of the regional problems. If there had been no meeting of minds, these relatively minor bilateral issues could have become major irritants. I am hopeful that we can keep our differences down to their true proportions and importance, by placing them against the background of our larger common interests."

Prime Minister Lee Kuan Yew's Visit to Malaysia, August 1982

Prime Minister Lee Kuan Yew paid a two-day official visit to Malaysia in late August 1982, accompanied by a 20-man delegation which included a strong team of ministers: Mr Goh Chok Tong, Mr S. Dhanabalan, Mr Lim Chee Onn and Dr Ahmad Mattar. The size of the Singapore delegation reflected the desire on both sides to give younger leaders, both political and administrative, more personal contact with their opposite numbers.

During Mr Lee's discussions with Dr Mahathir, seen as part of the ongoing process of consultation between two close neighbours, they were also expected to touch on a number of joint projects deemed to be of benefit to both countries. Among the bilateral matters they discussed[2] was the Malayan Railways land in Keppel Road. It was agreed that the Singapore government could go ahead and gazette the acquisition of the land required for the East Coast–Jurong Expressway even as officials of the two sides negotiated other matters in detail. The amount of compensation to be paid to Malaysia for the land was believed to be one of the matters to be settled.

Another important issue that was addressed was that of water from the Johor River. It was agreed that as Johor needed more water, arrangements should be made for the state to draw water from the river. They, however,

---

[2] *The Straits Times*, 24 August 1982.

had to take into account the 1962 agreement whereby Singapore had a right to draw a maximum of 1.1 billion litres daily from the river. There was also the agreement that more water would be supplied to Singapore if the republic needed it. New facilities to draw more water could be developed jointly, said Dr Mahathir. The price to be paid for the raw water was an issue that would prove troublesome for years in the future but it was not brought up at this stage.

The third major issue discussed was that of aircraft overflying the Johor Straits. Dr Mahathir disclosed that a problem might arise with planes landing and taking off from Changi Airport having to pass over the waterways used by ships moving into Pasir Gudang port in south Johor. This could be a major problem when the number of flights from Changi increased concurrently with an extension of Pasir Gudang. Some interruptions in air traffic might result. "We had not decided how to resolve this problem but it is agreed that a satisfactory solution will be worked out," Dr Mahathir said. "In any case, we expect this problem to come only around 1985, so there is plenty of time for us to work out a solution."

The two prime ministerial visits were conducted in a spirit of mutual understanding and cooperation which augured well for both countries.

Other Ministerial Visits, 1982–1983

Dr Mahathir's highly successful visit to Singapore in December 1981 was followed by a number of exchange visits of ministers in 1982 and 1983, which culminated with the visit to Singapore of Datuk Musa Hitam, the Malaysian deputy prime minister in February 1983. The main purpose of the ministerial visits was for the ministers to get to know each other as well as for several members of Malaysia's second echelon leadership to meet their Singapore counterparts as they were likely to succeed the present cabinet ministers in the future.

Immediately after Dr Mahathir's visit, the Malaysian minister of welfare services, Datin Paduka Hajjah Aishah Ghani, paid a three-day visit to Singapore in January 1982 as the guest of Dr Ahmad Mattar, acting minister for social affairs. Her main purpose was to learn how Singapore dealt with the drug problem. She said that drug abuse was a serious social problem in Malaysia. She was keen to study our attempts to solve the problem. She visited the Drug Rehabilitation Centre at Sembawang but thought that our "cold turkey" treatment would be too drastic for Malaysia at that time. Drug addicts there were allowed to take a less potent substitute drug to ease their withdrawal symptoms.

Datin Aishah was also interested in the childcare centres which Singapore had established as Malaysia planned to set up such centres in the major towns. She visited the NTUC Child Day Care Centre at Toa Payoh. As reported in *The Straits Times* on 8 January 1982, she said, "Before, domestic help was cheap and easy to get, and fewer mothers worked. Now, the situation is different, especially in Kuala Lumpur. We now need more such centres, especially in the bigger cities and near factories. We must make sure their children are given proper care. We want our centres to be more than just a place women leave their children at, we want them to be child development centres like those you have here. We are also looking into the legal aspect, to see how we can supervise and control the few private commercial crèches. For example, how we can prevent the child minders from taking in more children than they can handle."

In 1983, Mr Ong Pang Boon, Singapore's minister for the environment and Mr Teh Cheang Wan, minister for national development, also visited Malaysia. Mr Ong's three-day visit in January 1983 was part of a regular exchange of visits to promote cooperation and mutual understanding on environmental issues of common interest between the Singapore and Malaysian ministries. Mr Teh's two-day visit in early February 1983 was, according to the government statement of 5 February 1983, a follow-up of the agreement by the prime ministers of Malaysia and Singapore to establish closer personal ties between the leaders and officials of the two nations.

Datuk Musa Hitam's Visit, February 1983

In February 1983, Malaysian deputy prime minister Datuk Musa Hitam paid a three-day official visit to Singapore at the invitation of the second deputy prime minister (foreign affairs), Mr S. Rajaratnam. He arrived on 9 February accompanied by a powerful 25-member delegation which included the chief secretary, Tan Sri Datuk Haji Hashim Aman, six deputy ministers, several members of Parliament and senior civil servants. Among the six deputy ministers was the up-and-coming Anwar Ibrahim from the Prime Minister's Department. The visit was seen as an effort to foster relations between politicians and senior civil servants on both sides as the delegation included several members of Malaysia's second echelon leadership. Datuk Musa was reported in *The Straits Times* of 11 February 1983 as saying, "I have brought along with me on this trip a cross-section of the personalities who in all probability will take over progressively from the current crop of leaders in Malaysia. Needless to say, we have quite a few more at home. While we want to expose Singapore leaders to them, we also hope to expose them to those who are presumably being groomed to take over in Singapore. We hope that close personal contacts could be established and in the long run ensure that what we erect today will be further built upon by them tomorrow."

Datuk Musa's visit, the first since he took office in July 1981, "demonstrates Malaysia's desires that relations between Malaysia and Singapore will continue to prosper for the mutual benefits of the people of both countries". Speaking at a lunch organised by the Foreign Correspondents Association (FCA), he emphasised the mutuality of interests between the two nations. Datuk Musa said that although Malaysia and Singapore were two independent countries, each with its own national interests, "we still cannot alter the fact that we are inter-dependent".[3] He said that the emotions and unhappiness generated by the separation in 1965 were now over. "Let us ride out the storms and enjoy the good times together." He added, "Anything we can do to accommodate Singapore's interest, we shall try our best." He said that Singapore, on its part, had come a long way to accommodate the Malaysian point of view.

The *Business Times* on 12 February 1983 reported that, speaking at a press conference at the end of his three-day visit, Datuk Musa said that a number of areas of cooperation and collaboration between Malaysia and Singapore had been "resolved, satisfied and reassured" during his

---

[3] *Business Times*, 11 February 1983.

official visit. Apart from the supply of water from Malaysia to Singapore, the other areas included tourism, manufacturing and processing.

He said Singapore had been reassured that Malaysia would honour the existing agreement on water supply and that more importantly, there was already agreement on joint exploitation of water resources from Johor in the long term. On the question of the supply of an additional 60 million gallons of water daily to Singapore by 1985, Datuk Musa said this would be made available to Singapore and that it was only a question of how to facilitate the increased capacity. This, he added, involved the question of where to lay the pipeline and how it was to be done. The price of water, however, was not discussed, which in later years would be a bone of contention.

Datuk Musa was keen to promote tourism, particularly in Johor. He said that although there was a joint tourism committee, it was not effective. Johor Bahru should be developed to cater to Singapore visitors as well as other foreign tourists as there were at least 15 to 20 busloads of tourists daily. Tourists from Singapore even had to bring packed lunches as there were no amenities to cater to their needs. He suggested that perhaps a suitably sited terminal be built where the tourists could relax, shop and eat. On manufacturing and processing ventures, Datuk Musa said Malaysia welcomed Singapore investment, including those which preferred being located closer to home — in Johor Bahru.

Prime Minister Lee hosted a private dinner at the Istana for Datuk Musa and his wife at which only Mrs Lee, my wife and myself were present. At the end of the dinner when we were leaving, Mrs Lee asked me whether Datuk Musa had enjoyed the dinner. I told her that from my observation of Datuk Musa's body language and his being unusually quiet, he was not happy. The reason for this I found out later when Datuk Musa told me that at the "four-eyes" meeting with Prime Minister Lee when they were discussing a number of issues, particularly the supply of water, from time to time Mr Lee seemed to forget that Datuk Musa was the deputy prime minister of Malaysia and not one of his subjects in Singapore. Prime Minister Lee Kuan Yew even sounded threatening. He said that a few times during the course of their conversation he thought of getting up and walking out. Since that would be too discourteous, he simply sat through the whole session. Datuk Musa was unhappy about the treatment he had received during the meeting.

Datuk Musa and I were on friendly terms and he could confide in me. He had been one of the top Malay scholars who studied at the University of Malaya in Singapore in the late 1950s until 1962 when the University of Malaya was established in Kuala Lumpur. The scholars were required to do a course in English Language studies for a year. I had organised the special classes for them so most of them who later became top civil servants were very helpful to me as Singapore's high commissioner to Malaysia. Datuk Musa was the only one who became a politician. In 1971, during my first posting as high commissioner to Malaysia, Datuk Musa returned from the United Kingdom. By then the Tunku had resigned and Tun Razak had become prime minister. One night at a cocktail party in the Soviet Embassy he came up to me and said, "I don't think you'll remember me but I know you! You were my guru!" He always treated me as a friend.

Later on, I told our minister for foreign affairs, S. Dhanabalan, about what Datuk Musa had told me about what had occurred during the "four-eyes" meeting, and he must have conveyed this to our prime minister who, within days, wrote a private apology which I delivered to Datuk Musa who was obviously pleased with it although he murmured that it was really unnecessary.

Goh Chok Tong's Visit to Malaysia, August 1985

1985 saw a number of visits by Singapore ministers to Malaysia which included the Minister for Foreign Affairs S. Dhanabalan. The culminating point was a visit by Mr Goh Chok Tong, the newly appointed first deputy prime minister, when he was invited by the Harvard Club of Malaysia to speak on "Singapore and the Region: Challenge and Response" at a dinner hosted by the club president Dr Goh Cheng Teik, Malaysia's deputy minister of agriculture.

Earlier, at the press conference on his arrival, Mr Goh was asked his views regarding the downturn in Singapore's economy. He replied that the downturn was partly due to the slowdown of the US economy. He hoped it would be temporary "for two to three years". Singapore aimed to exercise wage restraints, as wages were high compared to Hong Kong and South Korea, and to focus on measures to increase productivity.

In his dinner speech, Mr Goh pointed out that politically major changes were in the offing as leaders of the previous generation were all getting on in years. "Not only Singapore but most of the other countries in ASEAN will soon be seeing leadership changes and an era of familiar faces and long-standing personal relationships is coming to an end. This is the challenge I see for Singapore in the years ahead. This is the challenge I see for ASEAN. Can the new players keep the golden age of ASEAN going?"[4] Thus it was necessary for the new generation of ASEAN leaders to start building bridges of understanding to link the six member countries. Touching on economic cooperation, he said there were economic rivalries between ASEAN countries as they had to compete with each other. Nevertheless, it was important to maintain good relations. Singapore's restructuring of its economy had benefited neighbouring countries, especially Malaysia. Spin-offs included Philips, General Electric and Hewlett-Packard relocating to Malaysia.

Mr Goh Chok Tong spoke for 30 minutes. The one hour question-and-answer session that followed was the most interesting part of the meeting. Responding to Malaysia's Minister of Works Datuk Samy Vellu's remarks that the ties between the older leaders seemed to be a thing of the past, Mr Goh said that the younger Singapore leaders welcomed more exchanges between the two countries. When asked whether he supported the proposal to amend Singapore's Constitution to give the elected president veto powers on the spending of the nation's reserves and was the move a reflection of Prime Minister Lee Kuan Yew's lack of confidence in the younger leadership, Mr Goh replied that indeed he supported the constitutional amendment for a two-key concept to safeguard Singapore's reserves. He explained that the two-key system was an arrangement for the government in charge to hold one key and the president to hold the other key. It did not reflect a lack of confidence in the younger leadership nor was the election of two opposition MPs to Singapore's Parliament that prompted the PAP government to consider it. It was rather the fear

---

[4] *The Straits Times*, 22 August 1985.

of the possibility of freak election results under the one-man-one-vote system when the popular vote might be used to raid the nation's reserves.

There was an interesting question when someone pointed out that at the separation of Singapore from Malaysia in August 1965, Prime Minister Lee Kuan Yew had said that it would be a temporary separation, and he asked whether Mr Goh thought the same. Mr Goh replied "In politics, anything can happen. It depends on how you define temporary. If the people of Singapore and Malaysia will it, it will be so."[5] This was warmly applauded by the audience.

Mr Goh's reply to a question on the economic downturn and the government's response to it was to hold wages, to work harder for high productivity and to hope for the best. "Can we do it? That is the real test for Singapore's younger leaders. If we can get management and workers to come to a consensus, we will signal to investors that we are rational and can adjust to a wage level according to the economic weather."[6] He expressed his confidence that Singapore will get over the difficult period.

To another question regarding the strict control of newspapers in Singapore and the collapse of the *Singapore Monitor*, Mr Goh said, "Newspapers are like politicians. They try to influence public opinion ... we can't allow two forces to contend for public opinion."[7] He said that the collapse of the *Singapore Monitor* was because it failed as a commercial venture and not because it was shut down.

The audience of about 400 people, politicians, bankers, professionals and businessmen, applauded many times during the course of his speech and the question-and-answer session that followed. Mr Goh's wit and charm worked well with the audience and his intelligent replies were warmly received and well-applauded.

On the second day of his visit, Mr Goh met his Malaysian counterpart Datuk Musa Hitam in the morning and discussed matters of mutual interest. As it was a courtesy call, there was no formal agenda. He was expected to meet with more Malaysian ministers. For a start, I arranged a lunch for him to meet Education Minister Datuk Abdullah Ahmad

---

[5] *The Straits Times*, 23 August 1985.
[6] *The Straits Times*, 23 August 1985.
[7] *The Straits Times*, 23 August 1985.

Badawi, Finance Minister Daim Zainuddin, Deputy Foreign Minister Abdul Kadir Sheikh Fadzir, Deputy Finance Minister Datuk Dr Tan Tiong Hong, Minister in the Prime Minister's Department Datuk Dr James Ongkili and Minister for Energy, Telecommunications and Post Datuk Leo Moggie. Dr Goh Cheng Teik, the deputy minister for agriculture, was also present.

The Tan Koon Swan Affair, January 1986

In late January 1986, the President of the Malaysian Chinese Association (MCA) Mr Tan Koon Swan was arrested in Singapore and charged with 15 counts of criminal conspiracy, cheating and fraud in connection with the financially troubled Pan-Electric Industries (Pan-El) which had collapsed in November 1985 with debts amounting to some $350 million. According to the *Straits Times* report of 8 December 1985, panic spread throughout the financial circles as forward dealings in Pan-El shares accounted for another $200 million amongst the brokers. Consequently, the Pan-El crisis led to a three-day closure of the stock market. Apparently, Mr Tan had come down to Singapore to try and settle the matter but found himself arrested. Immediately, the MCA reacted emotionally and organised a demonstration in front of the Singapore High Commission in Kuala Lumpur to show their unhappiness regarding the arrest of their leader and demanded that he be released or at least treated with respect because of his position as president of the MCA. Tan Koon Swan himself, in Singapore, issued a statement in which he asked the members of the MCA not to demonstrate and not to protest against his arrest as it was a private matter. He regretted that he had been involved in such a situation but the demonstrations would not help to resolve the issue. He offered to resign from the MCA but his resignation was rejected by the party's Central Committee. MCA members continued to protest in Malacca and in Ipoh. Some 70 MCA members in Johor gathered at the Causeway and tried to stop Singaporean cars from entering Malaysia. The demonstrators dispersed after the arrival of the police. The MCA Youth Political and Publicity Bureau, Federal MCA Youth and the MCA Central Committee issued a joint statement advocating a total boycott of goods and services from Singapore unless Mr Tan was released. The Johor MCA threatened not to support any increase in the water supply should the Singapore government request for it.

It so happened that Singapore's first Deputy Prime Minister Mr Goh Chok Tong was speaking at a forum on 29 January 1986 organised by Singapore Polytechnic students, when he was asked whether relations between Singapore and Malaysia would be affected by the MCA threat not to support a renewal of the water agreement between Singapore and Johor. Mr Goh, in response, remarked that "The MCA is not in charge of Malaysia. If they were in charge and our water supply is cut, I think we will be in deep trouble."[8]

Immediately, the issue became political because the MCA interpreted Mr Goh's remark as a denigration of their position in the Malaysian government. The Malaysian cabinet issued an official statement on 5 February 1986 calling Mr Goh's remark "irresponsible and an interference in the affairs of Malaysia".[9] An official protest note would be sent to the Singapore government by Foreign Minister Tengku Ahmad Rithauddeen Ismail. Even Dr Mahathir reacted when he said that "It is not right for anybody to make such a remark".[10]

Earlier, Dr Mahathir had made it clear that the Malaysian government would not interfere in any way with the judicial processes against Mr Tan Koon Swan in Singapore. He had also sent Minister of Finance Daim Zainuddin to talk to Mr Tan and to get the latest information on the case. Daim Zainuddin, on his return, said that the relations between the two countries would not be affected by the arrest of Tan Koon Swan. Singapore's Minister for Foreign Affairs Mr Dhanabalan on a one-day private visit to watch the semifinal match between Singapore and Malaysia in the Salem Asian Team Squash Championship in Kuala Lumpur in February 1986, said that there was no crisis in relations between the two countries as portrayed by press reports. In fact, the Malaysians had been very good to the Singapore team.

---

[8] *The Straits Times*, 30 January 1986.
[9] *Business Times*, 6 February 1986.
[10] *The Straits Times*, 7 February 1986.

I met Foreign Minister Tengku Ahmad Rithauddeen Ismail on 5 February 1986 and he expressed the hope that the good relations between the two countries would continue. I responded, "We share this hope." Later, an official protest note against Mr Goh Chok Tong's remark about MCA was delivered by Malaysian Deputy Foreign Minister Datuk Abdul Kadir Sheikh Fadzir to Mr Lin Chung Ying, our counsellor in Kuala Lumpur.

The threat not to support Singapore's request for more water supply was made by a Johor MCA official. As water was a very important matter to Singapore, Mr Goh had tried to reassure the students that there was really nothing to worry about. It was never his intention to give any offence as he was aware that the MCA was one of the ruling parties in the Barisan Nasional. Mr Goh's reply was put in such a way as not to cause alarm. The misunderstanding which arose from misinterpretation was unfortunate.

The MCA said that the Singapore government's official reply to the Malaysian protest note was "acceptable on diplomatic terms"[11] but it fell short of an apology. The MCA added that it felt that no one should do anything to damage the good relations between Malaysia and Singapore.

Tan Koon Swan was subsequently tried and sentenced by the Singapore High Court to two years' jail and fined S$500,000 for abetment of criminal breach of trust. After serving 16 months in Changi Prison he was released in December 1987. He was extradited to Malaysia to face another charge relating to the misuse of funds belonging to Multi-Purpose Holdings Berhad. He was sentenced to 30 months' jail and fined RM 1 million. An appeal reduced the jail term to 18 months without the fine. He was released after serving 12 months due to good behaviour.

Datuk Musa Hitam's Resignation, March 1986

Deputy Prime Minister Datuk Musa Hitam's resignation from the Mahathir cabinet on 16 March 1986 came as a big surprise as both Dr Mahathir Mohamad and Datuk Musa appeared to be working very well together and had, in fact, been close allies since the 1960s.

---

[11] *The Straits Times*, 15 February 1986.

Picture 27: MB having tea with Tengku Ahmad Rithauddeen Ismail, Minister of Foreign Affairs in Kuala Lumpur, Malaysia, in Kuala Lumpur, 1986.

After the May 13 riots, Musa Hitam was appointed by the Tunku as assistant minister of national development. But not long after, in August 1969, the Tunku removed him from the post because of an unfavourable report that the Tunku had received which questioned Musa's loyalty to the government. Shortly after his dismissal, Musa left for England to take a masters degree in international relations at the University of Sussex.

When I was first posted to Malaysia as high commissioner, Minister of Home Affairs Tun Dr Ismail told me that whereas Musa Hitam was sent off to be out of the Tunku's way, it would be difficult to forgive Dr Mahathir for what he had done to the Tunku. However, Tun Razak who was the deputy prime minister thought very highly of Dr Mahathir and brought him back into UMNO later when he became prime minister.

When Tun Hussein Onn took over as prime minister after Tun Razak's death, he selected Dr Mahathir as his deputy although at that time Ghafar Baba and Tengku Razaleigh had more votes as UMNO vice-presidents and Dr Mahathir was only the third man. When he resigned in 1981, Dr Mahathir succeeded him as prime minister.

Musa Hitam was the son of a Malay father and a Chinese mother; Dr Mahathir's paternal grandfather was Indian-Muslim, his father was a Jawi Peranakan and his mother was Malay.[12] There was a rumour that one of the Sultans was heard to have remarked privately, "What is this country coming to when we have a half-Indian and a half-Chinese running it!" However, they were both very efficient and highly regarded by people.

At first, Datuk Musa and Dr Mahathir worked closely together. When Musa challenged Tengku Razaleigh Hamzah in 1981 for the UMNO deputy president's post, he had Mahathir's support.

In 1984, Tengku Razaleigh was defeated by Datuk Musa for the second time when they vied for the same post. "Publicly, Mahathir's government had been labelled, probably by the press, the '2M', that is, 'Mahathir–Musa' administration. ... To all public appearances, Musa was Mahathir's heir apparent."[13]

So it came as a shock when on 27 February 1986, Datuk Musa's political secretary, Sulaiman Aris, handed Musa's letters of resignation from the posts of deputy prime minister, minister of home affairs and UMNO deputy president to Prime Minister Dr Mahathir. Datuk Musa would, however, remain as a member of Parliament and UMNO Segamat division head. Datuk Musa had left for Mecca to perform the *umrah* (minor haj) the night before.

Although their relationship was considered as highly successful, there were rumours that there were serious policy differences. It was known, for instance, that Datuk Musa did not like the appointment of Datuk Sanusi Junid, minister of national development, as UMNO secretary-general and he opposed the appointment of Tengku Razaleigh to the cabinet as minister of trade and industry. In fact, feelings between Datuk Musa and Tengku Razaleigh were very bad during that period. It was also known that Datuk Musa was opposed to the policy of Dr Mahathir to put Malaysia on the international map: for instance, to produce its own car, the Proton

---

[12] Wain, Barry (2009). *Malaysian Maverick: Mahathir Mohamad in Turbulent Times*. Basingstoke, UK: Palgrave Macmillan, pp. 4–5.

[13] Khoo Boo Teik (1995). *Paradoxes of Mahathirism: An Intellectual Biography of Mahathir Mohamad*. New York: Oxford University Press, pp. 228–229.

Saga, and to build the Penang Bridge. Datuk Musa thought that money should be spent more on the rural areas to help the peasants and workers rather than spending money on grandiose projects. However, these facts did not receive any publicity because Datuk Musa believed that in the cabinet whatever major decisions were made should be supported without any disagreements in public.

Datuk Musa's decision to leave office shocked UMNO party members. While he had many supporters, so did Dr Mahathir and the split between the two top leaders "unprecedented in 29 years of independence"[14] was the first crisis faced by UMNO since the early 1950s.

Datuk Musa cited the lack of trust in him as the main reason for his action.[15] In his seven-page letter to Dr Mahathir in his capacity as UMNO president with copies to UMNO Supreme Council members, Datuk Musa referred to the fact that, although he had questioned certain policies, he had accepted the principle of collective responsibility. He reminded Dr Mahathir that he had told him several times that he wished to retire because he was fed-up with money politics and the misuse of power for political reasons. He gave five reasons for his decision to step down: His commitment had declined as he was not trusted; whatever his actions, he would always be afraid of being accused of acting out of his own political interest; statements circulated by people that although Dr Mahathir and Musa could not work together any more, Dr Mahathir could not do anything about it because Musa had become too powerful; it was his intention to resign earlier but the timing was not right because of Dr Mahathir's visit to Johor on 20–21 February; his resignation would allow Dr Mahathir to choose another person to be his deputy, someone whom Dr Mahathir had complete faith in.

Datuk Musa's resignation from the deputy premiership could not have occurred at a worse possible time for the government of Dr Mahathir. The Bumiputra Malaysia Finance (BMF) affair, the MCA's financial scandals and the ensuing political crisis, the resurgence of Parti Islam Se-Malaysia (PAS) through younger more aggressive leaders, accompanied by falling commodity prices coupled with steadily rising unemployment were but

---

[14] *Business Times*, 1 March 1986.
[15] *The Straits Times*, 1 March 1986.

some of the problems faced by Malaysia which threatened to undermine the authority of the government.

Fearing that the rift between the leaders would cause a split in UMNO ranks because of conflict between their supporters, the UMNO Supreme Council decided to send a delegation of four "menteris besar" to London to persuade Datuk Musa to change his mind. The delegation — Datuk Amar Haji Wan Mokhtar Ahmad (Terengganu), Datuk Abdul Ajib Ahmad (Johor), Datuk Najib Tun Razak (Pahang) and Datuk Seri Ramli Ngah Taib (Perak) — returned with the news that, although Datuk Musa had withdrawn his resignation as deputy president of UMNO, he had refused to withdraw his resignation from his cabinet posts as deputy prime minister and minister of home affairs. In his statement, Datuk Musa said that he decided to return to the party's leadership because UMNO's Supreme Council and his own supporters had appealed to him to reconsider his decision. "I would like to urge all UMNO members ... to stop all activities that threaten the party and set aside their differences."[16]

While the politicians took one side or the other, Tengku Razaleigh Hamzah, minister of trade and industry, made it clear to his supporters that he was not involved in the conflict between Datuk Musa and Dr Mahathir. But later, at the opening of an exhibition, he remarked to reporters covering the event that "we should ... rally behind the leadership of Dato' Seri Dr Mahathir Mohamad."[17]

The one person who benefited from this conflict between the two leaders was a young man, Anwar Ibrahim, who had been selected by Dr Mahathir as a very promising leader and who had, in fact, won the position as UMNO Youth leader, defeating the incumbent by a very slim margin. Anwar's rise was a meteoric one. He had been very friendly with the opposition Islamic party, PAS, and it appeared as if he would join that party but he was dissuaded from doing so despite their close relationship. From then on, his rise in UMNO was very significant and he took advantage of the situation and early on declared that UMNO Youth was on Dr Mahathir's side. The following year at the UMNO party elections

---

[16] *The Straits Times*, 15 March 1986.
[17] *The Straits Times*, 15 March 1986.

he stood for one of the three vice-president posts and was elected along with Abdullah Badawi and Ghafar Baba.

The Herzog Visit, November 1986

There were some issues that created a great deal of controversy between Singapore and Malaysia. One of these was the state visit of the President of Israel, Chaim Herzog in November 1986. The visit was first requested by the Israeli Embassy in December 1984. Singapore had agreed but the visit, originally scheduled for May, was postponed by Israel. In April 1986, Singapore agreed to a visit from 18 to 20 November, as part of President Herzog's tour of Australia, New Zealand, Fiji, Tonga and the Philippines. Singapore had requested that President Herzog should visit at least one ASEAN country before coming to Singapore and this had been accepted. But at the last moment, President Corazon Aquino changed her mind and said that internal problems made it difficult to receive Herzog. He had to fly from Fiji to Hong Kong and bypass the Philippines. It was very astute of the Philippines because it anticipated that Muslim elements would be very upset if Herzog had visited the country despite having agreed earlier to receive him. Suddenly Singapore found itself alone among the ASEAN countries as Indonesia, Malaysia and Brunei did not have diplomatic relations with Israel.

The second problem was that whereas normally the government that extends the invitation announces the visit, the Israeli Embassy in Singapore jumped the gun and made the announcement about a month before the actual visit. This gave Indonesia and Malaysia ample opportunity to protest. The intention of the Singapore government was to delay the announcement for as long as possible until the last few days so that the matter would soon be over and there would be as little trouble as possible. But the Israeli embassy was determined to get the maximum publicity out of the event. This upset the Singapore government but there was nothing that could be done about it.

Once the announcement was made, UMNO Youth led by its Kedah branch protested that, due to the Israeli treatment of the Palestinians, its refusal to abide by UN resolutions and its inhuman behaviour, Singapore should cancel the visit. Dr Mahathir initially responded by saying that the

Malaysian government could not protest at what was really an internal affair of Singapore. However, as domestic pressure grew, Dr Mahathir had to back down. Daim Zainuddin warned me that it would be necessary to recognise the domestic pressure in some way. It must be admitted that the protests were genuine. Even Tunku Abdul Rahman, who had retired, and Tun Hussein Onn, the former prime minister, joined the hullabaloo. Although the feelings against the visit were genuine, UMNO Youth, for political reasons, loved to have Singapore as its target in order to improve its own position among the Malays.

Eventually many protests and demonstrations were organised against the Singapore High Commission. But the police protected the High Commission from any potential violence. The situation was safe but there were personal abuses, especially over the telephone at my office and also at home until the police redirected calls to the police station so that they could handle the abusive calls. The demonstrations escalated and effigies of Herzog and even the Prime Minister Lee Kuan Yew were burnt in front of the Singapore High Commission. But the police protection was complete. Some of the protesters threw stones at the American Embassy which was located opposite the Singapore High Commission but we were not harmed.

The situation was very tense as the protests continued. There were many letters in the newspapers and there were even suggestions that Malaysia should break off relations with Singapore and recall their high commissioner. This was done, but the Malaysian Ministry of Foreign Affairs explained that it was a routine matter and tried to play down the situation as much as possible. As far as Singapore was concerned, it was impossible to cancel the visit simply at the demand of a neighbouring country as this would discredit the government. Indonesia was also upset by the Herzog visit but not to the extent of Malaysia.

Later on, the Singapore government made its position clear to the Israelis during the speech given by President Wee Kim Wee at the dinner for President Herzog. President Wee said that Israel must return to the Arab countries the territories it occupied as a result of the June 1967 war; it must be prepared to recognise the right of the Palestinians to self-determination and to a homeland of their own; and Israel must rescind the illegal measures it had taken to change the character and status of the

City of Jerusalem.[18] This was the position of the other ASEAN members and the United Nations and it was necessary for President Wee to make it very clear that the Singapore government stood by the resolutions of the United Nations.

I was called up by the Malaysian Ministry of Foreign Affairs, first by Tengku Ahmad Rithauddeen Ismail, the acting minister of foreign affairs who was an old friend from college days in England. We had a chat about the situation and he explained why the Malaysian government was more or less compelled to act as it did due to domestic pressures. Later, I was called up by the deputy minister of foreign affairs, an up-and-coming young man who wanted perhaps to show his enthusiasm and gain popularity with UMNO Youth. I had to explain the situation to him. In the midst of these visits, Datuk Rais Yatim, the minister of foreign affairs who was in London at the time, sent me a huge bouquet of flowers with his good wishes. I returned home after a hard day at the mission and was surprised to see this beautiful bouquet in the house. I was very touched by the gesture of sympathy. I sent a message to Singapore mentioning this and Mr S. Dhanabalan, our minister for foreign affairs, acknowledged its significance.

During the Herzog visit, the Malaysian Ministry of Foreign Affairs did its best to play down the issues. The police certainly gave full protection to the Singapore High Commission and the high commissioner's residence was under guard by plain clothes policemen.

In the middle of December 1986, Prime Minister Lee Kuan Yew made an interesting statement on the Herzog visit. He said that the visit had been requested in December 1984 and he was not informed about its renewal in 1986. During 1986, there had been in the Malaysian press statements about Zionism, and the alleged manipulation of the commodities market of Malaysia by the Zionists in order to disrupt its economy. Dr Mahathir had made a statement in Parliament on 11 October 1986 referring to this alleged attempt by the Zionists to damage the commodities market of Malaysia. Press officers at the Singapore Ministry of Foreign Affairs had not paid any attention to these statements and Prime Minister Lee said that

---

[18] *The Straits Times*, 6 December 1986.

Picture 28: MB with Datuk Rais Yatim, Minister of Foreign Affairs, Malaysia at the Singapore High Commission in Kuala Lumpur, 1986.

if he had known in the light of these statements, he would have arranged for the visit to be postponed to a less sensitive time as his relationship with Dr Mahathir was a very good one, a very mature one. But of course, once the announcement was made, it would have been impossible to change the date or cancel the visit as no country would be able to maintain its reputation if it had done such a thing. When Dr Mahathir was asked by reporters to respond to Lee Kuan Yew's statement, the *New Straits Times* reported his comments/remarks: "Let's forget about it."

Malays in the Singapore Armed Forces (SAF), early 1987

Within three or four months after the Herzog visit, another problem arose. UMNO Youth was up in arms once again. This time it occurred when Minister for Trade and Industry Brigadier-General (Res) Lee Hsien

Loong on a visit to the Yuhua constituency, in reply to a suggestion at a forum that there should be a proportion of certain jobs, say, fighter pilots reserved for Malays, said, "We live in Southeast Asia. If there is a conflict, if the SAF is called to defend the homeland, we don't want to put any of our soldiers in a difficult position where his emotions for the nation may be in conflict with his emotions for his religion. These are very strong fundamental feelings and if they are incompatible, then there will be two strong destructive forces." This was the more serious of two reasons why the government could not reserve certain jobs in the armed forces for Malay Muslims. But BG Lee said that as Singaporeans gradually developed a sense of national identity, this would be less of a problem. The second reason was because jobs were not reserved for a particular section of the people but were allotted according to merit. Those who fitted the jobs best got them.[19]

UMNO Youth, driven by the struggle for leadership within the party, had taken every opportunity to attack Singapore on issues, as it had done leading the opposition in criticising the Herzog visit. This time, they seized upon the opportunity to criticise Minister Lee's statement which was a frank expression of his views — that Singapore is in the midst of Southeast Asia, surrounded by Muslim countries, and certainly Islam is a very strong religion and, as subsequently prove in other matters, Muslims are often torn between their support for their religion and their political attitudes.

What was more serious was that some Malaysian ministers also responded to BG Lee's statement. Malaysian Minister of Defence and UMNO Vice-President Datuk Abdullah Ahmad Badawi said that BG Lee's statement concerned the problem in Singapore. "But since it touches on the integrity of the Malays, my own race, therefore I regret the statement," he added. Malaysia's Minister of Foreign Affairs Datuk Rais Yatim, in response to a question from journalists after a function at Pemadam, the national association against drug abuse, said he regarded BG Lee's recent statement as an internal affair of Singapore therefore, "I have not reacted and I have no comment." Asked if the remark could have an impact on

---

[19] *Business Times*, 23 February 1987.

Malaysia–Singapore relations, he declined to say anything except that "we should avoid treading on dangerous ground."[20]

But less than two weeks later, for the second day in a row, Datuk Rais criticised BG Lee's statement. He said that the statement was a "serious threat" to the Malays, the *New Sunday Times* reported. Speaking at the Padang Terap (Kedah) division UMNO Youth annual general meeting, he said the statement showed that others assume that the "Malays have weakened considerably and are taking full advantage of it". Earlier, he had expressed regret over the statement and said that it was insensitive and might affect relations within ASEAN countries, especially Indonesia, Malaysia and Brunei. He told UMNO division delegates meeting in Labis, Johor that "UMNO must voice its concern as it is a serious statement. It involves the question of the Malay race." Datuk Rais also told the Labis delegates that he could not give a "diplomatic answer" as BG Lee made the statement "outside diplomatic ambits" as a politician and a PAP leader. "Therefore, we should give a political answer instead of commenting [on] it through diplomatic or other channels," Datuk Rais added. He said that the statement came from a "young man who is relatively new in politics and international relations. However, it shows that they are becoming more daring. This statement came after Singapore had invited the Israeli President to visit the country. We regard this as racial discrimination." Datuk Rais said the feelings of the Malays had been generally hurt by BG Lee and the recent visit by Israeli President Chaim Herzog to Singapore.[21]

Privately, he and other ministers held the view that whereas they understood the attitude of Singapore, just as in Malaysia no Indian or Chinese would ever be in command of the armed forces or be given key positions in the military, there was no need to proclaim these sensitive issues and bring them up for discussion in public. Whereas Singapore ministers' view was that problems should be thrashed out in public and discussed frankly before solutions could be found.

Dr Ahmad Mattar, minister for environment and minister in charge of Muslim affairs, in response to criticisms of some Malaysian ministers,

---

[20] *The Straits Times*, 6 March 1987.
[21] *The Straits Times*, 15 March 1987.

said that Malaysians should not drag Singapore into their domestic and political rivalries and that such interference was damaging to the relationship of the Malays with the other races in Singapore. *The Straits Times* on 29 March 1987 quoted Dr Mattar saying, "Do not use us, Malay Singaporeans, as expendable ammunition in your domestic political in-fighting. It is us, not you, who will have to cope with the consequences of your political adventurism. As a result of the racial tirade that you have directed at the elected government of Singapore as being racialist, an enemy of Islam and a base for Zionism, Malay Singaporeans have, for no rhyme or reason and through no fault of theirs, been made the objects of suspicion among the non-Malays here. Your actions can lead to the isolation of Malay Singaporeans." Dr Mattar stressed that the Herzog affair showed that racial harmony in Singapore could not be taken for granted. He also made it clear to Malay Singaporeans that, once the political in-fighting in Malaysia was over, Malaysian politicians would not help repair the damage they caused. And while the challenges of bringing Malay Singaporeans into the mainstream of national life were formidable, the community would be able to overcome the difficulties with the cooperation of non-Malay political leaders.

Dr Ahmad Mattar's toughly worded speech, made at the opening of a PAP seminar on challenges in nation-building, was the strongest reaction yet from a Singaporean minister to the criticisms from across the Causeway sparked off by the Herzog visit. That visit, he argued, was a matter of the past for many Singaporeans, including the Malays here who, like the non-Muslims in Malaysia, had also accepted the economic and political realities in their country. But the Malaysian Malays had stepped up their attacks and even accused Singapore of wanting to invade Johor. "In fact, Malaysia is the only ASEAN partner which has allowed its political leaders to openly intervene in our sensitive domestic issues which, as you and I well know, can lead to social chaos and, if unchecked, even to bloodshed."[22]

Later, Datuk Rais Yatim met Singapore's Minister for Foreign Affairs S. Dhanabalan privately to discuss the issues. Datuk Rais told reporters in

---

[22] *The Straits Times*, 29 March 1987.

Kuala Lumpur that he had extended Malaysia's views to Mr Dhanabalan and that "we agreed not to exchange discourse on public issues that could harm bilateral relations".[23]

BG Lee, responding to MPs in Parliament in the course of debating budgetary provisions for the Defence Ministry, referred to the controversy over the remarks he made regarding Malay representation in the SAF. He asserted that he had spoken more openly and frankly than before because Singapore society was more mature and ready to discuss important and sensitive issues. Indeed, as early as 1977, the then defence minister, Dr Goh Keng Swee, spoke about the "important yet delicate" subject of ethnic representation in the SAF. Since then, there had been substantial progress. For example, since March 1985, every eligible Malay citizen had been called up for national service, the proportion of Malays among the enlisted men had doubled since 1977 and Malays were being posted more widely within the SAF. For instance, they were now in the Commando Battalion; as more Malays gained A-levels, more had become officers; and four Malay Muslim officers had been given SAF scholarships to study at NUS. But BG Lee said that the SAF must integrate with caution because a mistake could lead to racial and religious disharmony within the armed forces. He quoted the Malay proverb *sedikit, sedikit, lama-lama, menjadi bukit* (a little over a long time makes a hill) that patience was required in dealing with this issue.[24]

BG Lee made no direct reference to his critics across the Causeway beyond saying that he agreed with the view that it was a Singapore problem to be solved by Singaporeans themselves.

Semangat 46, 1987

In February 1987, Musa Hitam made known his intention to defend his deputy president's post at UMNO's party election. Meanwhile, Tengku Razaleigh Hamzah, who was twice defeated by Musa for the deputy presidency in 1981 and 1984, declared that he would run for president against Dr Mahathir. Although former rivals, Musa took the first step in burying

---

[23] *Business Times*, 3 April 1987.
[24] *The Straits Times*, 18 March 1987.

the hatchet by inviting Tengku Razaleigh to officiate at the opening of his Segamat (Johor) division assembly. There, he threw his support behind Tengku Razaleigh. Three weeks later on 20 March 1987, Tengku Razaleigh invited Musa to inaugurate the opening of his Gua Musang (Kelantan) division assembly.

The contest for the posts of president, deputy president, three vice-presidents and the 25 Supreme Council seats split the party's leadership into two camps. UMNO cabinet ministers and their deputies were either supporters of Team A, the Mahathir–Ghafar Baba camp, or Team B, the Razaleigh–Musa camp. By late February 1987, all UMNO state chief ministers had pledged their support for Dr Mahathir. Among the UMNO cabinet ministers on Team A's side were Abu Hassan, Anwar Ibrahim, Daim Zainuddin, Rafidah Aziz and Sanusi Junid while Abdullah Badawi, Ajib Ahmad, Rais Yatim and Shahrir Samad went over to Team B. Wanita UMNO and Pemuda UMNO sided with Team A. Former prime ministers and ex-UMNO presidents, Tunku Abdul Rahman and Tun Hussein Onn supported Team B. The campaigning was intense; charges and counter-charges were made. The forecast was that Dr Mahathir would probably win by a very narrow majority. Although Dr Mahathir expected the outcome to be a narrow one, he made it very clear that even if he were to win by a single vote he would still remain as prime minister unless Parliament passed a vote of no confidence to remove him.

The excitement reached a climax on 24 April 1987 at the UMNO General Assembly. As the voting turned out, indeed Dr Mahathir had won by a narrow margin. He had 761 votes (51.45 per cent) against Tengku Razaleigh's 718 (48.55 per cent), a slim majority of 43 votes (2.9 per cent). Ghafar Baba defeated Musa by 40 votes. He had 739 votes to Musa's 699, but there were 41 spoilt votes. Of the three vice-president posts, Team A took two, Wan Mokhtar was first and Anwar Ibrahim third. The second place went to Team B's Abdullah Badawi. Of the 25 Supreme Council seats, Team B members won eight.

As Team B was defeated, Tengku Razaleigh and Rais Yatim resigned from the cabinet. Three ministers — Abdullah Badawi, Ajib Ahmad and Shahrir Samad — and four deputy ministers — Abdul Kadir Sheikh Fadzir, Radzi Sheikh Ahmad, Rahmah Othman and Zainal Abidin Zin — were purged from the cabinet, even though Abdullah Badawi had won one of the three vice-presidencies with the second highest number of votes and the rest had won six Supreme Council seats. Anwar Ibrahim supported Dr Mahathir's action as the prime minister would want "a cabinet that has confidence in him and in whom he has confidence."[25]

Party dissidents in Team B resorted to legal action to challenge the validity of the party elections. Team B claimed that as some of Team A's UMNO branches were not properly registered, their representatives should not have voted at the General Assembly. Their "illegal" votes would have impacted on the election results taking into consideration the narrow majority of votes for the top UMNO posts.

On 4 February 1988, Justice Harun Hashim ruled that the presence of unregistered UMNO branches made UMNO an illegal party under the Societies Act. Since UMNO had been declared illegal, it had to be deregistered.

Team B's efforts to form a new party with the support of the Tunku were rejected by the Registrar of Societies (who came under the Ministry of Home Affairs of which Dr Mahathir was the minister in charge) as being premature since the old UMNO was not technically deregistered yet. Instead, Dr Mahathir's application to register a new party, UMNO Baru (New UMNO), was approved by the Registrar of Societies. Dr Mahathir succeeded in outmanoeuvring his opponents in Team B.

In a bid to revive the old UMNO, UMNO-11 (as the Team B litigants were known) appealed against Justice Harun Hashim's ruling on 4 February 1988 on the deregistration of UMNO which was scheduled to be heard by the Supreme Court on 13 June 1988, to be presided over by Tun Salleh Abas with eight other judges. However, Tun Salleh was suspended as Lord President on 27 May 1988 and subsequently sacked from his post on 8 August 1988. On 9 August, the UMNO-11 appeal, which had been postponed when Tun Salleh was suspended, was heard in the Supreme Court and dismissed.[26]

By early February 1989, Musa Hitam had joined UMNO Baru. One of the reasons he gave for returning to the party was the acceptance by

---

[25] Khoo Boo Teik (1995). *Paradoxes of Mahathirism: An Intellectual Biography of Mahathir Mohamad*. New York: Oxford University Press, p. 271.

[26] Khoo Boo Teik (1995). *Paradoxes of Mahathirism: An Intellectual Biography of Mahathir Mohamad*. New York: Oxford University Press, pp. 292–293.

the Supreme Council of the six-point Johor unity formula of which he was the chief architect. The unity agreement included automatic acceptance of all the former Johor UMNO members as registered members of UMNO Baru and the reinstatement of UMNO leaders elected at division and branch levels in 1987. The other important consideration was the leadership's more compromising attitude towards the dissidents. UMNO Baru had decided to accept all Malays including those branded as troublemakers and traitors whom Dr Mahathir had initially barred from joining the new party as they had opposed him.[27] Regarding Tengku Razaleigh with whom he teamed up to run against Dr Mahathir and Ghafar Baba during the 1987 party elections, *The Straits Times* on 1 February 1989 reported that Musa said they always had their differences "I was never really accepted in the "46 group."

The split in the leadership of Team B was thus triggered by the fact that Musa and his supporters, Shahrir Samad in particular, were never accepted by Tengku Razaleigh. What Shahrir Samad told the Malaysian newspaper, *China Press*, was reported by *The Straits Times* on 5 February 1989: "Many people support him [Tengku Razaleigh] not because of a hunger for power and personal gains. He should keep these people. Unfortunately, he only believes in his own people, like Othman Saat. As long as he continues to take Othman Saat as a confidant, I'll not attend their meetings." Shahrir Samad said that he and Musa were not consulted by Tengku Razaleigh when the latter appointed Othman Saat as Johor UMNO '46 leader. He added that both were also not consulted before Tengku Razaleigh held talks with Abdul Razak Ahmad, the acting chairman of Parti Socialis Rakyat Malaysia.

Tengku Razaleigh and his supporters refused to join UMNO Baru. Instead, they formed a new political party, calling it Parti Melayu Semangat 46 (Spirit of '46) which they claimed represented the original UMNO founded in 1946. The Registrar of Societies approved its registration on 5 May 1989. By June 1989, Semangat 46 together with the opposition Parti Islam Se-Malaysia (PAS) and two Islamic-based parties, Berjasa and Hamim, formed a coalition known as Angkatan Perpaduan Ummah (APU) or Islamic United Front, in order to break UMNO's hold over

---

[27] *The Straits Times*, 1 February 1989.

the Malay population.²⁸ By September 1989, Semangat 46 had 3,000 approved branches with 300,000 members; another 2,000 branches were waiting for approval by the Registrar of Societies. According to Tengku Razaleigh, total membership was expected to increase to 500,000 by the end of the year.²⁹

Tengku Razaleigh agreed to hold talks with Dr Mahathir on 12 December 1989 to discuss the question of Malay unity but the meeting ended in deadlock. As reported in the *Business Times* on 13 December 1989, Dr Mahathir said that both had differing views on how Malay unity could be achieved. "He [Tengku Razaleigh] claims that there is a new and old UMNO. What I am saying is that there is only one UMNO. His view is that unity is only possible by reviving [the original] UMNO. I disagreed."

Although Tengku Razaleigh vowed from the outset not to join UMNO Baru, it was not to be. On 6 October 1996, with a unanimous show of hands, delegates at the special assembly of Parti Melayu Semangat 46 agreed to dissolve their seven-year-old party and made preparations to return to UMNO en-bloc. As reported in the *New Straits Times* on 7 October 1996, Tengku Razaleigh told party members to accept the fact that UMNO was now supported by the majority of Malays and therefore, in the interest of their religion, race and country, they had to join the party, adding, "It is for the entire future generation."

At a historic ceremony at the Putra World Trade Centre on 8 October 1996, Tengku Razaleigh handed his application form to Dr Mahathir in a symbolic gesture to signify the mass joining of UMNO by 200,000 former Semangat 46 members. Dr Mahathir received the other application forms in 26 boxes together with a cheque for RM 200,000 for the membership fee.³⁰

The Chinese Primary Schools Controversy, October 1987

After the UMNO election of 24 April 1987 which split the party into rival factions, another crisis, the Chinese primary schools controversy,

---

²⁸ *The Straits Times*, 16 November 1989.
²⁹ *The Straits Times*, 3 October 1989.
³⁰ *New Straits Times*, 9 October 1996.

followed in October 1987. The question of Chinese education is an extremely sensitive issue among Malaysia's ethnic Chinese population. Under the country's education system, Bahasa Malaysia, Chinese (i.e., Mandarin) and Tamil are the three mediums of instruction at primary school level. Although the Education Act 1961 guaranteed the existence of Chinese and Tamil primary education and it was endorsed by the Barisan National's 1986 election manifesto, a clause in the Education Act empowered the Education Minister to convert Mandarin and Tamil medium primary schools to national-type primary schools where the medium of instruction was Bahasa Malaysia, the national language, should the Minister wish to do so.

Prior to October 1987, four incidents involving the Education Ministry contributed to growing ethnic tensions. In April, Chinese associations and political parties objected to the practice of having all school children in Malacca take an Islamic-style pledge during school assembly. In June, the University of Malaya decided to discontinue using English, Mandarin and Tamil in the first-year elective courses in the English, Chinese and Indian Studies departments; instead, such courses would be taught in Bahasa Malaysia. From July to August, the Malaysian Chinese Association (MCA) protested against the use of the *songkok* and the *tudung* as headgear for all graduands, non-Malays and non-Muslims included, at the Universiti Teknologi Malaysia convocation. In September, UMNO Youth urged the government to withdraw financial aid to the Tunku Abdul Rahman College operated by MCA mainly because it did not use Bahasa Malaysia as its medium of instruction.[31] To the Chinese community, such incidents represented attempts to edge closer towards the national language policy of which the Education Minister Anwar Ibrahim, was a staunch advocate.

Amid such misgivings, the Education Ministry's administrative decision to promote 100-plus non-Mandarin-speaking ethnic Chinese teachers to be headmasters or senior assistants, posting them to Chinese primary schools in Malacca, Penang, Selangor and the Federal Territory, escalated into an ethnic controversy, and a dangerous situation

---

[31] Khoo Boo Teik (1995). *Paradoxes of Mahathirism: An Intellectual Biography of Mahathir Mohamad.* New York: Oxford University Press, p. 281.

began developing which could have led to a racial flare-up with dire consequences.

The promotion decision, seen as a ploy to erode Chinese primary education in the country, created a furore among the Chinese community and its leaders. MCA President Datuk Ling Liong Sik said that the move went against the solemn promise contained in the Barisan National's election manifesto. He said that the MCA could not accept the postings of such teachers. Chinese school teachers and parents as well as Chinese political and community leaders described the ministry's action as the first step towards changing the character of Chinese primary schools. They feared that if headmasters and senior assistants not proficient in Mandarin were appointed to administer the schools, they would eventually change the medium of instruction. Moreover, not being proficient in Mandarin meant that they would be unable to carry out their duties efficiently, affecting the day-to-day running of the schools, eventually threatening their very existence and leading to the demise of Chinese language education in Malaysia. Protest meetings were held simultaneously in Kuala Lumpur and Malacca. Several Chinese school teachers' associations resolved to organise a boycott of classes in Chinese primary schools nationwide.

At a meeting with MCA leaders to resolve the controversy over the promotions and postings to Chinese primary schools, Education Minister Anwar Ibrahim said that the government would not change its decision and "that his ministry would not bow to 'political pressures' on the appointments."[32]

On 11 October 1987, a meeting was held at the Thean Hou Temple in Kuala Lumpur comprising several thousand participants. It was organised by 15 Chinese guilds and associations, the MCA, Gerakan and the opposition Democratic Action Party (DAP). It was the first time MCA and Gerakan had participated in a rally against their coalition partners in the Barisan Nasional government. It was also the first time that the three Chinese-based political parties had joined hands to fight for a common cause together with the Chinese guilds and associations. MCA Deputy President Datuk Lee Kim Sai speaking at the meeting said, "The MCA

---

[32] *The Straits Times*, 6 October 1987.

takes an uncompromising stand to swim or sink with Chinese primary schools whether in the Cabinet or outside."[33]

The protesters, the National Save Chinese Education Joint Action Committee (JAC), set 14 October 1987 as the deadline for the ministry to transfer teachers from the affected schools. Otherwise, they threatened a boycott of classes in Chinese primary schools in Malacca, Penang, Selangor and the Federal Territory from 15 to 17 October. The appointment by Deputy Prime Minister Ghafar Baba of a five-member ministerial committee, chaired by Anwar Ibrahim with committee members Datuk Lee Kim Sai (MCA deputy president), Datuk Lim Keng Yaik (Gerakan president), Datuk Samy Vellu (MIC president) and Datuk Najib Tun Razak (acting UMNO Youth leader), enabled the MCA and Gerakan to persuade the JAC to call off the boycott. The assurances given by the MCA and Gerakan, both members of the ruling Barisan Nasional coalition, convinced the JAC that the government was sincere in wanting to resolve the issue by the end of the year.

Many UMNO members and their leaders were enraged at the MCA and Gerakan for supporting the opposition DAP and the Chinese guilds and associations. Photographs published in the press which showed Datuk Lee Kim Sai sitting next to DAP Secretary-General Lim Kit Siang made matters worse.

UMNO Youth, led by Datuk Najib Tun Razak, organised a rally on 17 October in retaliation to underline support for Anwar Ibrahim and to demand the resignation of MCA Deputy President Datuk Lee Kim Sai as minister of labour. About 5,000 youths attended the event. Banners and placards at the rally had slogans proclaiming "Do not repeat May 13", "Do not question Malay dominance", "Defend Malay honour" and "Malay dignity must be preserved". In his address, Datuk Najib said that UMNO Youth could not keep quiet if others tried to belittle the Malays or question their political dominance.[34] There were no incidents, probably due to the heavy police presence and heavy rain.

UMNO planned to hold a rally in Kuala Lumpur on 1 November for about 300,000 members and another 200,000 Malay supporters to

---

[33] *Business Times*, 12 October 1987.
[34] *The Straits Times*, 18 October 1987.

commemorate UMNO's birth. Ghafar Baba, Sanusi Junid and Megat Junid felt that such a rally would be "peaceful" despite police hesitation to issue a permit. Fortunately, Dr Mahathir returned from Montreal after attending the Commonwealth Heads of Government Meeting at the end of October 1987. In his capacity as minister of home affairs he banned all rallies nationwide, including that planned for 1 November. At an interview with *Asahi Shimbun* one week later, Dr Mahathir said "… the rally was to show that the grassroots are one group. But unfortunately the character of the rally changed from being an UMNO rally into an anti-Chinese rally. Because of that, I had to stop it." At another interview with *Asiaweek*, on 11 November, he said "… because of this 'triggering' by the issue of school teachers, we were about to have another May 13. I was not going to allow that … There was even talk about fighting, about coming with weapons. I cannot allow that kind of thing to go on."

From 27 October 1987, the police launched Operation Lalang, and made many arrests under the Internal Security Act (ISA) to defuse racial tensions. DAP MPs, second echelon MCA leaders, Chinese educationists, university lecturers including politicians from UMNO Youth (three of them, all from Team B), Gerakan and PAS, were detained. Newspapers *The Star*, *Watan* and *Sin Chew Jit Poh* were suspended indefinitely.[35]

The ISA detentions and the cancellation of the November UMNO rally prevented racial tensions from exploding. The Chinese primary schools controversy reflected the extent to which ethnic relations in Malaysia had deteriorated. There was mutual distrust. The issue of Chinese education in Malaysia would continue to be a serious bone of contention in years to come.

Lord President Tun Salleh Abas, 1988

As I was preparing to say farewell to Malaysia after more than seven years, relations between Prime Minister Dr Mahathir Mohamad and his government and the judiciary deteriorated drastically, culminating in the impeachment of the lord president, Tun Salleh Abas, and his ultimate

---

[35] Khoo Boo Teik (1995). *Paradoxes of Mahathirism: An Intellectual Biography of Mahathir Mohamad*. New York: Oxford University Press, pp. 284–285.

dismissal from office. Since I retired from diplomatic service in April 1988, much of what happened occurred after I had already left Malaysia. I thus had to rely on press reports from *The Straits Times* and *Business Times* for details of the Tun Salleh affair.

There were problems that led to the conflict between the government and the judiciary. The judiciary in Malaysia had a good reputation for independence in the British tradition and it tended to be proud of its independence. It so happened that in the five cases involving the government and its opponents, the government lost four of the lawsuits and this tended to create the impression that perhaps the judiciary, determined to prove its reputation for independence, might have made unfair decisions. The whole question was controversial and the prime minister's remarks, which reflected his impatience with the independence of the judiciary, did not help matters. When I called on Tun Salleh Abas on my farewell rounds, known to be a very strict and upright man, he said to me, "Let it not be said that during my term as Lord President that the courts bowed to executive pressure." He was very proud of the fact that the Malaysian courts had always upheld justice independently, unlike in most developing countries where decisions went in favour of the government when

Picture 29: At a dinner party at the High Commissioner's residence in Kuala Lumpur, Malaysia. From left: Tun Salleh Abas, Lord President; Tun Raja Mohar; Tan Sri Justice Eusoffe Abdoolcader (standing).

there was a conflict between the government and other bodies. Whereas in Malaysia, as I mentioned earlier, the decisions often went against the government. Tun Salleh said that during his term he was going to ensure that the judiciary should not be challenged and that it should continue to uphold its decisions in a fair manner.

The Tun Salleh Affair

After UMNO was declared illegal and subsequently deregistered in February 1988, the rivalry between Dr Mahathir and Tengku Razaleigh Hamzah for the leadership of the Malays intensified with Dr Mahathir successfully forming a new party, UMNO Baru, and Tengku Razaleigh and his Team B supporters going back to court to appeal against the deregistration of UMNO. Their case was scheduled to be heard by the Supreme Court on 13 June 1988 to be presided over by Tun Salleh Abas with eight other judges.

On 17 March 1988, Dr Mahathir tabled the Constitution (Amendment) Act 1988 in the Dewan Rakyat explaining that it was because the government realised the importance of the people having confidence in the judicial system that it had sought the amendment to the Constitution. *The Straits Times* article on 18 March 1988 also reported what Dr Mahathir said about the judiciary, that it should devote its attention to the dispensation of justice without favouring any side or being involved with any political party: "… justice will not be served if judges were more concerned with showing an attitude that is independent of the government."

For more than a year prior to this speech, Dr Mahathir had made several statements which Tun Salleh considered to be repeated attacks on the judiciary. As they were becoming more intense and frequent, Tun Salleh was concerned that the public impression of the judiciary would be affected. It was in this context that he made a series of speeches to clarify the proper role and function of the judiciary. After Dr Mahathir's latest speech, Tun Salleh called a meeting on 25 March 1988 attended by 20 judges. He later drafted a letter to the Yang di-Pertuan Agong.

Tun Salleh, appointed lord president in 1984, was suspended on 31 May 1988. According to a statement issued by the Prime Minister's Office, he was to be tried for misconduct by a tribunal. *The Straits Times* reported on 1 June 1988 that Tun Salleh had met Dr Mahathir on 27 May and the latter explained to him that the Agong wanted Tun Salleh to be replaced as lord president because of the letter Tun Salleh wrote which the Agong took exception to. "As constitutionally, this was not possible, the Prime Minister had advised the Yang di-Pertuan Agong to set up a tribunal to advise his Majesty after the tribunal had held its hearing." *The Straits Times* on 23 July 1988 elaborated on this aspect of the Federal Constitution: "According to the Constitution, judges can only be removed by the King on the advice of a tribunal, made up of no fewer than five serving or retired judges, including those of the Commonwealth."

The Straits Times article on 1 June 1988 also reported on the Malaysian Bar Council's reaction to Tun Salleh's suspension as lord president: "[It] expressed deep shock. It said in a statement that the present development would affect public confidence in the doctrine of the separation of powers, the administration of justice and the independence of the judiciary."

Both the *Business Times* and *The Straits Times* on 22 June 1988 reported on the allegations of misconduct against the suspended lord president. The government's case, set out in a 12-page document, was released on 21 June 1988. It listed five allegations of misconduct against Tun Salleh. He was accused of trying to influence the Malay Rulers in his letter of 26 May 1988 to the Yang di-Pertuan Agong expressing concern over the attacks made against the judiciary by the prime minister and falsely claiming that the letter had the support of the country's judges. The charges said that his action was likely to give rise to misunderstanding which could have adversely affected the good relations between the rulers and the government. "Such action has rendered you unfit to continue in the office of Lord President," the government document stated.

Tun Salleh faced four other charges of misconduct over a 20-month period relating to two public speeches he made, his judgement to adjourn indefinitely a case involving a minor's choice of religion in 1986, and his statements to the media following his suspension, in particular, his statement to the BBC which was regarded as the crucial point in the government's allegation that he did so in order to politicise the matter and to discredit the government.

The six-member tribunal, which included Chief Justice K.A.P. Ranasinghe of Sri Lanka and Justice T.S. Sinnathuray of the Singapore

Supreme Court, completed its investigation on 7 July 1988. Tun Salleh had boycotted the closed-door hearings of the tribunal. The tribunal's recommendation in a 52-page main report to the Yang di-Pertuan Agong on the five charges could not be submitted as Tun Salleh succeeded in getting the Supreme Court to issue a restraining order on 2 July challenging the constitutionality of the tribunal. *The Straits Times* on 29 July 1988 reported that the restraining order was lifted by a reconstituted five-man Supreme Court on 22 July. The five Supreme Court judges who issued the restraining order were themselves suspended on 6 July for "gross misbehaviour".

The *Business Times* on 9 August 1988 reported that the tribunal had found Tun Salleh guilty not only of misbehaviour but also of misconduct which rendered him unfit to properly discharge the functions of his office. It held that Tun Salleh had behaved in such a way as would destroy public confidence in his impartiality, honesty, integrity and ability to make decisions as a judge. Acting on the recommendations of the tribunal, the Yang di-Pertuan Agong ordered Tun Salleh to be dismissed both as a judge and lord president with effect from 8 August 1988 and that the tribunal's report be made public.

The *Business Times* on 11 August 1988 reported Tun Salleh's reaction to the tribunal's report: "All I need to say is that I totally disagree with the findings made in the report." The *Business Times* article commented that "Lawyers and opposition legislators view the sacking of Tun Salleh and the subsequent suspension of five other Supreme Court judges who will also face a tribunal on charges of 'misbehaviour' as the culmination of a government campaign to emasculate the judiciary and bring it under the control of the legislature." It was, as the *Business Times* noted on 10 October 1988 quoting Malaysian lawyers, "the worst crisis in Malaysia's judiciary."

Postscript

The Straits Times on 28 September 2006 reported that the Malaysia Bar Council was pushing for a review of the sacking of former Lord President Tun Salleh Abas 18 years ago in August 1988.

Earlier, on 23 August 2006, *The Straits Times* reported that Tun Salleh said that he hoped his sacking and the suspension of five other judges 18 years ago would be reviewed by the Abdullah administration. In response to Tun Salleh's call for a review, Minister in the Prime Minister's Department Datuk Seri Mohamed Nazri Abdul Aziz said that the government would not reopen the matter. He said in a Bernama news agency report that as far as he was concerned, all avenues for a review were closed and the matter was no longer an issue.

Almost two years later, everything changed after the general elections in March 2008 when the ruling Barisan Nasional lost its two-thirds majority in Parliament as well as control of five states to opposition parties. On 17 April 2008, it was reported in *The Straits Times* that Prime Minister Abdullah Ahmad Badawi had signalled that judicial reform was his key priority when he appointed prominent lawyer Datuk Zaid Ibrahim to his new cabinet to push his reform agenda. The reform agenda, announced during a special dinner that night hosted jointly by the government and the Malaysian Bar Council, saw the prime minister make an expression of regret over the 1988 judicial saga that led to the sacking of the country's top judge.

The Straits Times on 19 April 2008 reported that at the dinner, Tun Salleh, seated at the same table as the prime minister, expressed satisfaction with Datuk Seri Abdullah's announcement. "I waited 20 years and my prayers have been answered. I know that I could not win legally before the previous government, but my prayers were answered today, as I was given the moral victory," he said.

Chapter 8

Retirement in Singapore
1988–present

WHEN MY SECOND term as high commissioner to Malaysia ended in April 1988, I was offered the position of an ambassador-at-large with the Ministry of Foreign Affairs. I was also invited by the Institute of Southeast Asian Studies to be a Senior Research Fellow. I declined both offers. In 1989, I was appointed pro-chancellor at the National University of Singapore (NUS) and held it for 10 years. I was required to preside over some of the multiple commencement ceremonies held annually for graduands of NUS.

All along my passion had been reading and it is to this that I devoted much of my time since leaving diplomatic life. I decided to write my memoirs after Mr Robert Yeo approached me to participate in a series of books for younger readers to convey to them what it was like to grow up before the Second World War, up to the Japanese invasion and the fall of Singapore. My book *A Time of Fireflies and Wild Guavas* was published in 1995 and it is now out of print. A second edition was issued later in 1999. It is now republished with a new title *Growing Up in British Malaya and Singapore: A Time of Fireflies and Wild Guavas*.

This book completes my memoirs.

Picture 30: MB as Pro-Chancellor, National University of Singapore (NUS), presiding at a commencement ceremony for graduands of NUS, 1999.

www.ingramcontent.com/pod-product-compliance
Lightning Source LLC
Chambersburg PA
CBHW052056230426
43662CB00037B/1903